A Practical Treatise On The Office And Duties Of Coroners In Ontario, With An Appendix Of Forms...

William Fuller Alves Boys

A PRACTICAL TREATISE

ON THE

OFFICE AND DUTIES

OF

CORONERS IN ONTARIO,

WITH AN APPENDIX OF FORMS.

SECOND EDITION.

BY

WILLIAM FULLER ALVES BOYS, LL.B.

OF OSGOODE HALL, BARRISTER-AT-LAW.

TORONTO:

HART & RAWLINSON, 5 KING STREET WEST.

1878.

DEDICATED

TO

THE CORONERS OF THE PROVINCE OF ONTARIO,

WHOSE KIND RECEPTION OF THE FIRST EDITION OF THIS WORK

ON THE OFFICE OF CORONER

HAS RENDERED

THE PUBLICATION OF A SECOND EDITION NECESSARY,

BY

THE AUTHOR.

PREFACE TO SECOND EDITION.

In consequence of the First Edition of this treatise having been exhausted for some time past, and the very general desire on the part of Coroners for a new issue of the work, I have concluded to publish a Second Edition. I trust it will be found an improvement on the last, and that it will meet with the same approval as its predecessor. I have now added a chapter on ANTIDOTES, as likely to be of service to Coroners, and have made such corrections and additions as experience has suggested or changes in the law have rendered necessary. In referring to the Revised Statutes of Ontario, recently published, I merely give the page, and not the chapter and section, as is usually done in law books. I think this will be found more convenient for persons not accustomed to the daily use of statutes.

In preparing this edition, I again received valuable assistance from Professor Croft, of Toronto. Henry Totten, Esq., Auditor of Criminal Justice Accounts, Treasury Department, Ontario, also gave me material aid in revising the Schedule of Fees. To these gentlemen I desire to offer my thanks.

W. B.

BARRIE, *Hilary Term*, 1878.

PREFACE TO FIRST EDITION.

In submitting to the public the following work on the Office of Coroner, the writer must state that free use has been made of the standard English works of Umfreville, Impey, Jervis, Sewell, Grindon, Baker, and others; and were it not for the recent changes in the law which governs inquests in England, and for the provisions of our own statutes relating to Coroners and their duties, which render English text books unreliable in this country, some apology would be required for adding to the number of works already published on the subject. The writer is aware that Mr. Keele in his *Provincial Justice* has given a useful chapter on Inquests, and that a series of articles in the early numbers of the *Upper Canada Law Journal* supplied, to a certain extent, the want of a Canadian work on the Office of Coroner; but no book has yet appeared in Canada which purports to treat of the whole subject, with its connections, in a concise yet comprehensive and practical way: and while this fact has greatly influenced the writer in publishing the following pages, it has also caused him no little uneasiness for fear of his having overlooked any portion of the Canadian Law.

In addition to the information which might naturally be looked for in a work of this kind, chapters will be found treating of OFFENDERS—of CRIMES—of POISONS—of WOUNDS AND BRUISES—of the HYDROSTATIC TEST—of BLOOD TESTS—and of EVIDENCE—many of which subjects are not dealt with in any of the English works on Coroners, and yet a knowledge of them all is indispensable to an efficient discharge of duty. A careful perusal of the section on INFANTICIDE, and the remarks on death from negligence, is particularly recommended to Coroners.

The general arrangement of the book is the same, with slight variations, as that of Jervis's Office of Coroner—a work which has been most freely used by the writer.

In preparing the *medico-legal* portions, the well-known works of Drs. Taylor and Beck have been principally consulted.

The writer cannot close this preface without acknowledging the kind assistance he has received from the learned gentleman to whom the work is dedicated (1), from Professor Croft, of University College, Toronto, and from several other gentlemen, whose knowledge of the subjects treated of, or whose official positions, placed it in their power to lighten his labours, and at the same time to lessen that anxiety which is naturally felt for the success of a first effort.

W. B.

BARRIE, *Easter Term*, 1864.

---

(1) The first edition was dedicated to His Honour Judge Gowan.

TABLE OF CONTENTS.

PART I.

THE OFFICE AND DUTIES OF CORONERS GENERALLY.

CHAPTER I.

OF THE OFFICE AND APPOINTMENT OF CORONERS.

		PAGE.
SEC.	1. The Antiquity of the Office	1
	2. Qualifications	2
	3. Mode of Appointment	3

CHAPTER II.

OF THE DUTY AND AUTHORITY OF CORONERS GENERALLY.

SEC.	1. As Conservators of the Peace	5
	2. In Inquests of Death	6
	3. To Inquire into the Origin of Fires	9
	4. To Return Inquisitions	11
	5. To Execute Process	12
	6. Other Duties	17

CHAPTER III.

OF THE JURISDICTION OF CORONERS IN INQUESTS OF DEATH.

SEC.	1. Their General Jurisdiction	18
	2. Their Jurisdiction in Particular Cases	18
	3. Supreme Jurisdiction	20

CHAPTER IV.

OF THE RIGHTS OF CORONERS.

SEC.	1. General Remarks	21
	2. Their Right to Fees	21
	3. Their Exemption from Serving Offices	22
	4. Their Privilege from Arrest	22
	5. As to their other Rights and Privileges	23

CHAPTER V.

OF THE LIABILITIES OF CORONERS.

PAGE.

SEC. 1. For Misconduct 24
2. To be Removed 26
3. For the Acts of Co-Coroners........ 26

PART II.

THEIR OFFICE AND DUTIES IN PARTICULAR.

CHAPTER I.

OF OFFENDERS.

SEC. 1. Who may Commit Crimes—Infants 27
2. Persons Non compos mentis 28
1. Dementia Naturalis........ 28
2. Dementia Accidentalis 29
3. Dementia Affectata........ 29
3. Persons in Subjection to the Power of Others 29
4. Ignorance 30
5. Misfortune 30

CHAPTER II.

OF PRINCIPALS AND ACCESSORIES.

SEC. 1. Principals in the First Degree 31
2. Principals in the Second Degree 31
3. Accessories Before the Fact 32

CHAPTER III.

OF CRIMES WHICH COME UNDER THE NOTICE OF CORONERS.

SEC. 1. Of Felo de se:
1. Definition 34
2. Practical Remarks 35

2. Of Murder:
1. Definition 37
2. Practical Remarks 37

SEC. 3. Infanticide: PAGE.
1. When is a Child born 48
2. The Hydrostatic Test 50
3. Of the Uterine Age of a Child 51
4. Monstrosities 52
5. Legal Points 52
6. Cautions 54
7. Evidence 55

4. Manslaughter:
1. Definition 57
2. Practical Remarks 57

5. Excusable Homicide:
1. Per infortunium 59
1. Definition 59
2. Practical Remarks 59
2. Se et sua defendendo 60
1. Definition 60
2. Practical Remarks 60

6. Justifiable Homicide:
1. Definition 61
2. Practical Remarks 61

CHAPTER IV.

OF POISONS.

Classification of Poisons.

Irritants.

Mineral..
- Non-metallic ..
  - Acids (Sulphuric).
  - Metalloids (Phosphorus).
- Metallic ......
  - Alkalic Compounds (Potash).
  - Heavy Metals and Compounds .... (Arsenic).

Vegetable (Savin).
Animal (Cantharides).

Neurotics.

Cerebral (Morphine).
Spinal (Strychnine).
Cerebro-spinal (Coniine).

PAGE.

Sulphuric Acid 65
Nitric Acid 66
Hydrochloric Acid 66
Oxalic Acid 66
Phosphorus 66
Alkalies 67
Ammonia 67
Arsenic 67
Chloride of Mercury or Corrosive Sublimate 68
Salts of Lead 69
Copper 69
Antimony 70
Zinc 71
Iron 71
Tin 71
Nitrobenzole 71
Aniline 71
Carbolic Acid 72
Savin 72
Colchicum 72
Cantharides 72
Opium, Laudanum 73
Prussic Acid 73
Alcohol 74
Tobacco 74
Strychnine 75
Cicuta Maculata 76
Conium Maculatum 76
Æthusa Cynapium 76
Sium Lineare 76
Aconitum Napellus 76
Datura Stramonium 76

CHAPTER V.

OF ANTIDOTES.

General Remarks 77
Sulphuric Acid 77
Nitric Acid 77
Oxalic Acid 77
Phosphorus 78
Alkalies 78

	PAGE.
Arsenic—Arsenious Acid	78
Corrosive Sublimate	78
Lead	78
Copper	79
Antimony	79
Zinc	79
Cantharides	79
Tin	79
Nitrobenzole (Essence of Mirbane)	79
Aniline	79
Carbolic Acid	79
Prussic Acid	79
Strychnine	79

CHAPTER VI.

OF WOUNDS AND BRUISES.

SEC. 1. Examination of Wounds	80
2. Characters of a Wound Inflicted during Life	81
3. Characters of a Wound Made after Death	82
4. Practical Remarks	82

CHAPTER VII.

OF THE HYDROSTATIC TEST	91

CHAPTER VIII.

BLOOD TESTS	92

CHAPTER IX.

OF DEODANDS	95

CHAPTER X.

OF FLIGHT AND FORFEITURE	96

CHAPTER XI.

OF EVIDENCE.

SEC. 1. Competency of Witnesses	97
1. Idiots	98
2. Lunatics	98
3. Children	98
4. Infidels	99
5. Prisoners	99
6. Husband or Wife of Prisoner	99

PAGE.

SEC. 2. Primary Evidence 100
3. Presumptive Evidence 101
4. Matters of Opinion 102
5. Matters of Privilege 102
6. Hearsay Evidence 103
7. Relevancy of Evidence 105
8. Leading Questions 106
9. Proof of Handwriting 106
10. Proof of Documents 107

CHAPTER XII.

THE CORONER'S COURT.

SEC. 1. When and where Holden 109
2. Who may Attend 111
3. The Jury, and how Summoned 112
4. The Witnesses, and how Summoned 117
5. Counsel 120
6. Opening the Court 120
7. Viewing the Body 122
1. The Place where the Body is Found 123
2. The Position of the Body 124
3. The Marks and Spots upon the Body and Clothing 125
4. The Surrounding Objects 126
5. The Bearing and Conduct of the Parties in Attendance 127
8. Continuing and Adjourning the Court 127
9. The Medical Testimony 132
10. The Depositions 141
11. Obstructions—how Punished 142
12. The Inquisition 143
1. The Venue 144
2. The Place where Holden 145
3. The Time when Holden 145
4. Before whom Holden 145
5. The View 145
6. The Description of the Deceased 145
7. Where the Body lies 146
8. The Jurors and their Finding upon Oath 146
9. The Charge to Inquire 147
10. The Verdict 147
11. The Party Charged 147

PAGE.

12. The Addition 149
13. The Allegation of Time and Place 149
14. The Description of the Act 149
15. The Attestation 151

SEC. 13. Publication of Proceedings 151
14. Defraying Expenses 152

CHAPTER XIII.

PROCEEDINGS SUBSEQUENT TO THE INQUISITION.

SEC. 1. With Reference to the Trial 155
2. Of Bail 156
3. Of Amending and Taking New Inquisitions 156
4. Of Traversing Inquisitions 158
5. Of Quashing Inquisitions 159
6. Of Pleading to Inquisitions 160

CHAPTER XIV.

SCHEDULE OF FEES.

SEC. 1. The Coroner's Fees in Inquests of Death 162
2. The Coroner's Fees in Fire Inquests 163
1. In Cities, Towns and Villages 163
2. In Country Parts 164
3. The Coroner's Fees for Executing Civil Process 164
4. The Fees of the Medical Witness 166
5. The Chemist's Fees 166
6. The Jurors and Witnesses 166
7. The Constable's Fees 167

APPENDIX—Forms 169

INDEX 227

peace, commissioner for taking affidavits in the High Court of Justice, or notary public) setting forth briefly the results of such enquiry and the grounds on which the warrant for burial has been issued.

Fees of coroner for services under Act.

3. For such investigations and services as may be performed by any coroner under and by virtue of the two preceding sections of this Act, he shall be entitled to a fee of $5 besides mileage in each case in which the county crown attorney shall certify that there were sufficient grounds to warrant such investigations being made, and such fee shall be in lieu of all the fees to which the coroner would be entitled in respect of any proceedings taken by him towards holding an inquest. In all other respects the said fee shall be paid in the same manner and upon the same conditions as the fees of coroners are now payable in cases in which inquests are held.

Coroners not to act when personally interested.

4. It shall not be lawful for a coroner to conduct an inquest in any case where loss of life has been caused at or on railroads, mines or other works whereof he is owner or part owner, either as shareholder or otherwise, nor in any like case at or on works where he may be employed as medical attendant by the owner or owners thereof, or by any agreement or understanding direct or indirect with the employees at or on such works.

No. 116.] **BILL.** [1894.

BILL.

An Act respecting certain duties of Coroners.

HER MAJESTY, by and with the advice and consent of the Legislative Assembly of the Province of Ontario, enacts as follows :—

Warrant for burial where coroner deems inquest unnecessary after making declaration.

1. In any case in which the death of any person has been reported to a coroner, and he has in consequence of information received by him made the declaration required by section 4 of the *Act respecting Coroners*, if after viewing the body of such deceased person and having made such further enquiries as he deems necessary he comes to the conclusion as a result of such further enquiries that an inquest is unnecessary, he shall have the right to issue a warrant to bury, in the same manner as he would have power to do in case an inquest had been actually held, and to withdraw the warrant for the holding of an inquest in case he has issued such warrant.

Act not to affect case of prisoners dying in gaols, etc. Rev. Stat., c. 80.

5. Nothing in this Act contained shall apply to or affect the case of a prisoner dying in any penitentiary, gaol, prison, house of correction, lock-up house or house of industry, provided for by section 3 of the *Act respecting Coroners*, nor relieve any coroner from the performance of the duties imposed by the said section.

Act incorporated with Rev. Stat. c. 80.

6. The *Act respecting Coroners* and this Act shall be read and construed as one Act.

THE OFFICE

AND

DUTIES OF CORONERS.

PART I.

THEIR OFFICE AND DUTIES GENERALLY.

CHAPTER I.

OF THE OFFICE AND APPOINTMENT OF CORONERS.

SEC. 1.—*The Antiquity of the Office* 1
" 2.—*Qualifications* 2
" 3.—*Mode of Appointment* 3

SEC. 1.—*The Antiquity of the Office.*

The common law office of Coroner is one of great antiquity, and much learning and research have been expended in shewing its origin and high repute; but any lengthy remarks on these subjects would be unsuited to a work designed for practical use. It will suffice to state that the origin of the office is involved in obscurity, but it is supposed to be coeval with that of Sheriff, and to have been instituted to aid in keeping the peace when the Earls gave up the wardship of the county. It was certainly in existence in the time of King Alfred, and the Coroner is mentioned in the charter of Athelstan to Beverly, anno 925 (1).

(1) Jer. O. C. 3; Impey O. C. 473.

The precise designation of the officer appears to have varied from time to time. In the reign of Richard the First he was called *Coronarius;* in that of John, *Coronator,* or *Custos placitorum coronæ,* because originally he had the custody of the rolls of the pleas of the crown. In the reign of Henry the Second, he was called *Serviens regis,* and in the Scotch law, Crowner, an appellation still in use among uneducated persons (1).

SEC. 2.—*Qualifications.*

Formerly, the office of Coroner was of such high repute that no one under the degree of knighthood could aspire to its attainment (2), and in the reign of Edward the Third a Coroner was actually removed from the office because he was a *merchant!* It has, however, now fallen from such pristine dignity; and though still of great respectability, no qualifications are required beyond being a male of the full age of twenty-one years, of sound mind, and a subject of Her Majesty, and possessing the amount of education and mental ability necessary for the proper discharge of the duties (3.)

These qualifications are no more than what all public officers by the common law are supposed, and ought, to possess. The Coroner has often a very delicate and very important duty to perform, and it need hardly be said that the proper discharge of that duty depends almost entirely on his personal character and ability. Where these are deficient, scenes often occur at inquests which throw disgrace upon the office of Coroner.

---

(1) Jer. O. C. 2.

(2) 3 Ed. I., ch. 10.

(3) It is said a Coroner ought to have sufficient property to answer all such fines and duties as belong to him.

Before acting as Coroner, the oath of allegiance and the oath of office should be taken (1), since holding an inquest without taking these oaths would subject the Coroner to a penalty, although his acts would probably be legal.

Sec. 3.—*Mode of Appointment.*

In England, Coroners are of three kinds,—By virtue of office, by charter or commission, and by election. Those by virtue of their office are, the Lord Chief Justice of the Queen's Bench and the other judges of this Court, who are Sovereign Coroners, and have jurisdiction in all parts of the realm. But in Ontario Coroners must be specially appointed by the Lieutenant-Governor by commission, under the great seal; unless indeed the Chief Justice and Puisné Judges of the Court of Queen's Bench are Sovereign Coroners *virtute officii*, in a similar manner to the judges of the same court in England. One or more Coroners are first appointed for each county, city and town and for any provisional judicial, temporary judicial, or territorial district, or provisional county, or for any portion of the territory of Ontario not attached to a county for ordinary municipal and judicial purposes (2). The appointments are generally made upon the recommendation of a member of Parliament, or other person possessing influence with the Executive.

When one county separates from another, the municipal law requires the Lieutenant-Governor to appoint one or more coroners for the junior county, whose appointments take effect on the day the counties become disunited (3).

With regard to the number of Coroners for any county, city or town, there is no regulation. The number not

---

(1) See Forms, Nos. 2 & 3.
(2) Rev. Stat. 875.
(3) Rev. Stat. 1601.

being limited, the appointments are in part governed by the requirements of the locality, and possibly in part by the energy shewn by those seeking the office.

The Coroner, according to the definition at common law, is an officer of the King that hath cognizance of some pleas of the crown (1); but there are several duties imposed by statute. The tenure of office is during the Queen's pleasure and the Coroner's residence within the province (2); but practically he holds office for life. Like other officers, he may be removed for several reasons, which will be further noticed under Chapter V.

---

(1) Their power in proceeding to trial and indictment was taken away by *Magna Charta*, ch. 17.

(2) See the Commission Form, No. 1.

CHAPTER II.

OF THE DUTY AND AUTHORITY OF CORONERS GENERALLY.

SEC. 1.—*As Conservators of the Peace* 5
" 2.—*In Inquests of Death* 6
" 3.—*To Inquire into the Origin of Fires* 9
" 4.—*To Return Inquisitions* 11
" 5.—*To Execute Process* 12
" 6.—*Other Duties* 17

SEC. 1.—*As Conservators of the Peace.*

The duty and authority of Coroners generally will be considered in this chapter. Their particular duties and mode of proceeding will be treated of hereafter (1).

The powers of Coroners are judicial and ministerial. *Judicial*, as in the case of inquests upon bodies, and must be executed in person (2). *Ministerial*, as in the execution of process of the courts, and may be executed by deputy (3).

Coroners in former days were the principal conservators of the peace within their counties, and may now bind to the peace any person who makes an affray in their presence (4). It seems, also, from the English authorities on the subject, that they have power to cause felons to be apprehended, whether suspected of guilt, or found guilty after inquisitions, or if not guilty but present at the death (5). From the absence of precedent in this country, however, Coroners had better confine themselves to exercising the settled duties of their office as Coroners, and leave the magisterial functions to those more directly entitled to them.

---

(1) See Part II.
(2) Impey, O. C. 473; 14 Ed. I.
(3) Jer. O. C. 71.
(4) 1 Bac. Abr. 491; 2 Hawk, P. C. ch. 28, s. 5.
(5) Jer. O. C. 30.

Sec. 2.—*In Inquests of Death.*

When it is made to appear to any Coroner that there is reason to believe a deceased person came to his death from violent or unfair means, or by culpable or negligent conduct, either of himself or of others, under such circumstances as require investigation, *and not through mere accident or mischance*, or upon being notified by the proper authorities of the death, no matter from what cause, of any prisoner or lunatic confined in any private lunatic asylum, gaol, penitentiary, prison, house of correction, lock-up house, or house of industry, it is the duty of such Coroner to hold an inquest forthwith upon the body. This is the language of the Revised Statutes of Ontario, cc. 79 and 221, and it places the question of holding inquests in a clearer light than the old statute of Edward I., *De officio coronatoris*, which formerly regulated and defined the duties of Coroners. By this latter statute the Coroner was directed to hold an inquest on information of any "being slain or *suddenly dead*," and although dying suddenly was always interpreted as not meaning deaths from apoplexy, fever, or other visitation of God, yet it left room for the very improper practice to spring up of holding inquests on the bodies of all who died suddenly. There is now no excuse for such a custom; and the Coroners who hold unnecessary inquests, and the authorities who sanction their conduct by passing the accounts for them, are greatly to blame. The language of Chief Justice Jervis is very appropriate to the subject. He says: "Coroners ought not in such cases, nor indeed in any case, to obtrude themselves into private families for the purpose of instituting inquiry, but should wait until they are sent for by the peace officers of the place, to whom it is the duty of those in whose houses violent or unnatural deaths occur, to make immediate communication, whilst the body is fresh, and, if possible, whilst it remains in the same situation as when the person died." It is indeed very desirable, as will be seen hereafter, that an inquest (when there is occasion for one) should be held with as little delay as possible; yet nothing can be more reprehensible than *unseemly* haste, instead of waiting until properly acquainted with the necessity for an inquiry (1).

The power of justices to decline allowing items in Coroners' accounts for holding inquests, which in their opinions were unnecessary, was tried before the Court of King's Bench, in England, in *Rex* v. *Kent (Justices)*, 14 East. 229, when the court refused to compel the justices to allow an item in the Coroner's account, which had been struck out because there was no ground for holding the inquisition. And it has been held in this country, that if the justices audit the accounts before them at all, the Superior Courts will not review their decision (2).

Let it be borne in mind, then, that no inquest is now justifiable unless the deceased person came to his death from *violence* (3), or *unfair means* (4), or by *culpable* (5) or *negligent conduct* (6), either of himself or of others, *under*

(1) Coroners have been known to arrive before death has taken place, and to have watched the advent of that which gives them jurisdiction with an avidity far from being creditable. An inquest must always be a painful proceeding to those who generally have charge of the body, more particularly when accompanied by a *post mortem* examination; and Coroners who wantonly give additional pain to that which a sudden death has already caused, cannot be too strongly condemned.

(2) 22 U. C. Q. B. 405.

(3) In judging whether a death is comprehended under any of these terms, they must be read in connection with the words "under such circumstances as require investigation," for every death from violence, negligent conduct, &c., need not of necessity require investigation. For instance, if a man is chopping by himself, and in felling a tree it strikes and kills him, without there being any reason to suppose he wilfully placed himself in its way, there would be no circumstances connected with his death calling for investigation, although caused by "violence." On the other hand, if another man was chopping with him, an inquest might properly be held.

(4) See the previous note.

(5) See note 3.

(6) See note 3.

such circumstances as *require* investigation, unless the deceased was a prisoner or lunatic confined in a gaol or lunatic asylum, except a lunatic confined in the Provincial Lunatic Asylum. The jealous care with which the law watches over the safety of all imprisoned, renders it proper and necessary to hold inquests upon the bodies of such persons, whether they die a natural death or not; and the statutes above mentioned require those having charge of such prisoners and lunatics *immediately* to give notice of the death to a Coroner. When a patient dies in a private lunatic asylum, a statement of the cause of the death, with the name of any person present thereat, must be forthwith drawn up, and signed by the medical attendant of the house, and a copy, duly certified by the proprietor or superintendent, must, *within forty-eight hours* after the death, be sent by the proprietor or superintendent to the nearest Coroner (1).

Whenever judgment of death has been executed on any criminal, it is the duty of a Coroner of the district, county or place to which the prison where the offender was executed belongs, within twenty-four hours after the execution to hold an inquest and inquire into and ascertain the identity of the body, and whether judgment of death was duly executed on the offender. In these cases the inquisition must be in duplicate, and one of the originals is to be delivered to the sheriff. No officer of the prison or prisoner confined in the prison shall in any such case be a juror on the inquest (2).

In what manner Coroners should require the facts justifying inquests to be evidenced before they proceed to hold them, is not laid down by any positive enactment or decided case. By analogy to other legal proceedings, the informa-

---

(1) Rev. Stat. 2235.
(2) 32-33 Vic. ch. 29, ss. 115, 116.

tion should be on oath; and the Government now refuse to pay accounts for inquests unless they are accompanied by an information on oath, stating there was reason to believe the deceased person came to his death from violent or unfair means, or by culpable or negligent conduct, either of himself or of others, under such circumstances as require investigation, and not through mere accident or mischance, or that the deceased was a prisoner or lunatic as before mentioned. For form of information, see Form No. 130 (1).

The inquiry can only be taken upon view of the body (*super visum corporis*), and must be restricted to the cause of death of the person upon whom the inquest is taken, and to accessories *before* the fact: it should not extend to accessories *after* the fact (2), unless in the two instances mentioned in Chap. III.

Where there are several Coroners for the same place, an inquest may be taken by one or more; but when one proceeds in the matter, the acts of others will be void (3).

After receiving notice, the Coroner summons a jury, and proceeds with the inquest as directed in Chapter XII., Part II.

SEC. 3.—*To Inquire into the Origin of Fires.*

Coroners have authority, by Provincial statute, and it is their duty, to institute an inquiry into the origin of fires. The first statute on the subject (18 Vic. ch. 157), was limited to Quebec and Montreal, but this was repealed by 20 Vic. ch. 36, forming ch. 88 of the Con. Stat. Can., and now embodied in ch. 196 Rev. Stat. Ont., which enacts that

---

(1) The old statute of Ed. I. states: "When Coroners are commanded by the king's bailiffs, or by honest men of the county, they shall go to places where any be slain," &c.

(2) Moor, 29, pl. 95; 2 Hawk. P. C., ch. 9, s. 26.

(3) 2 H. P. C. 59.

whenever any fire has occurred whereby any house or other building has been wholly or in part consumed, the Coroner within whose jurisdiction the locality is situated, shall institute an inquiry into the cause or origin of such fire, and whether it was kindled by design, or was the result of negligence or accident, and act according to the result of such inquiry.

In the case of an investigation concerning any fire occurring in any place not within a city, town or incorporated village, the allowance to the Coroner is only five dollars for the first day; and should the inquiry extend beyond one day, then four dollars for each of two days thereafter, and no more; a remuneration considerably less than what is allowed for inquiries in cities, towns and incorporated villages.

It is not the duty of Coroners to institute inquiry into the cause or origin of all fires indiscriminately. They should first be satisfied that there is reason to believe the fire was the result of culpable or negligent conduct or design, or occurred under such circumstances as, in the interests of justice and for the due protection of property, require investigation (1).

In all cases the expenses of and attending fire inquests are to be borne by the party requiring them (2).

Formerly the Coroner was entitled to be paid his fees by the treasurer of the municipality, whether he made it appear to the authorities that an inquiry was proper or not (3). Now, no municipality is liable for any such expense, unless the investigation be required by an instrument under the hands and seals of the mayor or other head officer of the municipality, and of at least two other members of the

(1) Rev. Stat. 1990.
(2) Rev. Stat. 1991.
(3) Con. Stat. Can. ch. 88, s. 9.

council thereof (1); and such requisition is not to be given to charge any municipal corporation, unless there are strong special and public reasons for granting the same (2). And no expense of or for an adjournment of any such inquest is chargeable against or payable by the party, or municipal authorities, calling for or requesting the investigation to be held, unless it is clearly shown by the Coroner, and certified under his hand, why and for what purpose an adjournment took place, or became necessary in his opinion (3).

When investigating accidents by fire, a Coroner can in his discretion impannel a jury or not, unless he is required to do so on the written requisition of an insurance agent, or of any three householders resident in the vicinity of the fire (4). His duties and powers in these investigations, as to taking down the evidence, summoning jurors and witnesses, &c., are the same as in ordinary inquests (5).

The jury and witnesses in these investigations will be noticed in Chapter XII., and the fees in Chapter XIV.

SEC. 4.—*To Return Inquisitions.*

In every case of investigation found before Coroners, the inquisition, and every recognizance taken before them, with the written information (if any), and the depositions and statements (if any) of the accused, shall be forthwith delivered to the County Attorney for the county in which such inquisition has been found (6).

Under this section it will be proper to mention that Coroners are required to return lists of the inquests held by them, together with the findings of the juries, to the Provincial Treasurer, on or before the first day of January in

(1) See Form No. 127.
(2) 24 Vic. ch. 33, s. 2.
(3) 24 Vic. ch. 33, s. 3.
(4) Con. Stat. Can. ch. 88, sec. 4.
(5) Con. Stat. Can. ch. 88, ss. 5, 7.
(6) Rev Stat. 878.

every year (1), and the Coroner who holds an inquest, before the body is interred, should supply the Division Registrar of the Division in which the death took place, according to his knowledge or belief, with all the particulars required to be registered touching such death by the form provided in the Rev. Stat. (2).

Formerly the inquisitions were required to be engrossed on parchment, indented at the top; but this is not at the present day imperative. The usual custom now is to write them in the ordinary way on paper.

Sec. 5.—*To Execute Process.*

In addition to his judicial functions, the Coroner also acts ministerially as a substitute for the sheriff, and executes process when that officer is incapacitated by interest in the suit, or makes default (3). When so acting, the Coroner can do all lawful acts which the sheriff might have done (4).

When judgment is recovered against a sheriff and his sureties on their covenants, the plaintiff or his attorney must, by endorsement on the writ, direct the Coroner or other officer charged with the execution of such writ, to levy the amount thereof upon the goods and chattels of the sheriff in the first place, and in default of goods and chattels of the sheriff to satisfy the amount, then to levy the same, or the residue thereof, of the goods and chattels of the other defendant or defendants; and so in like manner with any writ against lands and tenements, upon a judgment on any such covenant (5).

If a sheriff forfeits his office and becomes liable to removal, he is still to execute process until his successor is appointed (6).

---

(1) Rev. Stat. 878.
(2) See Form No. 128.
(3) 4 Inst. 271.
(4) Hob. 85.
(5) Rev. Stat. 217.
(6) Rev. Stat. 217.

In case a sheriff dies, or is removed from office, or resigns his office and his resignation is accepted, process is not to be awarded to the Coroner, but to the under-sheriff or deputy (1).

When the process is awarded to the Coroner, the sheriff is no longer considered as an officer in the suit (2); and as judicial writs follow the course of their original, where the first process is awarded to the Coroners the execution must be directed to them also (3), even though a new sheriff be appointed in the meantime (4).

Interest in the sheriff who has executed the earlier proceedings in the suit, is no reason for directing final process to the Coroner; although, if the interest of the sheriff be suggested upon the roll, the court will award the *venire* to the Coroner (5).

Process against the deputy sheriff may, it seems, be awarded to the sheriff (6).

When the sheriff is interested in a suit the jury must be summoned by the Coroner under a *venire* awarded in the particular case. The number of jurymen summoned in such a case need not be over twelve, unless the writ of *venire* orders otherwise. See *Fraser* v. *Dickson*, 5 U. C. Q. B, 231.

In *Gilchrist* v. *Conger*, 11 U. C. Q. B. 197, it was held that where the sheriff is defendant a writ of replevin, under 14 & 15 Vic. c. 64, could be directed to the Coroners, though the statute does not provide for such a case, it being a well known rule of construction that a remedial statute shall be extended by equity to other persons besides those expressly named.

In a case where a Coroner has seized a note under a *fi. fa.* directed to him, and in suing for the note the declaration did

(1) Rev. Stat. 221. (2) Cro. Eliz. 894.
(3) 2 Hen. VI. 21 *a*; Bro. Exon. 110; 14 H. 8, 316; Jer. O. C. 52.
(4) Com. Dig. Officer, G. 13. (5) Jer. O. C. 52.
(6) *Gordon* v. *Bonter*, 6 *U. C. Law Journal*, 112.

not shew how the *fi. fa.* came to be directed to the Coroner, it was held that where a writ can under certain circumstances be properly directed to a Coroner, the court would assume those circumstances existed in the case before them. See *Brown* v. *Gordon*, 16 U. C. Q. B. 342.

Under our Act 48 Geo. III. ch. 13, s. 5, it was held the Coroner had no authority to summon a *special* jury; but it should have been done by some indifferent person appointed by the court, the sheriff being interested (1).

When a Coroner is required to arrest a sheriff, a difficulty must present itself in knowing what to do with the prisoner. If incarcerated in his own prison, he might dismiss the gaoler and turnkeys, who are all of his own appointment, and let himself out! and the Coroner would have no authority (in all cases at least) to take him into another county and imprison him there. If required to arrest a sheriff on a *habeas corpus*, and have his body before the court at Osgoode Hall by a day named, the Coroner might then perhaps start for Toronto immediately after the arrest, and lodge his prisoner in the gaol there until he was wanted; but when he arrests a sheriff on a *capias*, for instance, what can be done with him? In some cases he might no doubt be legally imprisoned in a private house, but in others no imprisonment would seem to be legal except in the common gaol of the county—imprisonment under the Division Court Act, for instance. Generally, from there being no danger of the sheriff absconding, the Coroner need only tell him he is his prisoner, and take a promise from him to appear when required. But if there is any likelihood of the sheriff keeping out of the way, perhaps the best method of securing him would be to confine him in the Coroner's or some other convenient house in charge of one or more bailiffs, according to

---

(1) 8 U. C. Rep. 281.

the necessity of the case. However, the writer knows of no authority by which to point out the proper course to be pursued.

Another difficulty occurs in the execution and return of writs directed to Coroners, which, however, more concerns the members of the legal profession than the persons for whom this work is specially written. It arises from the rule that where Coroners act ministerially, although one may execute the writ (1), the return must be in the name of all (2).

The practice in this country, as far as the writer is aware, is to direct the writ to the "Coroners" of the county, and to hand it to one Coroner, who makes a return in his own name; and if it is a writ of *fi. fa.*, it is endorsed on the back thus: "Mr. Coroner, levy and make," &c., &c. And the Coroner also makes the return simply in his own name. This general practice, if indeed it is such, seems clearly improper; for so inflexible is the rule mentioned, that in the case of *Rex* v. *Dolby* (3), the Coroners were directed to return a special jury, which was done; but a *tales* being required, it was returned by one Coroner, who happened to be in court. This was objected to on the ground that the return must be by all, and the validity of the objection was admitted. The difficulty does not appear to arise in England, for none of the practice books state how the return by all the Coroners is obtained. Probably they have no more than one or two Coroners for each county, and the return by all is easily effected. In this country, where Coroners are very numerous in every county, and some widely separated from others, it is impossible to comply with the law. Until a remedy is provided

(1) 2 H. P. C. 56.
(2) 2 Hawk. P. C. ch. 9, s. 45.
(3) Cited Umf. 144.

by Act of Parliament, no more can be done than to give the profession warning of the difficulty (1).

If the writ be directed to the "Coroners," where there are more than two Coroners in the county, it may be executed by the survivors, although one die before the return; but if one only survive, he can neither execute nor return the writ until another is appointed (2).

If the Coroner will not execute a writ, and an attachment is taken out against him, it must not be delivered to another Coroner to serve, but an elisor for that purpose will be appointed by a judge in chambers on affidavits stating the facts; who, if he accepts the writ and afterwards will not execute it, can also be attached. If he does not accept the writ he cannot be made to. More than one elisor will be appointed if required.

A writ of attachment should be personally delivered to the Coroner, in order to bring him into contempt (3).

Coroners, in their ministerial capacity, may do all such lawful acts as the sheriff might have done, and are subject to the same duties, process and penalties as the sheriff (4).

The ministerial duties of the Coroner need not be discharged personally, but, as in case of the sheriff, he may by warrant delegate his authority to another (5).

To trace all the law relating to the execution of civil process by Coroners, would be to write the office of Sheriff. Coroners are therefore referred to works on the duties of that officer for any further information they may require under the present heading.

---

(1) In adopting this course, the writer has followed the example of Mr. Harrison in the notes to the Common Law Procedure Act, p. 23.

(2) H. P. C. 56; F. N. B. 163; Cro. Jac. 383.

(3) 1 H. & W. 332, and see books of practice.

(4) Rev. Stat. 218.

(5) Jer. O. C. 71.

SEC. 6.—*Other Duties.*

As to the other duties of Coroners, it may be mentioned that the statute *De officio coronatoris*, 4 Ed. I. st. 2, gave authority to Coroners to inquire of other felonies besides homicide (though this, however, is doubted by some writers); to inquire of *treasure troves*, of *royal fishes*, and of *wrecks;* to receive an *appeal of felony* or *mayhem*, to take the *confession* and *abjuration of felons*, and to *pronounce judgment of outlawry*. Some of these duties have been expressly abolished by statute, and the others may be said to have become obsolete.

CHAPTER III.

OF THE JURISDICTION OF CORONERS IN INQUESTS OF DEATH.

SEC. 1.—*Their General Jurisdiction* 18
" 2.—*Their Jurisdiction in Particular Cases* 18
" 3.—*Supreme Jurisdiction* 20

SEC. 1.—*Their General Jurisdiction.*

The general jurisdiction of the Coroner is confined to deaths happening within the limits of his county, city, or town, and cannot be enlarged by any private Act or delegation from the crown (1).

When one county separates from another, or a city or town becomes incorporated, Coroners are appointed for the junior county, or the city or town, as the case may be, and the original Coroners should then confine themselves to the jurisdictions in which they reside.

SEC. 2.—*Their Jurisdiction in Particular Cases.*

In particular cases the Coroner has an extended jurisdiction. When any person, being feloniously stricken, poisoned, or otherwise hurt at any place in this Province, dies of such stroke, poisoning, or hurt, upon the sea, or at any place out of this Province, every offence committed in respect of any such case, whether the same amounts to murder or manslaughter, or to being accessory before the fact to murder, or after the fact to murder or manslaughter, may be dealt with, inquired of, tried, determined, and punished, in this Province, in the same manner in all respects as if such

---

(1) 2 Finch, 388.

offence had been wholly committed within the limits of this Province (1).

It will be observed that in these particular cases the accessories *after the fact* to murder or manslaughter can be inquired of. This is contrary to the power of the Coroner, when acting under his general jurisdiction (his duty then being to inquire into the *cause* of the death, which accessories after the fact could have nothing to do with), and suggests the idea that probably the provisions of these statutes were not intended to apply to inquests, although their language seems to include them. Indeed, when holding inquests under these statutes, Coroners had better leave the accessories *after* the fact to the magistrates to deal with.

And a murder or manslaughter committed on the boundary of two or more districts, counties or places, or within the distance of one mile of any such boundary, or in any place with respect to which it may be uncertain within which of two or more districts, counties or places it is situate; or if a murder or manslaughter is begun in one district, county or place, and completed in another, or if the murder or manslaughter was committed on any person in or upon any coach, waggon, cart or other carriage whatever, employed in any journey, or on board any vessel, boat or raft whatever, employed in any voyage or journey upon any navigable river, canal or inland navigation, every such murder or manslaughter may be inquired of in any one of the said districts, counties or places, or in any district, county or place, through any part whereof such coach, waggon, cart, carriage or vessel, boat or raft, passed in the course of the journey or voyage during which such murder or manslaughter was committed, in the same manner as if it had been actually committed in such district, county or place. And in all cases where the side, centre, bank or other part

(1) 32-33 Vic. ch. 30, s. 9.

of any highway, or any river, canal or navigation, constitutes the boundary of any two districts, counties or places, any such murder or manslaughter may be inquired of in either of such districts, counties or places, through or adjoining to or by the boundary of any part whereof such coach, waggon, cart, carriage or vessel, boat or raft, passed in the course of the journey or voyage during which such murder or manslaughter was committed, in the same manner as if it had been actually committed in such district, county or place (1).

Coroners of counties have jurisdiction concurrent with Coroners of the Admiralty over deaths happening in the arms of the sea (*infra corpus comitatus*) (2), and in great rivers (3), and in ships lying in harbour (4); but they have none upon the high seas, except in the cases above mentioned.

Coroners of counties have also jurisdiction when the death happens between high and low water mark upon the sea coast, when the soil is not covered with water (5).

In all these cases of extended jurisdiction the Coroner had better see that the body is brought within his county before holding the inquest.

SEC. 3.—*Supreme Jurisdiction.*

Coroners *virtute officii* have supreme jurisdiction everywhere (6).

---

(1) 32-33 Vic. ch. 29, ss. 8, 9, 10.
(2) 2 H. P. C. 15, 16, 54.
(3) 2 H. P. C. 15, 16, 54.
(4) 1 Str. 1097, 231.
(5) 3 Inst. 113; 5 Rep. 107.
(6) 4 Rep. 47.

CHAPTER IV.

OF THE RIGHTS OF CORONERS.

SEC. 1.—*General Remarks*.................................... 21
" 2.—*Their Right to Fees*.................................... 21
" 3.—*Their Exemption from Serving Offices*.................. 22
" 4.—*Their Privilege from Arrest*.......................... 22
" 5.—*As to their other Rights and Privileges*.............. 23

SEC. 1.—*General Remarks.*

Coroners, while acting judicially, have no right to appoint a deputy (1).

In England, this right has recently been conferred by statute (2), but we have no such enactment in Canada. The ministerial duties of Coroners may however be executed by deputy, but the return of process must be made in the name of all (3).

SEC. 2.—*Their Right to Fees.*

Their office was originally one of such great dignity, that Coroners *would* not take any reward for their services (4); and afterwards (when no doubt, the weakness of human nature began to get the better of our forefathers' pride) they were forbidden by statute to accept anything for executing their office, upon pain of heavy forfeiture (5).

It was not until the reign of Hen. VII. that Coroners were paid a regular fee for holding inquisitions, and then only in cases of persons slain, when they received 13s. 4d. (6).

---

(1) Cromp. Just. 227 *a*; 2 H. P. C. 58; 1 H. P. C. 388.
(2) 6 & 7 Vic. ch. 83.
(3) Jer. O. C. 71, and see p. 15.
(4) 1 Com. 347.
(5) 2 Inst. 210, 176.
(6) 3 Hen. VII. ch. 1.

Afterwards, they were paid for all inquests except those taken upon the view of bodies dying in a gaol or prison (1). And now, they receive remuneration in all cases.

If the authorities refuse to allow fees to a Coroner, his only remedy is to apply to one of the superior common law courts at Toronto (2) for a mandamus (3).

The writ must state all the circumstances of the case; must shew that he is entitled to the relief prayed; and that he had a right to require the auditors to do that, for the non-performance of which the writ was sued out (4).

For the execution of process and other acts incident to their ministerial character, Coroners are also entitled to fees.

For a Schedule of Fees, see Chap. XIV.

SEC. 3.—*Their Exemption from Serving Offices.*

Coroners are exempt from serving offices which are inconsistent with the duties of Coroner, and are not liable to be summoned as jurors (5).

SEC. 4.—*Their Privilege from Arrest.*

The same principle which exempts judges and officers of the superior courts from arrest while executing their judicial duties, seems to apply to Coroners; and in a case tried in

---

(1) 25 Geo. II. ch. 29.

(2) In England, the application can only be made to the Court of Queen's Bench, but in the complete co-ordinate jurisdiction given by Rev. Stat. 402, to both the superior common law courts in Ontario, sufficient authority will be found for the statement in the text.

(3) From the judgment of the Court of Queen's Bench, in *re Davidson and the Quarter Sessions of Waterloo*, 22 U. C. Q. B. 405, it seems the superior courts will only compel the Court of Quarter Sessions to audit. So if they do actually audit a Coroner's account, and disallow portions thereof, their judgments in the matter will not be interfered with.

(4) 7 T. R. 52.

(5) 2 Roll. Abr. 632, s. 4; F. N. B. 167; Rev. Stat. 535.

England, Mr. Justice Gaselee expressed his opinion that this exemption extended to Coroners, while going, remaining, or returning, for the purpose of taking an inquest.

Sec. 5.—*As to their other Rights and Privileges.*

In this place it may be stated that Coroners were formerly entitled to a copy of the Provincial Statutes of each session; but under the present regulations they are not so entitled, an order in council having been passed in 1859 discontinuing the practice which had theretofore obtained, of furnishing the statutes to Coroners, and a circular letter to that effect was addressed to the Clerks of the Peace in Upper Canada, on the 27th of June of that year. They ought to be furnished with lists of constables by the Clerks of the Peace, whenever ordered to be so furnished by the Justices in General Sessions (1).

---

(1) Rev. Stat. 905.

CHAPTER V.

OF THE LIABILITIES OF CORONERS.

Sec. 1.—*For Misconduct*.................................... 24
" 2.—*To be Removed*.................................... 26
" 3.—*For the Acts of Co-Coroners*........................ 26

Sec. 1.—*For Misconduct.*

If Coroners be guilty of any misconduct, either in their judicial or ministerial capacity, they are liable to be punished (1).

If a Coroner, after notice, do not view the body and take an inquisition in convenient time (2); if he conceals felonies, or is remiss in his duty through favour; if he misconducts himself in taking an inquisition; if he does not return the inquisition in proper time; or takes an inquisition without viewing the body; or if he do not reduce to writing the evidence given to the jury before them, or so much thereof as shall be material, and certify and subscribe the same, together with the recognizances and inquisitions before them taken; or if he do not return a list of inquests held by him, together with the findings of the juries, to the Provincial Treasurer, on or before the first day of January in every year; or if he does not supply the Division Registrar of the division in which a death takes place, and into the cause of which he makes inquiry before the interment of the body, with all the particulars required to be registered;—in any and all these cases he renders himself liable to punish-

---

(1) Jer. O. C. 98.
(2) See Form of Indictment, No. 4.

ment (1). And if a majority of the jurymen at an inquest are not satisfied with the evidence of the medical practitioner, or other witnesses examined in the first instance, and they name another equally qualified practitioner, in writing, to the Coroner, and he refuses to issue an order for his attendance, he will be guilty of a misdemeanor, and may be punished by a fine of $40, or by imprisonment for one month, or by both (2).

Coroners taking money to excuse any man from serving or being summoned to serve on juries may be fined (3).

Coroners, during the time they use or exercise their office, are not qualified to be justices of the peace; and if they act as such, their proceedings are void and of none effect, and they themselves become liable to be heavily fined (4).

If a Coroner forfeits his office for not returning writs, by the Common Law Procedure Act, and after such forfeiture continues to exercise his office without having been duly reappointed, he is liable to pay the sum of $400, to any person who sues therefor within twelve months (5).

If the body has been so long buried as to afford no information on view, a Coroner will not be justified in causing it to be disinterred; and if he do so, he may be fined (6).

If a Coroner inserts in the inquisition a material fact not found by the jury, he may be indicted for forgery (7).

All the witnesses who prove any material facts against the person accused, should be bound over by the Coroner, but not those called by the accused for the purpose of exculpating him. In every case the evidence given by each witness should be read over to him, and he should be requested to sign it.

---

(1) 2 H. P. C. 58; 3 Ed. I. ch. 9; 1 Leach, c. L. 43; Con. Stat. Can. ch. 102, ss. 62, 65; Jer. O. C. 90; Con. Stat. Can. ch. 33, s. 35; Rev. Stat. 378, 380.

(2) Con. Stat U. C. ch. 125, s. 9. & Rev. Stat. 376.

(3) Rev. Stat. 579.

(4) Rev. Stat. 845.

(5) Rev. Stat. 815.

(6) 2 Lev. 140.

(7) 3 Salk. 172.

By Stat. 1, Hen. VIII., justices of assize and justices of the peace within the county have power to inquire of, and punish the defaults of Coroners (1).

In their ministerial character Coroners are liable, like sheriffs in actions of debt, for an escape (2), case for a false return (3), or by attachment (4), according to the circumstances of the case.

Sec. 2.—*To be Removed.*

If a Coroner is convicted of extortion, wilful neglect of his duty, or misdemeanor in his office, the court before whom he is so convicted has power, under 25 Geo. II. ch. 29, to adjudge that he be removed from his office. Or a Coroner may be removed by being made a sheriff, or by the Queen's writ *De coronatore exonerando* (5), for a cause therein assigned (6); or he may forfeit his office by neglect in returning writs (7).

Confinement in prison out of the county is a sufficient ground for the removal of a Coroner from his office, although during his absence another Coroner of the same county has performed his duties (8).

Sec. 3.—*For the Acts of Co-Coroners.*

The default of one Coroner, when acting *judicially*, will not render his Co-Coroner liable; but when Coroners act *ministerially*, it is said they are all responsible for each other's acts civilly, although not criminally (9).

---

(1) And see 32-33 Vic. ch. 30, s. 63.
(2) 3 Lev. 399; 6 Mod. 37.
(3) Freem. 191.
(4) 2 Bl. 911, 1218.
(5) See Form, No. 5.
(6) Jer. O. C. 94.
(7) Rev. Stat. 815.
(8) *Ex parte Parnell*, 1 J. & W. 451.
(9) 1 Mod. 198; 2 Mod. 23; Freem. 91.

PART II.

THEIR OFFICE AND DUTIES IN PARTICULAR.

CHAPTER I.

OF OFFENDERS.

SEC. 1.—*Who may commit Crimes—Infants* 27
" 2.—*Persons non compos mentis* 28
1. *Dementia naturalis* 28
2. *Dementia accidentalis* 29
3. *Dementia affectata* 29
" 3. *Persons in Subjection to Power of others* 29
" 4. *Ignorance* 30
" 5. *Misfortune* 30

SEC. 1.—*Who may commit Crimes.*

The consent of the will is the great criterion by which to judge of the criminality of actions; hence, where there is no will there ought not to be any liability. Five heads contain all the causes which the law recognizes as exempting, in part or in whole, from liability by reason of defect in the will (1).

Infants.

Under seven years, no infant can be guilty of felony, or be punished for any capital offence (2).

Between the ages of seven and fourteen, the presumption of law is, that the infant is not capable of a mischievous

(1) 1 H. P. C. 14.
(2) Reg. 309 b; 1 H. P. C. 27, 28.

discretion; but this presumption can be rebutted by strong evidence of his capacity to judge between good and evil (1).

If, therefore, circumstances of malice be proved to the satisfaction of the *jury*, an offender between seven and fourteen years of age may be convicted and punished for a capital crime (2). Persons over fourteen are *prima facie* responsible for all their acts (3), and cannot escape punishmen except they are shewn to come under one of the other heads of exemption.

SEC. 2.—*Persons non compos mentis.*

The second class of persons who are not responsible for their actions by reason of want of will is the insane. All persons at the age of discretion are presumed by law to be sane, and, unless the contrary is proved, are accountable for their actions; and if a lunatic has lucid intervals, the law presumes the offence of such a person to have been committed in a lucid interval, unless it appears to the contrary (4). Those who are defective in the understanding and are over the age of discretion, are divided into three heads. 1. *Dementia naturalis*, Idiotcy, or natural fatuity. 2. *Dementia accidentalis*, Adventitious insanity. 3. *Dementia affectata*, Acquired madness.

1. *Idiotcy, or natural fatuity.*] An idiot is a fool or madman from his birth, without any lucid intervals. The deaf and dumb who cannot distinguish right from wrong are by presumption of law idiots, and are not answerable for their actions, but this presumption may be rebutted by strong evidence of understanding. Owing to the humane and successful efforts which have of late years been made to instruct this unfortunate class of persons, many of them have

---

(1) 4 Com. 23.
(2) 1 H. P. C. 25, 27; 4 Com. 23.
(3) 1 H. P. C. 25.
(4) 1 Hale, 33, 34.

been raised from a state of at least *legal* idiotcy to one of high intelligence, and are in consequence responsible for their actions (1). The question of idiotcy is one of fact to be decided by the jury (2).

2. *Adventitious insanity* may be either *partial*, its victims being insane on only one subject, or *total*, permanent (usually called madness) or temporary (the object of it being afflicted with the disorder at certain periods and under certain circumstances only), commonly called lunacy (3). While labouring under this disorder, no one is criminally responsible for his actions (4); although a partial aberration of intellect which does not prevent the party from distinguishing right from wrong will not excuse his guilt (5). Cases of much difficulty sometimes arise with this class of persons.

3. *Acquired madness* arises from drunkenness or the administration of something which produces frenzy. Voluntary drunkenness is no excuse for crime, but, on the contrary, aggravates it (6). Still the insanity caused by a habit of intoxication excuses from punishment (7). Intoxication, too, may be considered as a circumstance tending to shew a want of premeditation (8).

Sec. 3.—*Persons in Subjection to Power of others.*

Persons who do acts in obedience to existing laws or from the coercion of those under whom the private relations of

(1) 1 Hale, 34.

(2) Bac. Abr. Idiots (A.) Bro. Idiots 1.

(3) "In other cases reason is not driven from her seat, but distraction sits down upon it along with her, holds her trembling upon it, and frightens her from her propriety."—Erskine's Speech in defence of Hadfield, Vol. IV. p. 126, 3rd ed., by Rigway: and see the nice distinctions therein drawn with regard to insanity.

(4) 4 Rep. 125 Bac. Abr. Idiots (A).

(5) 1 H. P. C. 30.

(6) 1 H. P. C. 32; Co. Litt. 247.

(7) 1 H. P. C. 32.

(8) 1 Russ. 8, 7; C. & P. 817, 297, 145. But see Roscoe's Cr. Ev. 637.

society place them in subjection, are in many cases excused from the consequences of criminal misconduct. The classes of these persons usually requiring to be noticed are married women, children and servants. When the husband is actually present while the wife commits some crimes, the law presumes she is acting under his coercion; but this protection does not extend to the most heinous offences, and consequently a married woman cannot excuse her guilt, if convicted of treason, murder, homicide or the like, by shewing she was in company with or coerced by her husband (1). With regard to children and servants, their relation to their parents and masters will not excuse the commission of any crime, the command being void in law (2).

SEC. 4.—*Ignorance.*

Ignorance of the law is no excuse for crime, even in foreigners residing in Canada (3), unless an opportunity of acquiring a knowledge of it is wanting (4). Ignorance or mistake of *fact* may excuse in some cases, as where a man kills one of his own family in mistake for a burglar (5).

SEC. 5.—*Misfortune.*

If a person be doing anything *unlawful*, and a result ensue which he did not intend (as the death of another), the want of foresight is no excuse; but if accidental mischief follow from the performance of a *lawful* act, the party is excused from guilt (6).

---

(1) 1 H. P. C. 45, 47, 48, 516; 4 Bla. Com. 29.
(2) 1 H. P. C. 44, 516.
(3) 7 C. & P. 456; 1 H. P. C. 42.
(4) R. & R. 1.
(5) 1 H. P. C. 42, 43; 4 Bla. Com. 27.
(6) 4 Bla. Com. 27.

CHAPTER II.

OF PRINCIPALS AND ACCESSORIES.

SEC. 1. *Principals in the First Degree* 31
" 2. *Principals in the Second Degree*.......................... 31
" 3. *Accessories before the Fact*............................ 32

SEC. 1.—*Principals in the First Degree.*

Where two or more commit a felony they are: 1. Principals in the first degree; 2. Principals in the second degree; 3. Accessories before the fact; or, 4. Accessories after the fact. As Coroners are only to inquire into the *cause* of death, the three first classes are all this work need treat of.

Principals in the first degree are those who, with their own hands, or by means of an innocent agent, commit the offence. When the felony is committed by means of one aware of the consequences of his act, the inciter is either an accessory before the fact or an aider or abettor, according to the circumstances of the case (1).

SEC. 2.—*Principals in the Second Degree.*

Principals in the second degree, or aiders and abettors, are those who are present, aiding and abetting at the commission of the fact. They can now be punished, whether the principal offender has been first convicted or not. To constitute an aider and abettor, the person must be present aiding and abetting when the fact is committed, or intentionally near enough and ready to give assistance, if necessary (2).

---

(1) Fost. C. L. 349; R. & R. 363.

(2) Fost. C. L. 350; 2 Hawk. P. C. ch. 29, ss. 7, 8.

The felony need not of necessity be consummated in *presence* of the aiders and abettors, provided they are present assisting at its cause. For instance, if poison be laid for a man, those present and concurring in laying it are all principals in the second degree, although absent when the poison is taken (1).

The participation of aiders and abettors is either from a combination to commit the offence itself, or arising out of a combination to resist all opposers to the prosecution of some other unlawful purpose (2).

Principals in the second degree are punishable in the same manner as principals in the first degree (3).

SEC. 3.—*Accessories before the Fact.*

Accessories before the fact are those who, being absent at the time of the offence committed, do yet procure, counsel, command or abet another to commit a felony (4). The procuring is either direct, by hire, counsel, command or conspiracy; or indirect, by shewing an express liking, approbation or assent to another's felonious design of committing a felony (5). But he who barely conceals a felony to be committed is guilty only of misprision of felony (6).

Those who procure the commission of a felony, though by the intervention of a third party with whom they have no communication, are accessories before the fact (7).

If a man advise a woman to kill her child so soon as it is born, and she do so in pursuance of such advice, he is an accessory to the murder, though no murder could have been committed at the time of the advice (8).

---

(1) Fost. C. L. 349; Kel. 52.
(2) 2 Hawk. P. C. ch. 29, s. 9.
(3) 31 Vic. ch. 72, s. 3.
(4) 1 H. P. C. 615.
(5) 2 Hawk. P. C. ch. 29, s. 16.
(6) 2 Hawk. P. C. ch. 29, s. 23.
(7) 1 Fost. C. L. 125; 19 How. St. Tr. 746, 748, 804; 5 C. & P. 535.
(8) 2 Hawk. P. C. ch. 29, s. 18; Dyer, 168.

The act must be the probable result of the evil advice, and not substantially different from that advised. The test question, according to Mr. Justice Foster, being: "Did the principal commit the felony he stands charged with under the influence of the flagitious advice, and was the event, in the ordinary course of things, a probable consequence of that felony; or did he, following the suggestions of his own wicked heart, wilfully and knowingly commit a felony of another kind, or upon a different subject (1).

To manslaughter, it being sudden and unpremeditated, there can be no accessories before the fact (2).

An accessory cannot be guilty of a higher crime than his principal (3).

Accessories before the fact to felonies committed in this Province can be indicted and convicted either together with the principal felon or after the principal felon, or may be indicted for and convicted of a substantive felony, whether the principal has or has not been previously convicted or been amenable to justice (4). And it seems if the offence of counselling, procuring or commanding is committed within one county, and the principal felony within another, the accessory may be inquired of in either of such counties (5).

If the principal felon dies, or is pardoned, or is otherwise delivered before attainder, the accessory may notwithstanding be proceeded against in the same way as if the principal had been attainted (6).

It is not necessary that the principal felon should be in custody, or amenable to justice before accessories are charged with the substantive felonies (7).

---

(1) Fost. C. L. 372.

(2) 1 H. P. C. 347, 450, 616. Erle, J., in *R.* v. *Gaylor*, Dears & B. C. C. 288, said he thought Lord Hale was here speaking of manslaughter *per infortunium* and *se defendendo* only.

(3) 3 Inst. 139. (4) Con Stats. Can. ch. 97, s. 3; and 31 Vic. ch. 72, ss. 1, 2.

(5) Con. Stats. Can. ch. 97, s. 5. The Coroner's Court not having jurisdiction *to try* the principal felon, Coroners it is submitted have no jurisdiction under the fourth section of this Act. See 31 Vic. ch. 72, s. 8.

(6) 31 Vic. ch. 72, s 6. (7) 31 Vic. ch. 72, s. 7.

CHAPTER III.

OF CRIMES WHICH COME UNDER THE NOTICE OF CORONERS.

SEC. 1.—*Of Felo de se* 34
1. *Definition* 34
2. *Practical Remarks* 35
" 2.—*Of Murder* 37
1. *Definition* 37
2. *Practical Remarks* 37
" 3.—*Infanticide* 48
1. *When is a Child Born* 48
2. *The Hydrostatic Test* 50
3. *Of the Uterine Age of a Child* 51
4. *Monstrosities* 52
5. *Legal Points* 52
6. *Cautions* 54
7. *Evidence* 55
" 4.—*Manslaughter* 57
1. *Definition* 57
2. *Practical Remarks* 57
" 5.—*Excusable Homicide* 58
1. *Per infortunium* 59
1. *Definition* 59
2. *Practical Remarks* 59
2. *Se et sua defendendo* 60
1. *Definition* 60
2. *Practical Remarks* 60
" 6.—*Justifiable Homicide* 61
1. *Definition* 61
2. *Practical Remarks* 61

SEC. 1.—*Of Felo de se, or Suicides.*

1. *Definition.*] A *felo de se* is one who, being of the age of discretion and *compos mentis*, kills himself or commits some unlawful act the consequence of which is his own death (1).

(1) 1 Hal. P. C. 411; 1 Hawk. P. C. ch. 27, s. 4.

2. *Practical Remarks.*] It is not necessary that there should be an intention to commit self-murder to constitute this offence, provided there is an intention to do an unlawful act; for if one attempts to murder another and unintentionally kills himself, he is *felo de se* (1).

If two persons agree to die together, and one is persuaded by the other to buy poison, which both take, and the one who bought it survives and the other does not, the one who dies is *felo de se* (2). But if one desire or command another to kill him, the person killed is not *felo de se*, for his assent being against the laws of God and man, is void (3).

The person must die within a year and a day of the commencement of the cause of death, the whole day upon which the hurt was done being reckoned the first, to constitute the offence of *felo de se* (4). The offender must be of the age of discretion and *compos mentis* (5).

As many persons look upon all suicides as deranged, Coroners should caution the jury against being influenced by such a notion (6).

As one who commits the crime of self-murder, by the commission of the offence removes *himself* from the jurisdiction of human laws, the punishment can alone reach his fortune and reputation, and can only be inflicted as an example. An ignominious burial and forfeiture of property of the felon therefore form the appropriate means of deterring others from a like offence (7).

The burial, according to the rules of the Church of England, must be without the Christian rites of the Church, as the Rubric directs that the office for the burial of the dead "is not to be used for any who have laid violent hands upon

(1) 1 Hawk. P. C. ch. 27, s. 4. (2) Moor, 754; 1 Hawk. P. C., ch. 27, s. 6.
(3) 1 Hawk. P. C., ch. 27, s. 6. (4) 1 H. P. C. 411.
(5) 1 H. P. C. 30; 2 Hawk. P. C., ch. 27, s. 1.
(6) Jer. 142. (7) Jer. 143.

themselves." It seems that the body ought to be buried with a stake driven through it, in some public street or highway, in accordance with the ancient custom in England before 4 Geo. IV. ch. 52, by which statute Coroners were forbidden to issue warrants directing the interment in any public highway; and directing a private interment, without any stake being driven through the body, in the church-yard or other burial ground, within twenty-four hours from the finding of the inquisition, and between the hours of nine and twelve at night. This statute is not in force in Canada, and we must consequently be governed by the more barbarous law previously existing, unless Coroners are willing to depart from their strict duty, and issue process for the remains to be buried according to the less severe provisions of the later English enactment—a departure from duty which would have the sanction of humanity to support it. The Canadian law in this respect calls for amendment.

The forfeiture of *felo de se* it seems is of all chattels, real and personal, held in his own right, all chattels real held in right of his wife, or jointly with her, all bonds and other personal things in action belonging solely to himself, all entire chattels in possession, to which he was entitled jointly with another on any account except that of merchandise, and a moiety of such joint chattels as may be severed (1). His lands of inheritance are not forfeited, nor his wife barred of her dower (2).

With the finding of *felo de se* the jury should also find as to what goods the offender had at the time he committed the felony, and should specify them in an inventory annexed to the inquisition (3).

---

(1) 1 Hawk. P. C. ch. 27, s. 7; Jer. 144.
(2) 1 H. P. C. 413; Plowd. 261, 262; Jer. 144.
(3) 1 Saund. 272.

Goods held by the offender as executor, administrator or guardian, are not to be mentioned, as the forfeiture does not extend to them (1).

SEC. 2.—*Of Murder.*

1. *Definition.*] Murder is where a person of sound memory and discretion unlawfully kills any reasonable creature in being, and under the Queen's peace, by any means, with malice aforethought, either express or implied (2).

2. *Practical Remarks.*] In considering the general definition of murder, as given above, several things are to be noticed. *The person committing the crime must be a free agent,* and of sound memory and discretion, *i. e.*, he must not come within any of the classes of persons exempt from responsibility, before enumerated. Next—*The killing must be unlawful.* Consequently, when a criminal is executed by the proper officer, in pursuance of his sentence, this is justifiable homicide. But if done by any other person, or not according to the sentence, as by beheading when the sentence was hanging, it is murder. Officers of justice, gaolers and their officers, and others acting under authority, are protected in the proper execution of their duties; yet if they wilfully exceed the limits of their authority without just cause, and death follow, the law implies malice, and considers them guilty of murder. If they are resisted in the legal execution of their duty, they may repel force by force, but they must not kill where no resistance is made, or after the resistance is over, and time has elapsed for the blood to cool. And although justified in killing a *felon* who cannot otherwise be overtaken, yet for a *misdemeanor* they must not kill the accused, though there be a warrant to apprehend him, and he cannot otherwise be overtaken.

---

(1) 1 Plowd. 261; Co. Litt. 84, 88.
(2) 3 Inst. 47.

Killing a peace officer acting under legal authority is murder, whether the party killing be guilty or innocent of the felony charged against him (1). Parents, masters and others in authority may give reasonable correction to those under their care; and if death follow, it is no more than accidental death (2); but the correction in the manner, the instrument, or the quality, must not exceed the bounds of moderation (3).

The person killed must be a reasonable creature in being, and under the Queen's peace.] Outlaws or aliens, being under the Queen's protection, may be the subjects of this offence. Killing an alien enemy in the time of war is not murder (4). The person killed must be *in being;* therefore a child *in ventre sa mere* cannot be the subject of murder. But if the child be born alive, and afterwards dies from potions or injuries received while in the womb, it is murder in such as administered or gave them (5). The legal and other questions connected with infanticide being of much importance to Coroners, a section is devoted to their consideration alone, to which the reader is referred for additional information on the subject. (See Section 3, p. 48.)

The killing may be by any unlawful means.]—The means and manner of death being immaterial, provided there is a corporal damage to the party (6).

The means need not obviously tend to cause death, provided they apparently endanger life, and do ultimately occasion death, and are wilfully committed (7). Hence, carrying a sick person against his will, in a severe storm, from one town to another, by reason whereof he died, has been held to be murder (8). The injured person, however, must die within a year and a day to constitute murder, in

(1) Fost. C. L. 318.
(2) 1 E. P. C. 261.
(3) 1 H. P. C. 473.
(4) 3 Inst. 50; 1 H. P. C. 433.
(5) 1 Hawk. P. C. ch. 31, s. 16; Jer. 151.
(6) Jer. 152.
(7) 1 E. P. C. 225.
(8) 1 E. P. C. 225.

the computation of which the whole day upon which the hurt was done is to be reckoned the first (1). Murder may also be committed by means of an innocent agent, as by persuading a lunatic to kill another person, or by turning loose a furious animal with a knowledge of its disposition (2). If a physician or surgeon intending to do his patient good unfortunately kill him, this is only homicide by misadventure (3); and it makes no difference whether the party be a regular physician or surgeon or not, if he act honestly and use his best skill to cure (4). A medical practitioner must be guilty of criminal misconduct arising from the grossest ignorance or most criminal inattention, to render him guilty of manslaughter (5); and a person acting as a medical man, whether licensed or not, is not criminally responsible for a patient's death, unless his conduct shews gross ignorance of his art, or gross inattention to his patient's safety (6). The consent of the party killed does not extenuate the crime, such consent being merely void; one who kills another by his desire, or persuades another to kill himself, is a murderer (7.)

There must be malice aforethought.] This malice may be *express* and apparent, from the act being done with a deliberate mind, evinced by external circumstances; or it may be *implied* from the nature of the act or the means used, without any direct enmity being proved, as where one kills another on a sudden, without any considerable provocation, the law implies malice (8). So if a man deliberately strike another with a murderous instrument, without a sufficient cause, malice will be presumed. If the act intended to be done is founded in malice, the act done,

(1) 1 Hawk. P. C. ch. 31, s. 9; 4 Bla. Com. 197; 1 East. P. C. ch. 5, s. 112, pp. 343, 344

(2) 4 Bla. Com. 197; 2 Mood. C. C. 120; 9 C. & P. 356.

(3) 4 Bla. Com. 197; 1 Hale 429.

(4) 1 Hale P. C. 429.

(5) 3 C. & P. 635.

(6) 1 Russ. 497.

(7) 1 Hawk. P. C. ch. 27, s. 6.

(8) Jer. 161; Impey, 501.

although by accident, in pursuance of that intention, follows its nature (1). Hence if a man attempt to kill another, and accidentally kill himself, he is *felo de se* (2) ; or if in attempting to procure abortion death ensue, the person killing is guilty of murder (3).

Although malice is presumed in every case of homicide, it may be rebutted by the accused shewing:

1. *There was provocation.*] To clear himself of murder under this excuse he must prove—1. That the provocation was of a description of which he was unconscious ; 2. That it was unsought for, and was the immediate cause of the act ; 3. That it was commensurate with the act, and not an affront by word or gesture merely, or a trivial assault or blow ; 4. That the act was committed during the influence of the frenzy, and before the passion had a reasonable time to subside (4).

2. *That the party was killed in mutual combat.*] And this excuse will only avail or extenuate the offence where the occasion was sudden and unpremeditated, and not the result of preconceived malice, and where the parties at the onset were on an equal footing in point of defence. The quarrel must not be a mere cloak for the purpose of gratifying a concerted malicious design (5).

Deliberate duelling is murder, both in the principals and seconds, if death ensue (6); and no provocation, however grievous, will excuse the offender (7).

If two persons quarrel, and agree to fight a considerable time after, when the blood must have cooled, and death follows, it is murder (8) ; and it is the same in all fights where

(1) 1 E. P. C. 230.
(2) 1 Hawk. P. C. ch. 27, s. 4.
(3) 1 E. P. C. 230.
(4) Jer. 162.
(5) Jer. 169.
(6) 4 Bla. Com. 199.
(7) 3 East. 581 ; 1 H. P. C. 452.
(8) 1 Hawk. P. C. ch. 31, s. 32.

the circumstances shew that the parties do not commence in the heat of passion (1).

As boxing and sword-playing are *unlawful* acts, if either of the parties be killed, such killing is felony or manslaughter; and, in general, if death ensues from any idle, dangerous and unlawful sport, the slayer is guilty of manslaughter. To teach and learn to box and fence are equally lawful. They are both the art of self-defence; but sparring exhibitions are unlawful, because they tend to form prize fighters, and prize fighting is illegal (2).

3. *That the killing was occasioned by correction.*] Parents, masters, and other persons having proper authority, may give reasonable correction to those under their care (3); but the correction must not exceed the bounds of moderation, either in the manner, the instrument, or the quality of the punishment; or else, if death ensues, it will be manslaughter if not actual murder (4).

4. *That the killing was without intention, whilst doing another act.*] If the act is being done with a *felonious* intent, the killing which unintentionally follows is murder (5). If the act is not felonious but *unlawful*, it amounts to manslaughter only, except when death follows a *general combination* to resist all opposers in the commission of the unlawful act, when it is murder (6). And if the death ensue without intention from doing an act lawful in itself, with proper caution, according to its nature, it is generally homicide by misadventure (7).

An important class of cases which often comes under the notice of Coroners is that of deaths caused by negligent or wanton conduct, but without malice. This class includes

(1) 1 Lev. 180.
(2) *Hunt* v. *Bell*, 1 Bing. 1.
(3) 1 E. P. C. 261.
(4) 1 H. P. C. 473.
(5) Fost. C. L. 261.
(6) 1 Hawk. P. C. ch. 31, s. 51.
(7) Jer. O. C. 176.

deaths arising from furious or careless driving, from racing, from the want of competent skill to perform acts which the person holds himself out as capable of performing, from doing a duty imposed by law negligently, or omitting altogether to perform such duty, from neglect of ordinary precautions in the execution of lawful occupations, and indeed arising from all accidents which are the result of negligence, omission, or wanton conduct in the performance of lawful acts. If there is express malice discoverable in these cases, or if there is such a wanton indifference to the safety of others shown in them as to constitute malice by implication, of course the killing would be murder. But usually malice is wanting, and then the circumstances of each case must be considered to see if the offence is manslaughter or accidental death. No more can here be done than briefly to mention and illustrate the general principles which govern these cases.

The broadest principle perhaps that can be laid down as applicable to the whole class of cases is this: If the circumstances indicate a wanton and malicious disregard of human life, the killing may amount to murder; if they indicate negligence only, the killing will be manslaughter; and if they show an absence of even negligence, the killing will then be merely by misadventure or accident. And it seems that the death being partly caused by the fault of the deceased will not lessen the offence (1).

It seems also that the greatest possible care in performing the act is not to be expected or required, but there should be such care taken as is usual with persons in similar situations (2).

While a person is expected to anticipate and guard against all reasonable consequences, he is not expected to anticipate

(1) Per Pollock, C. B., in *R.* v. *Swindall*, 2 C. & K. 230; and see 1 C. & P. 320.

(2) 1 East. P. C. 263.

and guard against that which no reasonable man would expect to occur (1).

In the case of carriers of passengers for hire somewhat greater care may be required, for Hubbard, J., in *Ingalls* v. *Bell*, 9 Metc. 1, 15, is reported to have said "that carriers of passengers for hire are bound to use the utmost care and diligence in the providing of safe, sufficient, and suitable carriages, &c., in order to prevent those injuries which human care and foresight can guard against; and that if an accident happens from a defect in the coach, which might have been discovered and remedied upon the most careful and thorough examination of the coach, such accident must be ascribed to negligence, for which the owner is liable in case of injury to a passenger, happening by reason of such accident. On the other hand, where an accident arises from a hidden and internal defect, which a careful examination would not disclose, and which could not be guarded against by the exercise of a sound judgment and the most vigilant oversight, then the proprietor is not liable for the injury, but the misfortune must be borne by the sufferer, as one of that class of injuries for which the law can afford no redress in the form of a pecuniary recompense" (2).

With regard to *accidents from driving*, Garrow, B., said it is the duty of every man who drives any carriage to drive it with such care and caution as to prevent, as far as in his own power, any accident or injury that may occur (3).

A person driving a cart at an unusually rapid pace, drove over a man and killed him, and it was held manslaughter, though he called to the deceased to get out of the way, and he might have done so if he had not been in a state of intoxication (4).

---

(1) *Greenland* v. *Chapter*, 5 Ex. 248.

(2) *Readhead* v. *Midland*, R. W. Co., L. R. 2 Q. B. 412.

(3) *R.* v. *Walker*, 1 C. & P. 320. (4) *R.* v. *Walker*, 1 C. & P. 320.

If a person drives carelessly, and runs over a child in the street, if he sees the child and yet drives over him, it is murder; if he does not see the child, manslaughter; and if the child runs over the way and it is impossible to stop before running over him, it is accidental death (1).

What constitutes *negligence* in the case of driving must depend greatly upon the circumstances of each particular case (2).

Negligence is the omission to do something which a reasonable man, guided upon those considerations which ordinarily regulate the conduct of human affairs, would do, or doing something which a prudent and reasonable man would not do. Negligence includes two questions: 1. Whether a particular act has been performed or omitted; 2. Whether the performance or omission was a breach of legal duty (3).

As to *accidents from racing*, the test questions put to the jury in a case where death resulted to a person on an omnibus from the driver racing with another omnibus were these: Were the two omnibuses racing? And was the prisoner driving as fast as he could, in order to get past the other omnibus? And had he urged his horses to so rapid a pace that he could not control them? Patteson, J., told the jury that if they were of that opinion, to convict the prisoner of manslaughter (4).

If a driver happens to kill a person, and it appears he might have seen the danger, but did not look before him, it will be manslaughter for want of due circumspection (5).

The same rule applies to navigating a river as to travelling on a road. If death ensues from too much speed or negligent conduct in running a vessel, it will be manslaughter,

(1) 1 Hale, P. C. 476; Foster, 263. (2) Roscoe's Cr. Ev. 683.
(3) *Brown* v. *G. W. R. Co.*, 40. U. C. Q. B. 340.
(4) *R.* v. *Timmins*, 7 C. & P, 499. (5) Foster, 263.

just as if caused by furious driving or similar conduct on a public highway (1).

In order to convict the captain of a steamer of manslaughter, in causing a death by running down another vessel, some act of *personal* misconduct or negligence must be shown (2).

With regard to persons practising medicine or surgery, we have already seen (3) if they are guilty of criminal misconduct, arising either from gross negligence or criminal inattention in the course of their employment, and in consequence death ensues, it is manslaughter, and this whether they are licensed or not (4). In *R.* v. *Long* (5), Mr. Justice Bayley said, "It matters not whether a man has received a medical education or not. The thing to look at is, whether in reference to the remedy he has used, and the conduct he has displayed, he has acted with a due degree of caution, or, on the contrary, has acted with gross and improper rashness and want of caution."

A *chemist* who negligently supplies wrong drugs, in consequence of which death ensues, is guilty of manslaughter (6.)

Spirituous liquors are sometimes the cause of death without there being any intention of producing so unfortunate a result on the part of those causing them to be taken. In these cases, if they are given to a child in a quantity quite unfit for its tender age out of mere brutal sport, it is manslaughter (7). So also if a person make another excessively drunk with the view of carrying an unlawful object into effect, and the party dies from such drunkenness (8). But the simple fact of persons getting together to drink, or one

---

(1) 9 C. & P. 672. (2) 7 C. & P. 153. (3) See page 39.

(4) 3 C. & P. 635; 4 C. & P. 398; 5 C. & P. 333; Roscoe's Cr. Ev. 688, 661, and cases there cited.

(5) 4 C. & P. 440. (6) 1 Lewin, C. C. 169.

(7) 3 C. & P. 211. (8) 1 C. & Mars. 236.

pressing another to do so, and from which death ensues, will not be manslaughter (1).

Deaths from *exposure* or *the want of proper food* and *necessaries* are also included in the class of cases now under consideration. The neglect to supply food, shelter, and other necessaries, to wives, children, servants, apprentices, prisoners, or aged and infirm or other persons, on the part of those who are under legal obligation to so supply them, whether by law or contract, or by the act of taking charge of them, wrongfully or otherwise, and in consequence of which death ensues, is manslaughter (2). And if the neglect is wilful and deliberate, with the intention of bringing about death or of causing grievous bodily harm, it will even amount to murder (3). If the parties accused are husband and wife, before the latter can be convicted, it must be shewn that the husband supplied sufficient food, &c., and the wife did not give it (4). Except in the case of infants, when the mother is liable if the death was caused by her not suckling the child when she was capable of doing so (5). In which case it must be alleged it was the prisoner's duty to supply the child with food (6).

In the case of dropping infant children at doors, in streets, or on the highways, and thus causing their death, the question is whether the prisoner had reasonable ground for believing that the child would be found and preserved. If she had, the offence will only be manslaughter (7).

Where a gaoler, knowing a prisoner lodged in a certain room in the prison to be infected with small-pox, confined

(1) 1 C. & Mars. 286.

(2) 8 C. & P, 425; and see 1 C. & K. 600; 1 Den. C. C. R. 356; 3 C. & K. 123; 2 C. & K. 343, 368; Penge case, before Mr. Justice Hawkins, Sep., 1877.

(3) 1 East. P. C. 225. See Penge case, before Mr. Justice Hawkins, in England, Sep., 1877.

(4) 1 Russ. 490; 7 C. & P. 277. (5) 8 C. & P. 611. (6) 8 C. & P. 611.

(7) Carr & M. 164; see also 1 Den. C. C. R. 356; S. C. L. J. M. C. 53.

another prisoner, against his will, in the same room, and the latter prisoner who had not had the distemper (of which the gaoler had notice) caught it and died of it, it was held to be murder in the gaoler (1).

If a gaoler knows a prisoner in his charge is sick, and neglects or refuses to procure medical or other necessary assistance, in consequence of which the prisoner dies, he will be guilty of manslaughter or murder, according to the apparent necessity of the case, and the *animus* shewn by the gaoler.

But it is said where the death ensues from incautious neglect, however culpable, rather than from any actual malice or artful disposition to injure, or obstinate perseverance in doing an act necessarily attended with danger, regardless of its consequences, the offence will be reduced to manslaughter (2).

The numerous deaths resulting from *railway* and *steamboat* traffic, *machinery* of all kinds, *poisoning*, and in fact resulting from all other causes usually termed *accidental*, also come under this class of cases, and are all governed by the principles above referred to. But in these cases any wanton neglect of the statutory provisions for the inspection of railways (3) and steamboats (4), and for the safety of passengers travelling in the same; for regulating the sale of strychnine and other poisons (5), and for the prevention of accidents from machinery (6), ought to be considered in determining the degree of guilt of the persons by whose neglect or fault the deaths occur.

5. *That the killing happened from resistance to the execution of public duty.*] Officers of justice and others in authority may repel force by force in the legal execution of their

(1) 2 Str. 856; Foster, 322; 1 East. P. C. 331. (2) 1 East. P. C. 226; 1 Russ. 490.
(3) Rev. Stat. 1527. (4) 31 Vic. ch. 58 & ch. 65.
(5) Rev. Stat 1270. (6) Con. Stat. U. C. ch. 79.

duty (1); and if death ensue, the implied malice will be rebutted, unless no sufficient resistance was made, or sufficient time intervenes for the blood to cool (2).

Although it is said a felon may be killed who cannot be otherwise overtaken; yet one accused of a misdemeanor must not be so summarily dealt with, or it will be murder (3). Also the defendant in a civil suit, must not be killed for flying or escaping from arrest (4).

Sec. 3.—*Infanticide.*

Infanticide, or the criminal destruction of the fœtus *in utero*, or of the new-born child, might have been treated of in the previous section; but the importance of the subject to Coroners requires that it should be dwelt upon at greater length and with more particularity than would be appropriate to the heading, "General Remarks," and is therefore made the subject of a separate section.

Infanticide, medically speaking, contains two branches: 1. The criminal destruction of the fœtus *in utero*; 2. The murder of the child after birth. The latter branch is the only one which comes under the jurisdiction of Coroners, and alone requires notice in this work.

No *murder* can be committed of an infant in its mother's womb. It is not until actual birth that the child becomes "a life in being," so as to be embraced in the legal definition of murder (5).

Therefore, in considering the crime of infanticide in its second branch, the first question which presents itself is:

1. *When is a child born?*] A common test of live birth is the act of breathing; but a child may breathe during the

(1) Fost. C. L. 270, 271.
(2) 1 E. P. C. 297.
(3) Fost. C. L. 271.
(4) Fost. C. L. 271.
(5) 1 Hale, 433.

birth, and before the whole body is brought into the world, which would not be sufficient life to constitute it a life in being, and to make its destruction murder (1).

Again; a child may be wholly produced, and remain for some time without respiring, life being kept up from the fœtal circulation continuing, or from causes which appear to be involved in much obscurity (2). When a child is destroyed while remaining in this state, there are no certain medical signs by which it can be proved to have been living when maltreated (3); although some indirect evidence of the existence of life previous to respiration may be obtained from wounds and ecchymoses found on the body of the child (4). The child being seen to move or breathe, would of course be evidence of life (5).

Breathing is only *one* proof of life. Other proofs are admissible of life in a child before the establishment of respiration; and its destruction after being completely born in a living state, but before it has breathed, is murder (6).

Respiration is the *best* test of a child having been born alive; but in deciding whether or not it has respired, much skill is often necessary. Immersing the lungs in water—

(1) 5 C & P. 329. In these cases there is a very strong presumption against the probability of the child dying, unless through foul play, before being wholly born alive.—1 Beck, 496; Taylor, 332.

(2) Taylor, 326; 1 Beck, 448; see 6 C. & P. 349.

(3) Taylor, 324.

(4) 1 Beck, 448.

(5) Cases of this kind may be divided into two classes:—1. Where the child's life is merely a continuation of its fœtal existence, and is dependent on the life of its mother; and 2. Where the child's life is independent of that of its mother, yet there are no medical signs of its having been born alive to be discovered in the body after death. It seems, at least, doubtful if the destruction of a child coming under the first class would be murder. In *Rex v. Enock*, 5 C. & P. 539, Parke, J., said there must be an *independent* circulation in the child before it can be considered alive for the purpose of constituting its destruction murder. See also 9 C. & P. 754. And in *Reg. v. Christopher* (Dorset Lent Assizes, 1845) Erle, J., said the child must have an existence *distinct* and *independent* from the mother. But see 2 Moo. C C. 260.

(6) *Rex v. Brain*, 6 C. & P. 349; *Rex v. Sellis*, 7 C. & P. 850.

it being supposed that if they floated the child must have breathed—was, at one time, the usual test. It is now exploded; as air may have passed into the lungs by inflation, or they may have become permeated with air from decomposition. And even if respiration be proved, still it must be borne in mind that the child may have breathed during birth, before arriving at that stage of life when it may be the subject of murder (1). And on the other hand, children have occasionally lived for many hours, and even for days, without any signs of respiration being discoverable in their bodies after death (2).

Absence of the signs of respiration is no proof of natural dead birth; as the mother may cause herself to be delivered in a water-bath, or the mouth of the child may be covered in the act of birth.

If the child breathes and has an independent circulation of its own, it seems it is a "life in being," though the umbilical cord may not have been divided (3).

The presence of any marks of putrefaction *in utero* proves the child must have been born dead. The presence of marks of severe violence on *various parts* of the body, if possessing vital characters, renders it *probable* that the child was entirely born alive when the violence was inflicted (4). The presence of food in the stomach proves the child was entirely born alive (5).

2. *The Hydrostatic Test.*] Although employing this test as conclusive evidence of the child having breathed or not, is now exploded, yet when used by an intelligent physician, thoroughly acquainted with its real value, and who considers its result with other circumstances, it is a proper and im-

---

(1) This has been the case when the labour was long protracted after the waters have escaped, and the infant slow in descending through the passages.

(2) Taylor, 325, 327.

(3) 7 C. & P. 814; 9 C. & P. 25.

(4) Taylor, 352.

(5) Taylor, 358.

portant test to employ in many cases of infanticide. The mode of performing it will be found described in chapter VII., *post.*

A person using the hydrostatic test in cases of alleged infanticide, should remember that the lungs floating is not *a proof* that the child has been *born alive,* nor their sinking *a proof* that it was *born dead.* At most it can only prove the child has *breathed* or not. The fact of living or dead birth, has, strictly speaking, no relation to the employment of this test (1). The lungs may sink from disease (2); or they may sink, although the child has lived for hours and even for days (3): and they may float from putrefaction, either after the child is still-born, or after death *in utero* previous to its birth, or from artificial inflation (4); or from respiration before complete birth (5).

3. *Of the Uterine Age of a Child.*] In cases of premature birth, it is to be noticed as tending to narrow the difficulty of deciding the question of living production, that under the fifth month the general opinion is that no fœtus can be born alive; from the fifth to the seventh it may be born alive, but cannot maintain existence; and at the seventh it may be reared.

The following is a summary of the principal facts upon which an opinion respecting the uterine age of a child may be based, taken from Taylor's *Medical Jurisprudence*:

(*a*) At *six months*—Length, from nine to ten inches; weight, one to two pounds; eyelids, agglutinated; pupils, closed by membranæ pupillares; testicles, not apparent in the male.

(*b*) At *seven months*—Length, from thirteen to fourteen inches; weight, three to four pounds; eyelids, not adherent;

---

(1) Taylor, 325.
(2) Taylor, 325.
(3) Taylor, 327.
(4) Taylor, 330.
(5) Taylor, 339.

membranæ pupillares, disappearing; nails, imperfectly developed; testicles, not apparent in the male.

(*c*) At *eight months*—Length, from fourteen to sixteen inches; weight, from four to five pounds; membranæ pupillares, absent; nails, perfectly developed, and reaching to the ends of the fingers; testicles in the inguinal canal.

(*d*) At *nine months*—Length, from sixteen to twenty-one inches; weight, from five to nine pounds; membranæ pupillares, absent; head well covered with fine hair; testicles in the scrotum; skin pale; features perfect; these and the body are *well developed*, even when the length and weight of the child are much less than those above assigned.

(*e*) The point of insertion of the umbilical cord, with respect to the length of the body, affords no certain evidence of the degree of maturity.

There are no certain signs by which to determine how long a child has survived birth for the first twenty-four hours (1).

4. *Monstrosities.*] Some persons have the notion that monstrosities may be destroyed; but this is not correct. If destroyed under an impression of this kind, the want of malice might reduce the act below murder, although it would amount at least to manslaughter.

5. *Legal points.*] The onus of proving the child was born alive rests on the prosecution, as the law humanely presumes that every new-born infant is born dead; but if proved to have been born alive, further proof shewing its capacity to live is not necessary, for even if a want of viability or capacity to live be proved, its destruction would still be murder (2).

If a child is injured before birth, and dies from the injury *after* birth, this would be murder (3); but if injured when

---

(1) Taylor, 854. (2) *Reg.* v. *West*, Nottingham Lent Assizes, 1848.

(3) 3 Inst. 50; 1 Bla. Com. 129; Hawk. P. C. b. 1, ch. 31, s. 16.

partly born, and it dies in consequence before bei. born, the offence would not amount to murder (1).

Where there is wanton exposure of an infant withou intent to produce death, but with the expectation of shiftin its support upon some third person, and death ensues, it is manslaughter (2).

The better opinion seems to be, that the wilful prevention of respiration is murder, although no case to the point has yet been decided.

Causing a child to be born before the proper time, by reason of which it afterwards dies, is murder (3).

Causing the death of a child by giving it spirituous liquors in a quantity unfit for its tender age, is manslaughter (4).

The omission of a self-delivered woman to tie the umbilical cord, in consequence of which her child dies, is not murder, as her distress and pain may cause this neglect, or she may not be aware of the necessity for applying a ligature to the cord, or she may become insensible after delivery. But *wilfully* neglecting to perform this office for the child, if satisfactorily proved, would be murder.

As before stated (5), if a man advise a woman to kill her child so soon as it is born, and she do so in pursuance of such advice, he is an accessory to the murder, though no murder could have been committed at the time of the advice (6).

In a case of infanticide, the Coroner's jury should not find as to the concealment of birth, if any there be; for the concealment, under the present law, has no connection with the cause of death, to inquire of which is the purpose of the Coroner's inquest. An inquisition finding a concealment

---

(1) 6 C. & P. 349.
(2) Wharton & Stillé, 790.
(3) 1 Russ. 485, n. 1.
(4) 3 C. & P. 210.
(5) Page 32.
(6) Hawk. P. C. ch. 29, s. 18; Dyer, 168.

will neither put the party upon her trial, nor justify the Coroner in committing her, which can only be done by a magistrate's warrant for the misdemeanor (1).

6. *Cautions.*] A child may die from the cord becoming twisted round its neck *in utero*, before parturition. This cause of death sometimes gives rise to an idea that the child was strangled (2).

If death from suffocation is suspected, the mouth and fauces should be examined for foreign substances, which might give some clue to the means employed to produce it. Any peculiar smell about the body should be noted, in order to see if poisonous vapours were used to suffocate the child. In these cases it must be remembered that suffocation may arise from accident or unintentional neglect, particularly if the mother is delivered when alone, and is much distressed, or faints. Care should be taken to distinguish in these cases between means used simply to *conceal the birth*, and means used to *destroy the child*.

If the body is found in water, care should be taken to ascertain if the child was drowned, or killed before being placed in the water. The number of verdicts of "Found drowned" might doubtless be reduced by a proper attention to this caution.

The pains of labour may be mistaken for other sensations, and the child in consequence be born under circumstances which would inevitably cause its loss without any blame attaching to the mother. A careful examination of the ends of the cord, to see if it was cut or torn asunder, may afford important evidence in these cases. A lens should be used for the purpose, as the torn ends have sometimes been found nearly as sharp-edged and flat as if cut (3).

---

(1) Jer. O. C. 158.
(2) Taylor, 357.
(3) Med. Gaz. vol. xlviii. p. 985.

Severe injuries are sometimes unintentionally inflicted on infants suddenly born, while the mother is standing, sitting, or on her knees (1).

In deaths from starvation, mere neglect or imprudence, without actual malice, will not make them cases of infanticide.

Fractures of the skull, with extravasation, sometimes occur from natural causes during parturition, and may lead to a suspicion of criminal violence. These fractures and extravasations are generally of very slight extent, while those caused by criminal violence are commonly much more severe (2).

Tumours on the head, containing blood, arising from the same causes, sometimes lead to a suspicion of violence (3).

Severe wounds are sometimes accidentally inflicted upon children by clumsy attempts to sever the navel-string. In such cases the string is generally found cut (4).

Attempts innocently made by the female to aid her delivery, sometimes cause injuries to the child's body (5).

7. *Evidence.*] The consideration of evidence in general is reserved for another chapter (6).

A few points relating to infanticide in particular will here be noticed.

Mere appearances of violence on the child's body are not sufficient of themselves. The evidence must go further, and show intentional murder.

In order to connect the murdered child with the mother, sometimes an examination of the accused is necessary. Unless this takes place within twelve or fifteen days from delivery, no satisfactory evidence can in general be obtained (7).

---

(1) Taylor, 368.
(2) Taylor, 367.
(3) Taylor, 366
(4) Taylor, 365.
(5) Taylor, 372.
(6) See Chap. XI. *post.*
(7) Taylor, 382.

Whether a suspected female can be forced to furnish evidence against herself by submitting to an examination, seems doubtful. The spirit of our laws is opposed to such compulsory evidence.

The practice of frightening the accused into submission, if ever justifiable, is certainly not so before an examination is pronounced necessary by the Coroner. And a refusal to submit to such an examination should hardly be considered as implying guilt; for some innocent women, of delicate feelings, might naturally prefer lying under an imputation of crime, to submitting to a proceeding so revolting to them.

The concealment of birth is now no presumptive evidence of infanticide. In most cases of this nature the unfortunate woman has every reason to attempt concealment; and to imply guilt from conduct the innocent motives for which can be so easily understood, is shocking to human nature.

From the murder of bastard children by the mother being a crime difficult to be proved, at one time a special legislative provision was enacted for its detection (1), which made concealment of the birth almost conclusive evidence of the child's murder. But the severity of the statute (2) rendered its provisions fruitless, since few juries could be found willing to convict the unfortunate objects of accusation on such objectionable evidence, and it was repealed in England by 43 Geo. III. ch. 58. In Canada, this Act was repealed by Provincial Statutes now embodied in 32-33 Vic. ch. 20, s. 62; and the trial of women charged with the murder of their bastard children placed on the same footing as to the rules of evidence and presumptions as other trials for murder.

---

(1) 21 Jac. 1, ch. 27

(2) The reader will remember the story of Sir Walter Scott's, called "The Heart of Mid-Lothian," which is founded on a trial under a similar enactment in Scotland.

Sec. 4.—*Manslaughter.*

1. *Definition.*] Manslaughter is defined to be the unlawful killing of another without malice, either express or implied; and may be either voluntary, upon a sudden heat, or involuntary, ensuing from the commission of some unlawful act, or from the pursuit of some lawful act criminally or improperly performed (1). The main distinction between manslaughter and murder is the absence of "malice aforethought" (2).

2. *Practical remarks.*] All homicide is presumed to be malicious until the contrary is proved (3).

No insult by words or contemptuous actions or gestures, unless accompanied by some act indicative of actual and immediate violence, nor trespasses against lands or goods, will reduce the offence of killing to manslaughter where a malicious intention is manifested by the use of deadly weapons or other circumstances of the case (4). When no such malice accompanies the act, and the party provoked give the other a box on the ear or stroke with a stick or other weapon, not likely to kill, and death unfortunately ensues, it will be only manslaughter (5). But if the death result from a violent and unlawful restraint of personal liberty (6), or from the first transport of passion, arising from the detection by the husband of the adulterer in the act (7), the killing is reduced to manslaughter. So if one insults another, and gets a blow for his language, which he returns, and a scuffle ensues, and the party insulting is killed, it is manslaughter only, for his blow to the person insulted is considered a new provocation, on the principle that the

---

(1) 4 Bla. Com. 191.

(2) A distinction as venerable as the Mosaic Law. See Num. xxxv. 15 and following verses.

(3) 1 E. P. C. 224.

(4) Jer O. C. 185; Moir's case, Rosc. C. E. 717.

(5) Fost. 291.

(6) 1 E. P. C. 233.

(7) 1 H. P. C. 486.

second blow makes the affray, and the conflict a sudden, unpremeditated falling out (1). So an assault upon a man's person, accompanied with circumstances of great violence or insolence, which would reasonably cause a sudden transport of passion and heat of blood, will make the killing only manslaughter (2). Provocation of a slight kind will extenuate the guilt of homicide, where the party killing does not act with cruelty or use dangerous instruments (3); but if the instrument used is such that a rational man would conclude death would follow, it is reasonable for the jury to find death was intended (4).

Generally, all fighting, wrestling or other contests, *in anger*, are unlawful, and if death result, it is manslaughter at least (5).

Killing one who endeavours to commit a *felony* by force is justifiable homicide, if the intent to commit such crime clearly appears (6).

Lawful sports must be indulged in with due caution, according to their nature. For instance, death arising from accident, through shooting at a target placed in a position dangerous to persons passing along highways or other places commonly used, would probably be manslaughter (7).

In all cases of homicide upon provocation, if sufficient time has elapsed for the passion to cool and reason to regain its propriety, the killing is then deliberate, and amounts to murder (8).

Sec. 5.—*Excusable Homicide.*

There are two kinds of excusable homicide: homicide *per infortunium*, by misadventure, and homicide *se et sua de-*

---

(1) 1 Hale, 455.
(2) 1 Russ. 581.
(3) Fost. 291.
(4) 2 Lew. 225.
(5) 9 C. & P. 359.
(6) 1 H. P. C. 484; Jer. 192.
(7) Arch. C. P. 510.
(8) Fost. Cr. Law, 296. See also the remarks under the head of "Murder," sec. 2.

fendendo, in self-defence. Excusable homicide does not amount to felony, although some fault attaches upon the party by whom it is committed. Before 9 Geo. IV. ch. 31, s. 10, forfeiture of goods was a punishment for this offence; but now the party is entitled to be set free, without punishment or forfeiture.

I.—HOMICIDE PER INFORTUNIUM.

1. *Definition.*] Homicide *per infortunium,* or by misadventure, is where a man doing a lawful act with proper caution, and in a proper manner, without any intention of hurt, unfortunately kills another by mere accident or misadventure (1).

2. *Practical Remarks.*] In illustration of homicide by misadventure, the following may be considered: where the head of an axe accidentally flies off, while one is chopping, and kills a stander-by; when a person shooting at game, or at a mark, with due caution, undesignedly kills another; when a parent, moderately correcting his child, or a master his apprentice or scholar, and happens to occasion death. In such cases the death is only misadventure.

If poison is laid for vermin, and a person takes it and is killed, if it was laid in such a manner or place as to be mistaken for food, the better opinion seems to be, that it is manslaughter; but if laid with a proper degree of caution as to manner and place, it is misadventure only (2).

It seems killing a person by drawing the trigger of a gun in sport, supposing it to be unloaded, is homicide by misadventure, if the gun was tried with the ramrod, and the usual precautions taken to ascertain it was not loaded (3), or if there were reasonable grounds to believe that it was not (4).

---

(1) 4 Bla. Com. 182.

(2) 1 H. P. C. 431; Jer. 217.

(3) Jer. 218; 1 Russ. 658; Impey, O. C. 508.

(4) Fost. 265; 1 Russ. 659.

2.—HOMICIDE SE ET SUA DEFENDENDO.

1. *Definition.*] Homicide in self-defence is a kind of homicide committed in defence of one's person or property, or from unavoidable necessity, upon sudden affray, and is considered by the law in some measure blamable and barely excusable.

2. *Practical Remarks.*] Where a man is assaulted in the course of a sudden brawl or quarrel, and before a mortal stroke given, he declines any further combat, he may protect himself by killing the person who assaults him if such an act be necessary in order to avoid immediate death (1).

This kind of homicide is often barely distinguishable from manslaughter. The true criterion between them is this: when both parties are actually combating at the time the mortal stroke is given, the slayer is guilty of manslaughter; but if the slayer has not begun to fight, or, having begun, endeavours to decline any further struggle, and afterwards, being closely pressed by his antagonist, kills him to avoid his own destruction, this is homicide, excusable by self-defence (2).

To make the plea of self-defence good, it must appear that the slayer had no other possible or at least probable means of escaping from his assailant (3).

The plea of self-defence extends to excusing masters and servants, parents and children, husbands and wives, killing assailants in the necessary defence of each other (4).

In defence of a man's house, the owner or his family may kill a trespasser, who forcibly tries to dispossess him, and this without retreating to avoid the trespasser; but in forcible misdemeanors, such as trespass to goods, killing is not excusable (5).

---

(1) 1 Russ 661. (2) 4 Bla. Com. 184; Fost. 277.
(3) Impey, O. C. 506; Jer. 220. (4) 1 Hale, 484. (5) Jer. 222.

Killing from unavoidable necessity takes place in cases such as the following: Two persons being shipwrecked, got on the same plank, which, proving unable to save them both, one thrust the other from it, whereby he was drowned. That principle of self-preservation which prompts every man to save his own life in preference to that of another, where one must inevitably perish, excuses the homicide in such cases (1).

SEC. 6.—*Justifiable Homicide.*

1. *Definition.*] This kind of homicide is such as the law requires, or permits to be done; and is not only justifiable in all cases, but in some commendable. It is of three kinds. First, homicide in the execution of the law; second, homicide for the advancement of public justice; third, homicide in the just defence of property, or for the prevention of some atrocious crime which cannot otherwise be avoided. In all these cases the slayer is not blamable, and is entitled to his acquittal and discharge.

2. *Practical Remarks.*] 1. Killing in execution of the law must be done when, and in the manner, the law requires it. Therefore, wantonly to kill the greatest of malefactors is murder (2). Or, if an officer, whose duty it is to execute a criminal, behead the party when he ought to have hanged him, it is murder (3), unless, perhaps, when he acts contrary to the judgment upon a warrant from the Crown (4).

2. Killing in advancement of public justice can only be done when there is an apparent necessity for it: without the necessity it is not justifiable (5). If an officer of justice or other person is restricted in the legal execution of his

---

(1) 4 Bla. Com. 186. (2) 1 H. P. C. 497.
(3) 1 Hale, 433, 501; 2 Hale, 411; 4 Bla. Com. 179.
(4) Fost. 268; 4 Bla. Com. 405. (5) 4 Bla. Com. 180.

duty, he may repel force by force (1). But he must not kill after the resistance has ceased (2). And if the party merely *flies* to avoid arrest, the officer will not be justified in killing him unless he is a *felon*, and cannot otherwise be overtaken. This distinction is, therefore, to be noticed. If an officer or private person be *resisted* in the legal execution of his duty *by any one*, and there is an apparent necessity, he is justified in killing the person so resisting him; but if he is legally endeavouring to arrest a man, and he merely *flies* to avoid that arrest, he will not be justified in killing the person unless he is a *felon*, or has committed treason, or has given a dangerous wound. Killing a person who flies from arrest for a misdemeanor, or under civil process, would be murder or manslaughter, according to the circumstances of the case (3).

In the case of a riot (4), if the officers (and those commanded to assist them), endeavouring at the proper time (5) to disperse, seize or apprehend any of the persons committing the riot, happen to kill any such persons, they are justified and free from all blame (6). They would be justified also by the common law (7).

If a gaoler or his officer is assaulted by a prisoner, in gaol or going to gaol, or by others in his behalf, provided the assault is made with a view of the prisoner's escaping, he will be justified in killing the assailant, whether a prisoner in civil or criminal suits, and this without first retreating (8).

3. Homicide in defence of property, &c., is justifiable when the offence endeavoured to be committed amounts to

---

(1) 1 H. P. C. 494; 2 Ibid. Jer. 181. (2) 1 E. P. C. 297.

(3) Fost. 271; Hale, 481; Jer. 228.

(4) To constitute a riot, twelve or more persons must be unlawfully, riotously, and tumultuously assembled together, to the disturbance of the public peace.—See 31 Vic. ch. 70.

(5) *i. e.*, an hour after the Riot Act has been read. (6) 31 Vic. ch. 70.

(7) 1 H. P. C, 495; 1 E. P. C. 304. (8) Fost. 321; 1 Hale, 481, 496.

felony, and force is used. A mere endeavour to beat another, or to take his goods merely as a trespasser, would not reduce the killing below manslaughter (1). There must be a plain manifestation of a felonious intent (2).

The servants and other members of the man's family whose person or property is thus attacked, and even strangers present at the time, are also justified in killing the felon (3).

---

(1) 1 Hale, 485, 486.

(2) 1 Russ. 669.

(3) 1 H. P. C. 481, 484; Fost. 374.

CHAPTER IV.

OF POISONS.

Classification of Poisons.

The following classification and symptoms have been compiled from Dr. Taylor's work on *Poisons*—the best on the subject :

IRRITANTS.

Mineral ..	Non-metallic ..	Acids, Sulphuric.	
		Metalloids, Phosphorus.	
	Metallic	Alkalic compounds, Potash.	
		Heavy metals and compounds	(Arsenic).

Vegetable, Savin.
Animal, Cantharides.

NEUROTICS.

Cerebral, Morphine.
Spinal, Strychnine.
Cerebro-spinal, Coniine.

Irritant poisons occasion violent vomiting and purging, either preceded, accompanied or followed by intense pain in the abdomen, commencing in the region of the stomach. Effects are chiefly manifested by inflammation of the stomach and intestines. Many poisons of this class possess strong corrosive properties, and when swallowed produce an acrid or burning taste, extending from the mouth down the œsophagus to the stomach. Others possess no corrosive action, and are called pure irritants. These produce their characteristic symptoms less rapidly than those of the former class, the effects not becoming visible till after the lapse of half an hour from the act of swallowing, unless in some exceptional cases.

Neurotic poisons act chiefly on the brain and spinal marrow; the *cerebrals*, acting principally on the brain, producing stupor and insensibility, without convulsions; the *spinals*, acting on the spinal marrow, producing violent convulsions, sometimes of the tetanic kind, not necessarily attended by loss of sensibility or consciousness, and rarely inducing narcotism; the *cerebro-spinal*, acting both on the brain and spinal marrow, causing delirium, convulsions, coma and paralysis. The cerebral poisons have no acrid taste, and rarely give rise to vomiting or diarrhœa, and they do not irritate or inflame the viscera. Some of the irritant poisons will, however, occasionally produce narcotic effects, as has been observed with arsenic, while opium may sometimes produce pain and vomiting, with an absence of the usual symptoms of cerebral disturbance. Several of the cerebro-spinals, when taken in the form of roots or leaves, often have a compound action, producing their ordinary effects together with those of irritant poisons.

Irritant Poisons.

MINERAL IRRITANTS.

Sulphuric acid.—Cases generally referable to suicide or accident. The symptoms which commence immediately are violent burning pain, extending through the throat and gullet to the stomach; violent retching or vomiting, the latter accompanied by the discharge of shreds of tough mucus and of a liquid of a dark coffee-brown colour, mixed or streaked with blood; mouth excoriated, tongue and lining membrane white and swollen, hence difficulty in breathing; a thick, viscid phlegm is formed, rendering speaking and swallowing very difficult; abdomen distended and painful; any of the acid getting on to the lips or neck produces brown spots; any of the acid itself, or of the matter first vomited, falling on coloured clothes, produces yellow or red stains, and destroys the texture of the stuff; great exhaustion and general weakness; pulse quick and small; skin cold or clammy; great thirst, and obstinate constipation.

Nitric acid.—The symptoms are very similar to the above. Gaseous eructations are produced; the vomited matter has a peculiar smell; and the membrane of the mouth, &c., is at first white, becoming gradually yellow or brown. Stains produced by the acid are generally yellow.

Hydrochloric acid is rarely used as a poison. The symptoms are very similar to those above described.

Oxalic acid, although a vegetable substance, may be ranked with the preceding acids. Cases of poisoning by this acid are generally referable to suicide or accident. It produces a hot, burning taste, and causes vomiting almost immediately, unless taken in a diluted form; the vomited matters have a greenish brown, almost black appearance; burning pain in the stomach, with tenderness of the abdomen, followed by cold, clammy perspiration, and convulsions; pain is sometimes absent: there is in general an entire prostration of strength; unconsciousness of surrounding objects, and a kind of stupor; legs sometimes drawn up; pulse small, irregular, and scarcely perceptible; the lining membrane of the mouth, &c., is commonly white and softened; but often coated with the dark brown mucous matter discharged from the stomach.

Phosphorus.—The symptoms are slow in appearing: they may not occur for some hours or even days. A disagreeable taste resembling garlic is peculiar to phosphorus; the breath has a garlic odour; an acrid burning sensation in the throat; intense thirst; severe pain and heat with a pricking sensation in the stomach, followed by distension of the abdomen; nausea and vomiting continuing until death; the vomited matters are dark-coloured, emit the odour of garlic, and white vapours, and sometimes appear phosphorescent in the dark; purging is often caused, and the motions are luminous in the dark. Pulse small, frequent, prostration of strength, and other symptoms of collapse.

Alkalies.—These may be taken by accident, in the form of pearlash or soap-lees. They produce an acrid, caustic taste, and, if strong, soften and corrode the lining membranes; burning heat in the throat, extending down the gullet to the pit of the stomach; when vomiting occurs, the vomited matters are sometimes mixed with blood of a dark brown colour, and portions of the mucous membrane; purging, with severe pain in the abdomen, resembling colic; the lips, tongue and throat soon become swollen, soft and red.

Ammonia and its carbonate produce symptoms similar to the above.

Arsenic.—The symptoms may commence within a few minutes of the act of swallowing, or may be delayed for several hours; in general they commence within an hour; faintness, depression and nausea, with intense burning pain in the region of the stomach, increased by pressure; the pain in the abdomen becomes more and more severe, and there is violent vomiting of a brown, turbid matter, mixed with mucus, and sometimes streaked with blood; purging, more or less violent, accompanied by severe cramps in the calves of the legs; dryness and burning heat in the throat, with intense thirst; pulse small, irregular, scarcely perceptible; skin sometimes hot, at others cold; great restlessness, and painful respiration; before death, coma, paralysis and tetanic convulsions or spasms in the muscles of the extremities. The symptoms are generally continuous, but sometimes there are intermissions. The pain, which is compared to a burning coal, is sometimes absent, and there may be neither vomiting nor purging, although the former is seldom wanting. The intense thirst is sometimes absent, and occasionally the symptoms almost resemble those of a narcotic poison. In cases of recovery from the first effects, or of poisoning by repeated small doses, there will be inflammation of the conjunctiva, suffusion of the eyes, and intolerance of light. A peculiar eruption is often produced, resembling nettle-rash. Local paralysis, preceded by numbness or tingling of the fingers and toes, are of frequent occurrence. Salivation, strangury, exfoliation of the cuticle and skin of the tongue, with falling off of the hair, fœtor of the breath and emaciation, are all symptoms of chronic poisoning.

Chloride of mercury or corrosive sublimate.—The symptoms come on immediately, or after a few minutes, the poison exerting a chemical or corrosive action on the animal membranes. A strong metallic taste is perceived in the mouth; a sense of constriction of the throat during the act of swallowing, amounting almost to choking, and a burning heat in the throat, extending to the stomach; shortly a violent pain is felt in this organ, and over the whole abdomen, increased by pressure; frequent vomiting of long, stringy masses of white mucus, mixed with blood, together with profuse purging, the evacuations being of a mucous character, and sometimes streaked with blood; pulse small, frequent and irregular; tongue white and shrivelled; skin cold and clammy; respiration difficult; and death is commonly preceded by syncope, convulsions and general insensibility; urine often suppressed; salivation is sometimes produced in a few hours, but more generally only after the lapse of some days, if the patient survives so long; sometimes the mucous membranes of the mouth are uninjured, and pain on pressure is occasionally absent. When taken in small doses at intervals, colicky pains, nausea, vomiting and general uneasiness are produced; the salivary glands become painful, inflamed and ulcerated, the tongue and gums red and swollen, and the breath has a peculiarly offensive odour; difficulty in swallowing and breathing. Salivation often occurs, but this may be produced in some persons by very small doses of calomel. Calomel occasionally acts as a poison, even in small doses, apparently from the idiosyncrasy of the individual. Excessive salivation and gangrene of the salivary glands may be produced.

Salts of Lead.—Acetate and carbonate of lead produce colic and constipation of the bowels; the vomiting is commonly not very violent; pain in the mouth, throat and stomach are commonly observed; sometimes dragging pains in the loins, cramp and paralysis of the lower extremities, are produced. The symptoms often remain for a long time, returning again and again. The carbonate is not so poisonous as the acetate, requiring large doses to produce any very serious effect; but when swallowed in small quantities for a length of time, it produces the usual symptoms of lead poisoning (painter's colic). The pain in the stomach is generally relieved by pressure, and has intermissions. If any fæces are passed, they are usually of a dark colour. A peculiarly well marked character in cases of poisoning by lead, especially when the poison has been gradually absorbed during a considerable period, is a clearly defined blue line round the gums, where they join the teeth. Occasionally purging is produced, and sometimes the symptoms reappear after the patient has apparently recovered. Chronic poisoning by lead may occur among persons exposed to the powder of many preparations of that metal, especially white lead, and may also be caused to a certain extent by the continued use of some hair-dyes. Even handling articles containing lead may, under some circumstances, produce paralysis. Chronic poisoning may also be caused by the use of certain waters, when kept in leaden cisterns.

Copper.—Poisoning by the sulphate or acetate of copper (blue vitriol and verdigris) is not common, owing to the colour and strong taste of these salts; but serious effects may be produced by the use of pickles and other culinary preparations made in copper vessels. When a considerable quantity of either of the above salts has been taken, the following symptoms are usually observed:—Metallic taste; constriction of the throat; griping pains in the stomach and bowels; pain in the abdomen, increased on pressure; increased flow of saliva; purging and vomiting, the vomited matter being generally of a bluish or greenish colour. When the poison is absorbed, the breathing becomes hurried and difficult; quick pulse; weakness; thirst; coldness and paralysis of the limbs; headache; stupor and convulsions. A green paint made of the oxychloride of copper (Brunswick green) has sometimes caused death when taken into the stomach; and articles of food containing salt, if left in copper vessels, are apt to become injurious. When chronic poisoning ensues from the after effects of a large quantity of some preparation of copper, or from the gradual assimilation of small quantities, excessive irritability of the alimentary canal is established, with tenderness of the abdomen, and colicky pains resembling dysentery; frequent tendency to evacuate and to vomit; loss of appetite; prostration and paralysis.

Antimony.—Although several of the preparations of antimony, especially tartar-emetic, are largely used in medicine, and occasionally in large quantities, they may at all times, and under peculiar circumstances, act as poisons; children, for instance, having been frequently killed by comparatively small doses of tartar-emetic. When a large quantity has been swallowed a metallic taste is noticed, followed in a few minutes by violent vomiting; pain in the stomach and bowels; purging, and burning heat and choking in the throat; sometimes great thirst and flow of saliva; cramps in the arms and legs; sometimes severe tetanic spasms; coldness of the surface; clammy perspiration; congested state of the head and face; extreme depression; loss of muscular power; pulse small and feeble or barely perceptible; respiration short and painful; lips and face livid; eyes sunk; loss of voice; incapacity for exertion; wandering or delirium, with loss of consciousness. These symptoms do not all occur together: several may be entirely absent, even the vomiting and purging. Generally the quantity of urine is increased. Persons may recover after taking a large dose of tartar-emetic; but if subjected to repeated doses during recovery, fatal results may ensue. A peculiar eruption, resembling small-pox, is sometimes observed. When the poison has been administered in small and repeated doses, chronic poisoning is produced, which is principally characterized by nausea, vomiting, watery purging, loss of voice and strength; great depression; coldness of the skin, and clammy perspiration.

Zinc.—Sulphate of zinc in an overdose produces pain in the abdomen, and violent vomiting coming on almost immediately, and followed by purging. Death may result from the exhaustion caused by excessive vomiting. Chloride of zinc produces similar symptoms; but acts also as a corrosive, destroying the membranes and producing frothing.

Iron.—Green vitriol, or copperas, is sometimes used as an abortive, and may produce violent pain, vomiting and purging, sufficient to cause death.

Tin.—Chloride of tin, dyer's salts, may be accidentally swallowed.

Nitrobenzole (essence of mirbane).—This substance, when swallowed as a liquid or inhaled as vapour, acts as a violent poison, in its effects very much like prussic acid, but not nearly so rapid. A blue coloration of the skin, and more especially of the lips and nails, is very characteristic, resembling Asiatic cholera.

The essence of mirbane resembles oil of bitter almonds in its smell, and is sometimes used instead of it in scents, soaps, &c.

Aniline acts very much in the same way as nitrobenzole, the blue colour strongly marked. Inhalation of the vapour causes symptoms like intoxication. The aniline dyes are in many if not all cases more or less poisonous, partly from the dyes themselves, and partly from their often containing arsenic, used during their preparation.

Carbolic acid, when swallowed, causes a hot, burning sensation, extending from the mouth to the stomach. The lining membrane of the mouth is whitened and hardened. There is severe pain in the stomach, with vomiting of a frothy mucus. Skin cold and clammy; lips, eyelids and ears livid; pupils of the eyes contracted and insensible to light. The breath and the air of the room smell strongly of carbolic acid (tarry odour).

VEGETABLE AND ANIMAL IRRITANTS.

Savin is often used as an abortive, as from the violent pain in the abdomen, vomiting and strangury which it produces, it may sometimes have that effect. Purging and salivation are sometimes observed.

Colchicum, which has been used intentionally as a poison, produces burning pain in the gullet and stomach; violent vomiting, and occasionally violent bilious purging.

Cantharides, which is sometimes used as an abortive or as an aphrodisiac, produces burning in the throat, with difficulty in swallowing; violent pain in the abdomen; nausea, and vomiting of bloody mucus; great thirst and dryness of the throat, but in some cases salivation; incessant desire to void urine, which becomes albuminous. Purging is not always observed. The matters discharged are mixed with blood and mucus. After a time there is often severe priapism, and the genital organs are swollen and inflamed. Owing to the popular idea of its aphrodisiac properties, this substance is sometimes administered on sweetmeats, such as lozenges. The shining particles of the insect are easily recognizable under the microscope.

NEUROTIC POISONS.

These poisons affect principally the brain, spinal m. and the nervous system. They possess no corrosive properties; produce no local chemical action; rarely give ri. to vomiting or purging, and do not commonly leave any marked appearances in the stomach and bowels. Fulness of the vessels of the brain and its membranes is sometimes observed, as also a redness of the mucous membrane of the stomach, in cases of poisoning by prussic acid.

CEREBRAL.

Opium. Laudanum.—The symptoms are giddiness, drowsiness, tendency to sleep; stupor, succeeded by perfect insensibility. When in this state the patient may be roused, but not at a later stage, when coma has supervened with stertorous breathing. The pulse is at first small, quick and irregular; the respiration hurried; but later the pulse is slow and full; the breathing slow and stertorous. The expression of the countenance is placid, pale and ghastly; the eyes heavy, and the lips livid; vomiting and purging are sometimes observed; convulsions are sometimes produced, especially in children; and all secretions are suspended, except by the skin, which is often bathed in perspiration. The symptoms usually commence in from half an hour to an hour, but sometimes in a few minutes. All the preparations of opium and of poppies, as well as morphia, act much in the same way; the latter substance producing, in addition, excessive itching of the skin, followed by an eruption, and frequently causing convulsions.

Prussic acid.—The symptoms occasioned by a large dose of this acid may occur almost instantaneously, and are rarely delayed beyond one or two minutes. Hence the first symptoms are seldom seen, but when the patient is examined at the above period, he is found perfectly insensible; eyes fixed, prominent and glistening, pupils dilated and unaffected by light; limbs flaccid; jaws fixed; frothing at the mouth; skin cold and covered with clammy perspiration; convulsive respiration at long intervals; pulse imperceptible; and involuntary evacuations are occasionally passed. The respiration is slow, deep, gasping, and sometimes heaving, sobbing and convulsive. When a small quantity has been swallowed, the patient first experiences pain in the head, with confusion of intellect; giddiness, nausea; a quick pulse; loss of muscular power; shortness of breath and palpitation. There is generally frothing at the mouth, with a bloated appearance of the face, and prominence of the eyes.

Oil of bitter almonds, bitter almond water, laurel water, and cyanide of potassium may all produce effects similar to those caused by prussic acid. Owing to the extensive use of the last named salt by photographers, many serious accidents have happened. The kernels of peach, apricot and cherry stones may also produce similar symptoms if eaten in quantity.

Alcohol, when swallowed as raw spirits or high wines, may act as a poison. Death may be produced almost instantaneously, or the ordinary symptoms of intoxication may come on after a few minutes, ending in insensibility and convulsions, which latter are often absent. With diluted alcohol excitement may be produced before stupor, but with concentrated, profound coma may be induced in a few minutes.

Tobacco, when swallowed in a solid form or as an infusion, may produce faintness, nausea, vomiting, giddiness, delirium, loss of power in the limbs, relaxation of the muscular system, trembling, complete prostration of strength, coldness of the surface, with cold, clammy perspiration; convulsive movements; paralysis and death. Sometimes there is purging, with violent pain in the abdomen; sometimes a sense of sinking or depression in the region of the heart; dilatation of the pupils; dimness of sight, with confusion of ideas; weak pulse and difficulty of breathing are also observed. The poisonous principle of tobacco (nicotine) will cause death with almost the same rapidity as prussic acid, and with very similar symptoms.

SPINAL POISONS.

These poisons do not act on the brain, but on the spinal marrow, producing violent convulsions and rigidity of the muscles, resembling tetanus. The most remarkable among them is nux vomica, and the alkaloid strychnine which is contained in the berries.

Strychnine.—The taste of this substance is intensely bitter, and at an interval of time varying from a few minutes to one hour or more, the person who has taken it is seized with a feeling of suffocation and great difficulty of breathing. The head and limbs are jerked; the whole frame shudders and trembles; tetanic convulsions then suddenly commence; the limbs are stretched out, the hands clenched, the head is bent backwards, and the body assumes a bow-like form, supported on the head and feet (opisthotonos); the soles of the feet are curved; the abdomen hard and tense; the chest spasmodically fixed, so that respiration seems arrested; the eyeballs prominent and staring; the lips livid; a peculiar sardonic grin is noticed on the features. Between the paroxysms the intellect is perfectly clear; but there may be loss of consciousness before death. The fits are intermittent, whereby poisoning by strychnine is distinguished from tetanus; moreover, the symptoms come on suddenly, almost without warning. The attacks subside after a few minutes, but return again rapidly, and may be induced by very slight causes. The person generally dies within two hours, often in less than half an hour. The rigidity of the body and arched position of the feet often remain after death. Half a grain may be considered as a fatal dose.

But few of the other spinal poisons have been used for felonious purposes, but accidents have not unfrequently happened from the accidental use of the roots or leaves of certain plants. The following may be mentioned as occurring in this country:

Cicuta maculata, musquash root, beaver poison.—The roots of this plant are sometimes mistaken for parsnips. The symptoms are giddiness; dimness of sight; headache, and difficulty of breathing; burning pain in the stomach, with vomiting, and often convulsions preceding death.

CEREBRO-SPINAL.

Conium maculatum (naturalized) varies in its effects, producing sometimes stupor, coma and slight convulsions; at others paralysis of the muscular system. The first effects are like intoxication.

Æthusa cynapium (naturalized).—The roots may be mistaken for turnips, and produce symptoms resembling those of conium.

Sium lineare is a common plant in this country, and would probably produce similar symptoms.

Aconitum napellus, being often grown as a garden plant, may occasionally give rise to accidents. Numbness and tingling of the mouth and throat; the same feeling in the limbs; giddiness; loss of power; frothing; severe pain in the abdomen, followed by vomiting and purging, are the most common symptoms. Sometimes the patient is completely paralyzed, at others there is dimness of sight, and cerebral symptoms. The root is sometimes mistaken for horse radish, and the medicinal tincture may be taken by accident.

Datura stramonium (partly naturalized).—The seeds of this common plant are exceedingly poisonous, and often produce furious delirium, and, after a time, insensibility, which may terminate in death.

CHAPTER V.

OF ANTIDOTES.

General Remarks.—In many cases no antidotes are known, and, even if available, must be employed as soon after the administration of the poison as possible. In the case of mechanically corrosive poisons, little advantage can be expected. The use of demulcent drinks may in almost all cases be recommended, and also the administration of emetics or clearing out the stomach by means of appropriate apparatus, unless vomiting has already taken place. The chemical action of antidotes is either in neutralizing acids or by forming substances more or less insoluble in the juices of the stomach, whereby they become wholly or partly inert, and may be gradually removed.

Sulphuric acid.—Any substance that will neutralize the acid may be used, as the sulphates are mostly inert. Chalk, magnesia, bicarbonate of soda (baking powder), carbonate of soda (washing soda), soap suds, ammonia, or even pounded mortar may be used. The action of the strong acid on the passages is, however, so violent, that little benefit can be expected, and the same cause generally prevents the use of the stomach pump.

Nitric acid.—The above remarks apply equally to this corrosive poison.

Oxalic acid.—Finely pounded chalk or whitening is probably the best antidote; any substance containing carbonate of lime, such as mortar, may be used, but potash, soda or ammonia would be of no avail, as the oxalates of their bases are soluble and poisonous. In cases of poisoning by any of these salts, the most efficacious antidote would probably be chalk *partly* dissolved in vinegar.

Phosphorus.—No direct antidote is known. Probably the administration of emetics is all that could be of any service, with subsequent use of weak soda or lime water.

Alkalies.—Weak acids, such as vinegar, tartaric or citric acid (lemon juice) may be used. Mucilaginous drinks and sweet oil may be added.

Arsenic—Arsenious acid.—Hydrated peroxide of iron is undoubtedly a good antidote, administered by spoonfuls in milk every half hour. It cannot be said that the oxide will neutralize solid pieces of white arsenic, but it will act upon it as fast as it dissolves, and will thus give time for its removal from the bowels. When the poison has been a salt of arsenious acid, a solution of acetate of the peroxide of iron must be used at the same time, as when an overdose of Fowler's solution has been taken.

Hydrated oxide of magnesium, obtained by adding liquor potassœ to a solution of Epsom salts, may be used instead of the iron preparation; also, as above, the acetate of magnesia may be required, which is easily obtained by dissolving the carbonate in vinegar.

Of course, demulcents may always be recommended, and sometimes emetics and purgatives.

Corrosive sublimate.—The white of two or three eggs is perhaps the best remedy; it is not advisable to use a larger quantity. Finely divided metallic iron has been recommended as reducing the salt to the form of metallic mercury, which is comparatively inert.

A weak solution of liver of potash (sulphide of potassium) might form the insoluble sulphide of mercury, but this potash salt is not altogether harmless itself.

Lead.—Dilute sulphuric acid, when white lead has been swallowed, or a solution of Epsom salts or Glauber's salts, when any salt such as sugar of lead has been taken. For persons exposed to the dust of white lead, a lemonade made with sulphuric acid is a tolerably sure preventive of ill effects.

Copper.—Sugar, or rather honey, has been recommended as an antidote to salts of this metal, as the oxide may thereby be reduced to the form of suboxide; its action, however, is somewhat doubtful. Fine iron filings have also been proposed, by which the metal itself may be separated. Probably white of egg is the best substance that can be administered. Yellow prussiate (ferrocyanide) of potassium may be used.

Antimony.—Probably strong tea, coffee, or any astringent substance containing tannin, would be efficacious, if the vomiting caused by antimonial preparations did not prevent their retention. Hydrated peroxide of iron has been recommended.

Zinc.—There does not seem to be any direct chemical antidote for this poison, beyond ordinary medical treatment.

Cantharides.—No chemical antidote is known.

Tin.—White of egg may counteract the irritant effects of tin, dyers' salt.

Nitrobenzole (essence of mirbane).—No antidote is known.

Aniline.—No antidote is known.

Carbolic acid.—The speedy use of the stomach pump and washing out with water is probably the most effectual treatment.

Prussic acid.—For the organic poisons few, if any, antidotes are known. The action of prussic acid is so rapid that there would seldom be time to administer any. Possibly salts of iron with magnesia might be of service. When only a small quantity has been taken, or the vapour inhaled, dousing with cold water may be recommended.

Strychnine.—The almost equally poisonous alkaloid, curarine, has been recommended as overcoming the effects of strychnine in a remarkable manner. Strong coffee or other astringents may be used, and chloroform has been employed with success in some cases, enabling the system to get rid of the poison in a few hours.

CHAPTER VI.

OF WOUNDS AND BRUISES.

SEC. 1.—*Examination of Wounds* 80
" 2.—*Characters of a Wound inflicted during Life* 81
" 3.—*Characters of a Wound made after Death* 82
" 4.—*Practical Remarks* 82

SEC. 1.—*Examination of Wounds.*

The wounds on a dead body should be examined as to their situation, form, extent, length, breadth, depth and direction. And the presence or absence of effused blood, either liquid or coagulated, and of ecchymosis in the skin, should be noticed. The surrounding parts and edges of wounds should also be carefully examined, care being taken not to destroy the external appearances more than can possibly be helped, as these often afford valuable evidence in identifying the weapons used (1). The dissection, too, should not be confined to the injured part, particularly when the death would not apparently be caused by the wounds found on the body. All the organs and cavities should be carefully inspected, to see if any natural cause of death existed (2). Deaths apparently caused by violence have sometimes been really caused by poison. This was the case in an instance mentioned by Dr. Taylor. A girl died apparently from a severe chastisement inflicted by her father for stealing, but the death being rather more sudden than would be expected from the nature of the injuries, the surgeon examined the stomach, in which he found arsenic. The girl, to avoid her father's anger, had poisoned herself. Such cases shew the necessity of examin-

---

(1) Taylor, 183.
(2) Taylor, 183.

ing the stomach, no matter how unconnected with that cavity the apparent cause of death may be. By an examination of the stomach important evidence relating to the time of death is sometimes discovered from the absence or presence of food therein, and when present, from its nature and degree of digestion.

A medical witness who has examined the body should not only be able to prove he found wounds or injuries sufficient to account for death, but he should be able to go further, and prove that no other cause of death could be found. To do this he must examine all the organs and cavities.

SEC. 2—*Characters of a Wound inflicted during Life.*

Dr. Taylor says the principal characters of a wound inflicted during life are :—1. Eversion of the edges, owing to vital elasticity of the skin. 2. Abundant hemorrhage, often of an arterial character, with general sanguineous infiltration of the surrounding parts. 3. The presence of coagula.

It seems wounds which prove immediately fatal do not always present any characters by which to distinguish them from wounds made upon the dead body (1). Wounds which prove fatal within ten or twelve hours present throughout much the same characters (2).

The presence of gangrene, the effusion of adhesive or purulent matter, or swollen and enlarged edges, and the commencement of cicatrization, prove the wound was made some-time before death (3). A burn which has occurred during life will, *in general*, leave marks of vesication with serous effusion, or a line of redness, or both, about the burnt part (4).

(1) Taylor, 184 ; in note by the American editor.
(2) Taylor, 184.
(3) Taylor, 184.
(4) Taylor, 302.

Sec. 3.—*Characters of a Wound made after Death.*

The following are the chief characters of a wound made after death, as given by Dr. Taylor:—1. Absence of copious hemorrhage. 2. If there be hemorrhage, it is exclusively venous. 3. The edges of the wound are close, not everted. 4. There is no sanguineous infiltration in the cellular tissue. 5. There is an absence of coagula.

When wounds are inflicted soon after death, it becomes more difficult to distinguish them from those made during life, according to the length of time that has elapsed since the breath left the body. The characters of a wound upon the dead body, made twelve or fourteen hours after death, are distinctly marked, but if inflicted before twelve or fourteen hours have elapsed, they become less and less distinct, until medical testimony can prove no more than that the wound was made during life, or very shortly after death (1).

Cuts and stabs, if made during life, bleed profusely, but much less, if at all, when made after death, so that the quantity of blood lost is something to judge from in these cases. Lacerated and contused wounds, however, do not always cause much hemorrhage (2).

Sec. 4.—*Practical Remarks.*

The discoloration of the skin (called ecchymosis) which usually follows contusions and contused wounds, does not always take place around or even near the seat of injury. Sometimes it is found at some distance, and leads to mistakes as to the exact place of the injury, or to the number of injuries received. These discoloured parts are generally recognized as not being the immediate seat of the violence from the skin over them being smooth and unabraded (3).

---

(1) Taylor, 185, 186.
(2) Taylor, 185, 186.
(3) Taylor, 187.

This discoloration often proceeds from natural causes. Aged persons sometimes have it on their legs and feet (1). Persons severely afflicted with scurvy will get it on the slightest pressure (2). After death it repeatedly appears, particularly if the person died suddenly, in diffused patches, in stripes, traversing and intersecting each other in all directions, and in spots varying in size; and to the unprofessional observer presenting the appearance of being the effect of blows from a stick or other violence (3). But whether proceeding from infirmity or disease in the living, or from congestion or gravitation in the dead, a surgeon can pretty readily distinguish this kind of discoloration from that produced by blows. Almost invariably the cutis alone is found discoloured when the skin is cut into, and the extravasation of blood, compared to the size of the marks, is slight (4). Putrefaction will also produce suspicious-looking marks on dead bodies, but their general characters are well distinguished, and cannot easily be confounded with marks of violence (5).

While we bear in mind that apparent marks of violence found on dead bodies are often the result of natural causes, we must at the same time remember that severe internal ruptures and lacerations may occur from violence, without there being any external discoloration to indicate their cause (6). These ruptures can be distinguished from those occurring from natural causes by the absence of disease in the organ injured (7).

Wounds made with a cutting or stabbing instrument can generally be recognized by their appearance. The edges are clean and regular. The wound produced by a stab is apparently smaller than the instrument used, owing to the

(1) Taylor, 191.
(2) Taylor, 191.
(3) Taylor, 193.
(4) Taylor, 192, 193.
(5) Taylor, 194.
(6) Taylor, 195.
(7) Taylor, 195.

elasticity of the skin; but sometimes, from its mode of infliction, it is larger. When the weapon passes through the body, the exit wound is usually smaller than the entrance aperture (1).

Wounds are often accounted for by stating the party injured fell upon stones, glass, crockery or other sharp substance, and wounded himself. A careful examination of the wounds will generally expose any pretence of the kind. Accidental injuries of this nature present marks of laceration and irregularity.

Contused wounds are the most difficult to deal with. They can seldom be positively ascribed either to criminal violence or to mere accident, from an examination alone. The number, extent and position of the injuries may help to explain their origin. An accidental fall will seldom produce a *number* of wounds, nor will there be a very copious effusion of blood beneath the skin, nor will such a fall usually wound the top of the head. Contused wounds on bony surfaces sometimes look as though made with a cutting instrument (2).

An examination of the dress worn over the parts wounded may assist in discovering the nature of the injury. A cutting weapon will divide the dress with clean edges, but a dull instrument will seldom divide it at all, and if it does, the edges will generally be ragged. Any dirt or other substance near the injury to the dress should be noted, and the instrument by which the wound is supposed to be made examined for similar substances.

Evidence as to whether a wound is the result of suicide, homicide or accident, can sometimes be gathered from a close examination of its situation, direction, shape and extent. Coroners cannot be too particular in gathering the

---

(1) Taylor, 196.
(2) Taylor, 199.

minutiæ of wounds from a medical witness, for if anything important is omitted at the inquest, any further examination of the body is seldom practicable.

The weapon with which a wound is produced is not always covered with blood, particularly if the wound is a stab. Sometimes no blood is found on the weapon, or there is only a slight film, which, on drying, gives to the surface a yellowish-brown colour (1). When blood is found, the manner in which it is diffused over the weapon should be carefully noticed (2). Any hair or fibres adhering to the weapon, or imbedded in blood on the weapon, should be examined with a microscope or powerful lens, and its nature—whether human hair or not, or cotton, woollen or other fibres—ascertained (3). Foreign substances, such as wadding, paper, hay-seeds, &c., found in wounds, may afford strong evidence of their origin, if carefully examined (4). Mud found on clothing may serve to connect the accused with an act of murder, if there is anything peculiar in the soil where the murder is committed. The mud should be examined microscopically (5).

In all cases of death from violence or maltreatment, the mortal injury is not necessarily specific and well-defined, for death may result from shock, without there being any visible internal or external lesion. The shock may be occasioned by a single blow, or by many injuries, each comparatively slight (6). In such cases the age, constitution, and the previous state of health or disease may accelerate or retard the fatal consequences (7).

It is sufficient to constitute murder that the party dies of the wound given by the prisoner, although the wound was not originally mortal, but became so in consequence of

(1) Taylor, 213.
(2) Taylor, 213.
(3) Taylor, 213.
(4) Taylor, 213.
(5) Taylor, 215.
(6) Taylor, 226.
(7) Taylor, 226.

negligence or unskilful treatment; but it is otherwise when death arises not from the wound, but from unskilful applications or operations used for the purpose of curing it (1). In the one case death results from the wound by improper treatment, in the other from improper treatment irrespective of the wound. When death is owing to the wound, it matters not if more skilful treatment or more favourable circumstances would have prevented the fatal result.

It is sufficient to prove that the death of the party was accelerated by the malicious act of the prisoner, although the former laboured under a mortal disease at the time of the act (2). A man is not bound to have his body always in so sound and healthy a state as to warrant an unauthorized assault upon him.

Severe wounds of the head, heart, great blood-vessels of the neck, ruptures of the diaphragm and of the bladder, generally prove rapidly fatal, and immediately deprive the injured person of the power of volition and locomotion: but cases are on record of persons surviving for some time after receiving such injuries, and retaining the power of volition and locomotion, almost to the time of death. By bearing such cases in mind, difficulties arising from the body being found at a distance from where the injury could have been received, &c., may be removed (3).

A difficulty may also occur from persons who were near the scene of a murder at the time of its committal, not having heard any cries or noise, which can be explained in cases where the trachea is found divided. An injury of this kind produces a loss of voice (4).

A mortal wound, particularly when accompanied with much hemorrhage, will generally prevent all *struggling* (5).

---

(1) 1 Hale, 428.
(2) 1 Hale, 428.
(3) Taylor, 255, 256, 257.
(4) Taylor, 257.
(5) Taylor, 258.

This is important to know in some cases, in order to fix the time of wounding. As long as the injured party was struggling with his antagonist, it is pretty certain he was not thus wounded.

If the injured person has been stupid or insensible previous to death, strict inquiries should be made as to whether he was intoxicated or not.

When death ensues from rupture caused by unauthorized violence, care should be taken to ascertain if the part ruptured was in a diseased condition or not, for if previous disease is established, it may mitigate the offence of the assailant in some cases. Severe ruptures of the various organs may take place without there being any external signs of injury to account for them (1).

In cases of death from gunshot wounds it is sometimes very material to ascertain whether the piece was fired near to or at a distance from the injured person. If the muzzle of the piece is near the body, the edges of the aperture of entrance will be torn and lacerated, and will appear blackened. The clothes will also be found blackened, and sometimes burnt. If the muzzle is not in immediate contact with the body, the wound will be found rounded, or if the bullet strikes obliquely, oval. When the piece is fired at some little distance, the aperture of entrance will be round or oval, the skin slightly depressed, the edges appearing a little bruised, but no mark of burning will be found (2).

If possible, the projectile in cases of gunshot wounds should be carefully examined, and means adopted to preserve its identity, should a trial be at all likely to follow the inquest.

Several wounds may be produced on the same body by a single bullet, by its splitting on angular surfaces or project-

---

(1) Taylor, 273, 275.
(2) Taylor, 284.

ing ridges of bone. A case once occurred in which a ball, after entering a man's body, divided into two pieces, which, passing through one leg, lodged in the opposite one, thus making *five wounds!* three of entrance and two of exit. The ball may also divide, and one portion pass out of the body and the other lodge in it, leading a careless observer to suppose the whole ball had made its exit (1).

In cases of suicide by pistol shots, the marks indicating a near discharge of the pistol are usually found and the marks of gunpowder on one of the hands.

A gun fired near may cause death, although merely loaded with wadding or even gunpowder (2).

It seems an assailant may occasionally be identified from the flash of a gun on a dark night, but Dr. Taylor appears to consider that the man who declared he recognized a robber through the light produced by a blow on his eye in the dark (!) pulled the long bow.

It is possible that a chemical analysis of the projectiles found in gunshot wounds may be of service. Such an analysis may connect the projectiles with metal of a similar nature found on the accused or in his use.

Should it be material to ascertain whether a gunshot wound was received while retreating from or approaching towards a person who fired the shot, an examination of the wound itself will generally afford evidence on the point. If the bullet has entered the front of the body, the person must have been facing his antagonist, unless he was struck by a glancing or rebounding ball; and if it has entered the back part, the contrary must have been the case. When the projectile passes through the body, of course there may be a wound in front and behind also; it will then be necessary to find out which is the aperture of entrance and which

---

(1) Taylor, 286.
(2) Taylor, 292.

the aperture of exit. The former is generally three or four times smaller than the latter, the skin is slightly depressed, and, if the muzzle of the piece was close to it, blackened or burnt. On the other hand, the orifice of exit is never discoloured by the powder or flame, its edges are somewhat everted, and if there is any bleeding, it will most likely be from this aperture (1).

To determine the direction a ball came from with regard to the person struck, is occasionally more difficult. If the piece was fired upwards, the course of the ball through the body may still be downwards, owing to its striking a bone or other hard substance, and *vice versa*. And if fired on a level with the orifice of entrance, the course of the ball may also be deceptive from similar reasons.

The fact of the aperture of exit being immediately opposite that of entrance, does not necessarily prove the shot passed directly through the part struck, for balls have been known to enter the front of the head and come out at the back, without penetrating the bone, their course having been round the skull under the skin merely (2). In one case on record the ball struck the upper part of the *abdomen*, and passed out at the back nearly opposite, without traversing the abdominal cavity. It had deflected beneath the skin. This deflection of balls is most often met with when they strike obliquely a curved surface (3).

---

(1) Taylor, 284.

(2) A case of the nature referred to in the text was recently reported in a Toronto paper as follows:—"ANOTHER SHOOTING ACCIDENT.—A few days ago a boy, who refused to give his name or that of any of the parties concerned, came to Dr. Fisher's office on Queen Street to have a pistol bullet taken out of his head. It was found, on examining the wound, that the bullet had cut the skin on the left side of the head just above the ear, and that, failing to penetrate the skull, it had traversed the scalp and lodged between the skull and the skin, nearly opposite the place where the skin was first broken. The bullet was removed without any difficulty. On being asked how the shooting took place, the boy refused to give any particulars further than that it was 'accidental.'"

(3) Taylor, 287.

When the body of an individual who is suspected to have died from external violence, is not seen until some time after dissolution, the injuries will appear to be of a much more aggravated nature than they ought to be considered by the medical jurist (1).

(1) Taylor; Devergie; Beck.

CHAPTER VII.

OF THE HYDROSTATIC TEST.

This test, although now exploded as a reliable one, for the purpose of proving the live *birth* of infants, is still one which may afford important corroborative evidence on the subject, and its use should therefore not be neglected.

The mode of performing the hydrostatic test is as follows:

The lungs are removed from the chest in connection with the trachea and bronchi, and placed on the surface of water, free from salt or other ingredient which would increase its specific gravity—pure distilled or river water is recommended. If they sink, notice whether rapidly or slowly. Then try if each lung will sink separately; cut them into several small pieces, and see if these pieces float or sink. If the lungs float, note if they float high above the surface, or at or below the level of the water, and see if the buoyancy is due to the lungs generally, or only to the state of particular parts. By considering the general result of these experiments, an inference may be drawn as to whether respiration has taken place at all, or partially, or perfectly (1).

While performing this test, the remarks regarding it in Chap. III. s. 3, should not be lost sight of.

---

(1) Taylor; Beck.

CHAPTER VIII.

BLOOD TESTS.

Examination of blood stains should always be left to experienced professional men, if possible, but where such assistance cannot be obtained, the following tests of blood may be found useful.

The colouring matter of blood readily dissolves in distilled water, forming, if recent, a rich red solution (1). The red colour of this solution differs from all other known colouring matters, except kino and catechu, since it is not changed by ammonia, unless very concentrated or added in large quantity, when the red colour turns brownish (2).

Blood being heavier than water, will sink when placed in that liquid, descending in streaks. After ascertaining that the specific gravity of the suspected substance is greater than water (3), apply heat to it while in the water, and see if it coagulates. By this test the red colour of blood is destroyed, and a muddy brown precipitate is found. Heat seems to be the most reliable test of blood, as other red colouring matters do not lose their colour by its application.

Nitric acid and a solution of corrosive sublimate will both produce a precipitate in the red solution of blood.

The coagulum produced by boiling a solution of blood, when collected in a filter and dried, forms a black resinous-looking mass, quite insoluble in water (4).

---

(1) Taylor, 228.

(2) Taylor; Beck.

(3) If the stains have been subjected to heat before being placed in water, this test will fail, as heat when applied to dry blood, whether on clothing or weapons, renders it insoluble in water.

(4) Taylor, 228.

These tests, it must be remembered, can merely prove the matter to be *blood*. Whether *human blood* or not must be otherwise ascertained.

When the blood is on clothing endeavour to ascertain whether the articles examined were worn by the deceased or accused, as the case may be.

After the lapse of a week, Dr. Taylor states, it is extremely difficult to give an opinion as to the actual date of a blood stain on white or nearly colourless linen and other stuffs. And on coloured clothing no changes are observable in the stains from which to form an opinion as to their date of origin. Spots of blood on white stuffs, when recent, are of a deep red colour, which change to a reddish brown after a few hours (1).

When the suspected stain is on clothing, dip pieces of the stained part in a small quantity of distilled water, until it is charged with sufficient of the colouring matter to apply the tests above given. If the solution is too small in quantity to obtain coagula by heat, the chemical tests must be abandoned, and the microscope resorted to. If possible, it should be ascertained on which side of the clothing the blood fell, as this may be of importance. Generally, the side which first comes in contact with blood, will be more stained than the other.

If the stain is on plaster or wood, cut or scrape off a portion and soak it in water, and proceed in like manner. It is recommended in these cases to first of all examine a portion of the plaster or wood which is unstained.

Suspected spots on weapons may be tested by exposure to a heat of 77° to 86° Fahr. If of blood, they will come off in scales, but not so if they arise from rust (2).

---

(1) Taylor, 280.
(2) 2 Beck, 146.

To apply the tests above given to such stains, the following method is recommended:—Pour a stratum of water upon a piece of plate-glass, and lay the stained part of the weapon upon the surface. By this means the colouring matter of blood will be dissolved and a solution obtained to experiment upon.

The stains of blood on a weapon, if scraped off and heated, will give off a smell of burnt horn and evolve ammonia, which may be detected by its turning *red* litmus paper *blue*.

The better opinion seems to be that the blood of a man cannot be distinguished from that of a woman, or the blood of a child from that of an adult. Nor can *menstrual* blood be distinguished from that of the body generally (1).

Human blood may, however, in some instances, be distinguished from that of animals by means of the microscope; but this test requires so much experience and familiarity with the instrument, that few persons are capable of making use of it. To those who do possess the requisite knowledge, any information that could be given on the subject in this little work would be useless.

Other tests for blood have been proposed, such as the colour produced by guiacum and peroxide of hydrogen, and also by means of the spectroscope. These, however, can scarcely be employed except by experts.

Before closing this chapter, it is proper to repeat that the examination of blood stains should be intrusted to experienced professional men alone, where practicable, and in cases not requiring immediate investigation, the assistance of a chemist or surgeon possessing Provincial reputation should be obtained. The tests are all of them of a delicate nature, requiring judgment and experience to produce reliable results, and should not be left to inexperienced persons to deal with.

---

(1) Taylor, 236.

CHAPTER IX.

OF DEODANDS.

One species of homicide *per infortunium*, which does not arise from the killing of man by man, is occasioned by pure accident, without the default, concurrence or procurement of any human creature. This takes place when the death is occasioned by some beast or inanimate thing. By the common law the instrument which causes death in such cases was forfeited to the Sovereign for pious uses, under the name of a *deodand*. This singular custom appears to have had its origin in the days of Popery in England, and was designed as an expiation for the souls of such as were snatched away by sudden death. These forfeitures being founded rather in superstition and ignorance than in the principles of sound reason and policy, did not meet with much countenance from the courts in modern days, and at last, by 9 & 10 Vic. ch. 62, were entirely abolished in England, and in Canada by 32-33 Vic. ch. 29, s. 54.

CHAPTER X.

OF FLIGHT AND FORFEITURE.

Formerly it was the duty of Coroners to inquire what goods a person found guilty of murder had, and to cause them to be valued and delivered to the township. This part of their duty was abolished by 1 Rich. III. ch. 3, except, perhaps, in cases where the accused flies, when it is said the Coroner may, as formerly, seize the goods of the fugitive. It is not usual in this country for Coroner's juries to make any inquiry as to flight or forfeiture (1), except as to property forfeited by persons dying by their own hands. See page 36.

(1) Juries impanelled to try persons indicted for treason or felony are forbidden to inquire concerning their lands, tenements or goods, or whether they fled for such treason or felony, 32 & 33 Vic. ch. 29, s. 53, but this provision does not appear to apply to Coroner's juries.

CHAPTER XI.

OF EVIDENCE (1.)

SEC. 1.—*Competency of Witnesses* 97
1. *Idiots* 98
2. *Lunatics* 98
3. *Children* 98
4. *Infidels* 99
5. *Prisoners* 99
6. *Husband or Wife of Prisoner* 99
" 2.—*Primary Evidence* 100
" 3.—*Presumptive Evidence* 101
" 4.—*Matters of Opinion* 102
" 5.—*Matters of Privilege* 102
" 6.—*Hearsay Evidence* 103
" 7.—*Relevancy of Evidence* 105
" 8.—*Leading Questions* 106
" 9.—*Proof of Handwriting* 106
" 10.—*Proof of Documents* 107

SEC. 1.—*Competency of Witnesses.*

All persons of sound mind and of sufficient intelligence to understand the nature of an oath, and who believe in its religious obligation, not being the prisoner or the wife or husband of the prisoner, are competent and compellable to give evidence in every court of justice concerning the matters in issue.

The persons not competent to be witnesses pointed out by this rule are—

1. Idiots.

(1) It will be necessary to remind the professional reader that this work is intended for the practical use of *Coroners* alone, and consequently when it treats of any branch of the general law, no pretence is made to do more than give such portions of that branch as may be found useful to Coroners in the discharge of their duties.

2. Lunatics.
3. Children.
4. Infidels.
5. Prisoner.
6. Husband or wife of prisoner.

Each of these classes requires to be noticed separately; but it may be here stated that the question of competency of the witness is one to be decided solely by the Coroner on a preliminary examination. This preliminary examination is called the examination on the *voir dire*, and formerly it was held that no objection to the competency of witnesses could be made except upon the *voir dire;* but it appears that now a witness may be declared incompetent, and his evidence rejected at any time during the examination (1).

There are various causes which may affect the *credibility* of a witness, but a blemish of this kind must not exclude the witness, and the amount of credit due to his testimony the jury will be the judges of.

1. *Idiots.*] Those who never have had any understanding from their birth are incompetent to give evidence. Persons born deaf, dumb and blind are looked upon in law as idiots. But this is a legal presumption which may be done away with by proof of understanding and sufficient religious belief. Deaf and dumb persons, if found competent, may give evidence by signs, or through an interpreter, or in writing (2).

2. *Lunatics.*] Those who, having had understanding, have lost their reason by disease, grief or other accident, are only competent witnesses during lucid intervals.

3. *Children.*] The age of the child is immaterial, when judging whether or not he is competent of being a witness. The criterion is his religious belief. If he has such a know-

(1) Jervis C. C. 261.
(2) 1 H. P. C. 34; 1 Leach C. C. 455; 3 Car. & P. 127.

ledge of the obligation of an oath, as to understand the religious and secular penalties of perjury, he is competent—otherwise not.

4. *Infidels.*] Persons who do not believe in God, or if they do, do not think that He will either reward or punish them in this world or in the next, cannot be witnesses, as an oath is no tie or obligation upon them (1). The only means at the disposal of the Coroner for determining whether a proposed witness is such an infidel as to be incompetent to give evidence, is to question him upon the *voir dire,* as to whether he believes in God, a future state of rewards and punishments, and the sanctity of an oath. If his answers are orthodox, he must be admitted.

5. *Prisoners.*] The prisoner is not competent to give evidence for or against himself: but accomplices are admissible to give their evidence for what it is worth. A settled principle with regard to the evidence of accomplices is, that a prisoner ought not to be convicted upon the evidence of any number of accomplices, if unconfirmed or uncorroborated by other testimony (2). The testimony of the wife of an accomplice is not a proper confirmation of his statement (3). The confirmation need not be in every particular, as long as it is sufficient to satisfy the jury that the evidence is worthy of credit (4). The accomplice's evidence ought, however, to be corroborated with regard to the identity of the prisoner, so as to satisfy a jury that the prisoner is *the person* who committed the crime which is charged against him by the accomplice (5).

6. *Husband or Wife of Prisoner.*] In all cases which can fall under the notice of Coroners, husbands and wives are not competent to give evidence for or against each other,

---

(1) Willes, 538. (2) 5 C. & P. 236.
(3) 7 C. & P. 168. (4) Jervis O. C. 260.
(5) 8 C. & P. 107.

except in the case of a wife mortally injured by her husband, when her dying declarations, if not otherwise inadmissible (1), are evidence against him (2); as are also the dying declarations of the husband against the wife, under similar circumstances (3). And after a divorce *a vinculo matrimonii*, either husband or wife can give evidence for or against the other (4).

Sec. 2.—*Primary Evidence.*

It is an inflexible rule that the best evidence of which the nature of the thing is capable must be given. Hence a copy of a deed or will is inadmissible as evidence, so long as the original exists and is producible, no matter however indisputably authenticated.

On the same principle, so long as a written document can be produced, oral evidence of its contents is inadmissible, except when it is in the possession of an adverse party, who refuses or neglects to produce it; or when it is in the possession of a party who is privileged to withhold it, and who insists on his privilege; or when the production of the document would be, on physical grounds, impossible, or very inconvenient; or when the document is of a public nature, and some other mode of proof has been specially substituted for reasons of convenience (5). The preliminary question as to whether secondary evidence of a document should be admitted or not, is one for the Coroner to decide alone, after hearing all the evidence tendered on the point.

And a written statement of a witness is not to be admitted as equal to the oral evidence of the witness himself. Any evidence which has testimony of a more original kind

---

(1) See page 103.
(2) 1 East. P. C. 357.
(3) 1 East. P. C. 455.
(4) Peake's Evid. App. p. 39.
(5) Roscoe's C. Ev. 2.

behind it must not be received until the better evidence is shewn to be unprocurable. But if the original evidence cannot be produced, the next best need not be required, for there are no degrees in secondary evidence.

Sec. 3.—*Presumptive Evidence.*

On many investigations no *direct* proof as to the perpetrator of the crime can be obtained; but circumstances point so strongly in one direction, that it would be contrary to reason not to call upon the suspected person to contradict or explain this *evidence* against him. Evidence of this kind is called *presumptive*, and care must be taken not to draw too hasty conclusions from it.

A case may here be mentioned which will serve to illustrate the subject, and also, from its unfortunate result, to show the danger of placing too much reliance upon presumptive evidence. A man was apprehended with a horse in his possession which had recently been stolen, and as he could give no satisfactory explanation of how he came by the animal, and the thief was unknown, the law presumed he was the man who had stolen it. Horse-stealing was then a hanging matter, and the poor man was executed. Afterwards it came out that the real thief, being closely pursued, had overtaken the man and asked him to hold the horse for a few minutes, and in this way the thief escaped and the innocent man was found with the horse.

In this connection the following presumptions may be mentioned:

The law presumes innocence.

The law presumes in criminal matters that every person intends the probable consequence of an act which may be highly injurious.

The law presumes that a person acting in a public capacity is duly authorized to do so.

If a man by his own wrongful act withhold the evidence by which the facts of the case would be manifested, every presumption to his disadvantage will be adopted (1).

A presumption may be rebutted by a contrary and stronger presumption (2).

Sec. 4.—*Matters of Opinion.*

Ordinary witnesses must only state facts, and leave the judge or jury to draw all inferences from them. Their own opinions regarding the facts to which they testify should not be received. But the opinions of skilled or scientific witnesses are admissible to elucidate matters which are of a strictly professional or scientific character (3).

Sec. 5.—*Matters of Privilege.*

A witness may be *asked* any question, but there are many he need not *answer*.

A witness is not compellable to answer any question tending to criminate himself, and when such a result can be anticipated, the witness should be cautioned that he is not bound to answer.

Danger from a civil action is no ground for such a privilege.

Counsel, solicitors and attorneys cannot be compelled to disclose communications which have been made to them in professional confidence by their clients. This, however, is the privilege of the client, not of the legal advisers.

---

(1) Powell's Ev. 56.
(2) 5 Taunt. 326.
(3) Powell's Ev. 63.

Clergymen and medical men do not possess the same privilege with regard to confidential communications made to them in the performance of their professional duties; but the judges have shewn a disinclination to receive such communications made to clergymen.

A witness is not allowed to state facts, the disclosure of which may be prejudicial to any public interest.

In criminal cases no evidence can be excluded on the ground of indecency (1).

SEC. 6.—*Hearsay Evidence.*

Hearsay evidence, or the oral or written statement of a party who is not produced in court is, as a general rule, not admissible. The principal exceptions to this rule requiring notice are—

(*a*) When offered in corroboration of a witness' testimony, to shew that he affirmed the same thing before on other occasions (2).

(*b*) When it is essentially connected with a transaction and forms part of it.

(*c*) When given as popular reputation or opinion or as the declarations of deceased witnesses of competent knowledge, if made before the litigated point has become the subject of controversy, and without reasonable suspicion of undue partiality or collusion (3).

(*d*) When the evidence consists of dying declarations in cases of homicide. The death of the deceased must be the subject of the investigation, and the circumstances of the death the subject of the dying declarations. Here the feel-

(1) Powell's Ev. 83.
(2) Powell's Ev. 87.
(3) Powell's Ev. 94.

ing of responsibility on the approach of death is looked upon as equal to the effect of an oath upon the conscience. The sense or conviction of *approaching* death must be perfect and certain, although the declarant need not be *in articulo mortis*, or even *think* he is, provided he thinks there is no hope of a continuance of life, and is under an impression of almost immediate dissolution (1). The declarations must have been made by a person who, if alive, would have been a competent witness; therefore, the dying declarations of one who had no sufficient belief in a future state, and his religious responsibility for his actions in this life, are not admissible (2).

Before receiving dying declarations as evidence, the Coroner should inquire into the circumstances under which they were made, and exclude them if there is any reasonable doubt as to the veracity, sanity, consciousness or sense of religious responsibility and impending dissolution in the mind of the deceased (3).

(*e*) When a prisoner makes a statement of the circumstances of the crime with which he is charged, it is evidence against him, unless elicited by a person who had at the time actually or presumably power to forgive, or who in that capacity induced the prisoner to confess by holding out to him an offer or prospect of forgiveness.

If the prosecutor or his wife has obtained the confession by any threat or promise, it is inadmissible, or if the confession was made under similar circumstances to the master or mistress of the prisoner when the crime has been committed against either of them, or to the attorney of the person in authority, or to a constable or any one acting

(1) 3 C. & P. 629; Roscoe's C. Ev. 3; and see *Regina* v. *Howell*, Law Times, Jan. 25, 1845, 317.

(2) Powell's Ev. 124.

(3) Powell's Ev. 124.

under a constable, or to a magistrate. But the inducement must be held out by a person who has presumably power to shield the criminal. If the inducement be made in the presence of such a person who stands by and does not object, his silence will exclude the confession. But inducements held out by persons who have no authority in the matter will not make the confession inadmissible.

If a party accused wishes to make any statement, the evidence against him should be first read over, and then he should be cautioned in the following manner: "Having heard the evidence, do you wish to say anything in answer to the charge? You are not obliged to say anything unless you desire to do so; but whatever you say will be taken down in writing, and may be given in evidence against you upon your trial" (1). He may then make his statement, which should be read over to him, and be signed by the Coroner. He is not to be sworn.

(*f*) Statements having reference to the health or sufferings of the person who makes them, form another exception to the general rule rejecting hearsay evidence. If it becomes necessary to inquire into the state of health at a particular time of a person who is deceased, a witness may detail what the deceased person said on that subject at the time (2).

SEC. 7.—*Relevancy of Evidence.*

The evidence must be confined to the matter in issue, and must tend directly to the proof or disproof thereof. Under this rule, evidence that a prisoner has committed a similar crime before, or that he has a disposition to commit such

(1) This caution the writer has applied to Coroner's inquests by analogy, a similar caution being requisite at investigations before magistrates. See Con. Stat. Can. ch. 102, s. 32.

(2) Roscoe's C. Ev. 30.

crimes is inadmissible (1). Evidence of good character is admissible in criminal cases, but as Coroners' juries have no power to try the party suspected, such evidence need not be taken at inquests.

Sec. 8.—*Leading Questions.*

On an examination *in chief* a witness must not be asked leading questions; or, in other words, a witness must not be asked by the person calling him, questions so shaped as to suggest the answers he is expected to make. When he is cross-examined, that is, examined by the opposite party to the one who called him, he may be asked leading questions. Generally, questions which may be answered by "Yes" or "No" are leading questions. If, however, the witness proves hostile to the party calling him, the Coroner may, in his discretion, allow leading questions to be asked, or if a question from its nature cannot be put except in a leading manner, the Coroner should allow it to be put (2); or if the witness has forgotten a circumstance, and it cannot otherwise be recalled to his mind, it may be asked him in a leading form.

Sec. 9.—*Proof of Handwriting.*

If it becomes necessary to prove handwriting, the following methods are admissible:

(*a*) By a witness who saw the party write or sign the document.

(*b*) By a witness who knows the party's handwriting. Such knowledge may have been obtained merely by having seen him write once (provided it was not for the purpose of

---

(1) Powell's Ev. 225.
(2) Powell's Ev. 439.

making the witness competent to give evidence) or by having seen documents purporting to be written by him, and which, by subsequent communications with him, he has reason to believe are the authentic writings of such party.

(*c*) By the court or the jury comparing the questionable handwriting with a genuine document. The strict rule seems to be that the genuine document used for comparison, must come before the court in the course of the case, but in criminal trials this rule has been relaxed by 32-33 Vic. ch. 29, s. 67, and by a previous statute. Although those statutes do not appear to apply to inquests in all their provisions, still Coroners had better act in accordance with them.

Sec. 10.—*Proof of Documents.*

In the first edition of this work it was stated, that—"In "criminal cases where a private writing is subscribed by "one or more attesting witnesses, such attesting witnesses, "or one of them, must be called to prove its execution, "although the document may not be such as by law is "required to have the attestation of a witness. The admis-"sion of the party executing it will not be sufficient. To "this rule there are exceptions, of which the following may "be named: An instrument 30 years old proves itself. If "the attesting witness is proved to be dead, insane, beyond "the jurisdiction of the court, or otherwise not producible "after proper efforts to bring him before the court, it will "generally be sufficient if his handwritting is proved." But since the passing of the Act 32-33 Vic. ch. 29, s. 66, the necessity for calling an attesting witness to instruments, the validity of which does not require attestation, has been done away with, and such instruments may now be proved by such evidence as is admissible to prove documents without attesting witnesses. This statute is not expressly made applicable to inquests in all its provisions, and there is a question as to whether section 66 would govern investigations by Coroners. The writer would recommend Coroners not to insist on the necessity of calling attesting witnesses to documents which do not require to be witnessed to make them valid (1).

---

(1) A mere outline of the rules of evidence which Coroners will most commonly have to consider, has been attempted in the text. Further information on the subject of evidence can be found in the works of Taylor, Roscoe, Starkie, Powell, Phillips and others.

CHAPTER XII.

THE CORONER'S COURT (1).

SEC. 1.—*When and where Holden* 110
" 2.—*Who may Attend* 111
" 3.—*The Jury, and how Summoned* 112
" 4.—*The Witnesses, and how Summoned* 117
" 5.—*Counsel* 120
" 6.—*Opening the Court* 120
" 7.—*Viewing the Body* 122
1. *The Place where the Body is Found* 123
2. *The Position of the Body* 124
3. *The Marks and Spots upon the Body and Clothing.* 125
4. *The Surrounding Objects* 126
5. *The Bearing and Conduct of the Parties in Attendance* 127
" 8.—*Continuing and Adjourning the Court* 127
" 9.—*The Medical Testimony* 132
" 10.—*The Depositions* 141
" 11.—*Obstructions—how Punished* 142
" 12.—*The Inquisition* 143
1. *The Venue* 144
2. *The Place where Holden* 145
3. *The Time when Holden* 145
4. *Before whom Holden* 145
5. *The View* 145
6. *The Description of the Deceased* 145
7. *Where the Body lies* 146
8. *The Jurors and their Finding upon Oath* 146
9. *The Charge to Inquire* 147
10. *The Verdict* 147
11. *The Party charged* 147
12. *The Addition* 149
13. *The Allegation of Time and Place* 149
14. *The Description of the Act* 149
15. *The Attestation* 151
" 13.—*Publication of Proceedings* 151
" 14.—*Defraying Expenses* 152

(1) For the forms connected with this chapter, see the Appendix.

Sec. 1.—*When and where Holden.*

When the Coroner receives proper notice of a death having taking place under such circumstances as require investigation (1), he should procure the necessary information on oath (2) and proceed to hold his inquest forthwith, by issuing a precept or warrant (3) to summon a jury to appear at a particular time and place named. The inquest must be taken within a reasonable time after the death. Seven months has been held too late (4). But the time ought in each case to be governed by the state of the body. If it is so far decomposed as to afford no information on view, the inquiry should be left to the justices of the peace. Still it is difficult to say when the body will afford no information, for in some instances the bones alone might point out the cause of death; and in some cases of poisoning, traces of the poison might be found long after the body was decomposed; yet, it is said, the whole of the body should be inspected (5). However, in the comparatively few instances when a Coroner is called upon to hold inquests long after the death has happened, he must govern his decision in this respect by a judicious consideration of all the facts he can learn with regard to each case. If the body has been buried, the Coroner may lawfully take it up for the purpose of holding an inquest. It is a misdemeanor to bury a body on which an inquest should be held before or without sending for the Coroner; and, if possible, the body ought not to be moved in any way until viewed by the Coroner and jury (6).

The proceedings by inquisition, being judicial, must not be conducted on a Sunday (7).

---

(1) See page 6.

(2) See page 9, and Form No. 130.

(3) See Form No. 7.

(4) 1 Stra. 22; 1 Salk. 235 and 377.

(5) *R.* v. *Bond*, 1 Stra. 22.

(6) 1 Salk. 377.

(7) 9 Co. 66a.

It is not absolutely requisite that the inquest should be held at the same place where the body is viewed, provided it is taken within the same jurisdiction (1).

In olden days the impanelling of the Coroner's inquest and the view of the body was commonly in the street, in an open place, and in *corona populi* (2); but in modern times it has become usual to hold the inquest in any convenient building.

Sec. 2.—*Who may Attend.*

Much discussion has taken place as to whether the public have a right to attend inquests. It seems from the best authorities that they have not (3). The power of deciding who shall be present and who not rests with the Coroner, who, together with all persons who administer a public duty, has a right to preserve order in the place where it is administered, and to turn out whom he thinks fit, without rendering himself liable to an action of trespass (4). And the Coroner's court being a court of record (5), of which the Coroner is a judge, this is in accordance with the ancient rule that no action will lie against a judge of record for any matter done by him in the exercise of his judicial functions (6).

But however clear the power to exclude the public from inquests may be, and however proper for the sake of decency, or out of consideration for the family of the deceased, the exercise of that power in some instances may be, yet it

---

(1) 2 Hawk. ch. 9, s. 25; Latch. 166; Poph. 209; and see *ante* p. 18.

(2) Hist. of the Commonwealth, by Sir T. Smith, p. 96.

(3) Only those summoned, or who are suspected or interested in the result of the inquiry, or live in the neighbourhood where the body is found dead, at most have such a right. Jer. O. C. 241.

(4) 6 B & C. 611; and see 10 B. & C. 237; and see judgment of Lord Abinger in *Jewison* v. *Dyson*, 9 M. & W. 585.

(5) Some doubt is thrown upon this by Lord Abinger in his judgment just cited.

(6) 6 B. & C. 625.

should not be used in an arbitrary manner, nor for the mere sake of shewing a little authority. A Coroner had far better err on the side of publicity, than in conducting his proceedings too secretly. When any one is excluded, it should be for a just cause, and after due consideration.

SEC. 3.—*The Jury, and how Summoned.*

Inquests held by Coroners are expressly excepted from the operation of the Juror's Act (1), and Coroners left to make all inquests by jurors of the same description as they were used and accustomed to do before the passing of that Act.

No qualification by estate is necessary for jurors on inquests, but they should be "lawful and honest men" (2). Aliens, convicts and outlaws are not such, and if impanelled on the inquest, it seems the inquest may be avoided (3). They should be rejected by the Coroner, although, strictly speaking, jurors upon inquests are not challengeable (4).

Each juror should be able to write his own name.

Jurors ought to be persons indifferent to the subject-matter of the inquiry, and residents of the township near the place where the body is found, although jurors taken from the body of the county cannot be objected to. Householders should be preferred.

The jury upon inquests on prisoners ought to be a party jury, as it is called, that is, one-half prisoners (if so many there be) and the other half persons not prisoners (5), except when the prisoner was executed under sentence of

(1) Rev. Stat. 572. (2) Lord Raymond, 1305.
(3) 2 H. P. C. 60, 155; Lamb Just. 391. (4) Mir. ch. 1, s. 13; Brit. 6 a.
(5) Umfrev. 212, 213.

law, in which case the jury must not be composed of prisoners confined in the gaol, or of officers of the prison (1).

And in inquests upon fires, they are to be impanelled from among the householders resident in the vicinity of the fire (2).

No person appears to be exempted from serving on Coroners' juries, yet those who are exempted from serving on other juries had better not be summoned.

The following persons are absolutely freed and exempted from being returned and from serving as either grand or petit jurors in any of the courts (3).

1. Every person upwards of sixty years of age.

2. Every member of the Executive Council of Canada and of this Province.

3. The secretaries of the Governor-General and the Lieutenant-Governor; and

4. Every officer and other person in the service of the Governor-General or Lieutenant-Governor for the time being.

5. Every officer of the Dominion or Provincial Government; and

6. Every clerk and servant belonging to the Senate and House of Commons and the Legislative Assembly, or to the public departments of Canada or of this Province.

7. Every inspector of prisons.

8. The wardens of the Provincial Penitentiary, the Central Prison and Reformatory.

9. Every officer and servant in the said Penitentiary, Central Prison and Reformatory.

10. Every judge of a court having general jurisdiction throughout Ontario.

---

(1) 32-33 Vic. ch. 29, s. 116.
(2) Rev. Stat. 1990.
(3) Rev. Stat. 535.

11. Every judge of any county or other court (except the General Sessions of the Peace) having jurisdiction throughout any county.

12. Every sheriff, coroner, gaoler and keeper of a house of correction or lock-up-house.

13. Every priest, clergyman and minister of the gospel recognized by law, to whatever denomination of Christians he may belong.

14. Every member of the Law Society of Upper Canada, actually engaged in the pursuit or practice of his profession, whether as a barrister or student.

15. Every attorney and solicitor actually practising.

16. Every officer of any court of justice, whether of general, county, or other local jurisdiction, actually exercising the duties of his office.

17. Every physician, surgeon and apothecary, duly qualified to practise and being in actual practice.

18. Every officer in Her Majesty's army or navy on full pay.

19. The officers, non-commissioned officers and men of corps of volunteers, while they continue such.

20. Every pilot and seaman actually engaged in the pursuit of his calling.

21. Every officer of the post office, customs, and excise;

22. Every sheriff's officer and constable.

23. Every county, township, city, town and village treasurer and clerk.

24. Every collector and assessor.

25. Every professor, master and teacher of any university, college, collegiate institute, high school, public school or other school or seminary of learning, actually engaged in performing the duties of such appointment.

26. Every officer and servant of any such university, college, school or seminary of learning, actually exercising the duty of his office or employment.

27. Every editor, reporter and printer of any public newspaper or journal actually engaged in such employment or occupation.

28. Every person actually employed in the management and working of any railway.

29. Every telegraph operator.

30. Every miller.

31. Every fireman belonging to any regular fire company. But no fireman shall be exempt from serving as a juror, unless the captain or other officer of the fire company, at least five days before the time appointed for the selection of jurors, notifies to the clerk of the municipality the names of firemen belonging to his company, residing within such municipality, and claims exemption for such fireman.

Every member of the Senate and House of Commons and of the Legislative Assembly of this Province,—every warden and every member of any county council,—every mayor, reeve or deputy reeve of any city, town, township or village,—every justice of the peace, and every other member and officer of any municipal corporation,—is also absolutely freed and exempted from being selected to serve as a grand or petit juror in Her Majesty's inferior courts, and every such person is moreover absolutely freed and exempted from being returned upon any general precept to serve as a petit juror at any Sessions of Assize or *Nisi Prius*, Oyer and Terminer or General Gaol Delivery, and the name of any such person, if drawn in drafting such panel, should be set aside and not inserted in the same.

No man not being a natural-born or naturalized subject of Her Majesty is qualified to serve as a grand or petit juror in any of the courts aforesaid on any occasion whatever.

No man attainted of any treason or felony, or convicted of any crime that is infamous, unless he has obtained a free pardon, and no man who is under outlawry, is qualified to serve as a grand or petit juror in any of the said courts on any occasion whatever.

The jury may consist of any number of persons not less than twelve; and the verdict must be the opinion of the majority, provided that majority be composed of twelve jurymen at least (1).

If twelve cannot agree, the jury are to be kept without meat, drink or fire (2) until they return their verdict; and if this is ineffectual, no verdict can be taken by the Coroner, and he should adjourn them to the next assizes, when they may have the benefit of the opinion and direction of the judge (3).

The jury may at any time during the investigation call back witnesses and ask them further questions.

It is the province of the jury to investigate and determine the *facts* of the case, but they should take the *law* from the Coroner.

The jury are summoned by the Coroner issuing his precept or warrant to the constables of the county to summon at least twelve (4) able and sufficient men to appear before him at an hour and place named. This warrant, with a summons for each juryman (5), is given to a constable, who should serve the jurors personally, or at least leave the sum-

---

(1) *Reg.* v. *Golding*, 39 Q. B. 259.

(2) In modern practice this harsh law is mitigated, and the jurors are allowed reasonable accommodation and comforts while making up their decision. If, after some delay, there is evidently no chance of a verdict—the difference of opinion among the jurymen appearing to be permanent, without any hope of their being brought to unanimity—the Coroner should adjourn the jury to the assizes.

(3) Jervis C. C. 256; Comb. 386.

(4) Any number thought advisable, but not less than twelve, may be summoned. See Form No. 7.

(5) See Form No. 9.

mons at their dwelling house with some gro... of the family, and return the warrant to the Co... the names of the persons summoned (1). Where a ... jury is required, a warrant must also be issued to the gaoler of the prison (2).

If any person duly summoned as a juror does not, after being openly called three times, appear and serve as such juror, the Coroner may fine the delinquent person any sum he may deem proper, not exceeding four dollars (3). And he must thereupon make out and sign a certificate (4) containing the Christian and surname, residence and trade or calling of such person, the amount of the fine imposed and the cause of the fine, and transmit such certificate to the Clerk of the Peace for the county in which the person resides, on or before the first day of the General Sessions of the Peace then next ensuing, and cause a copy of such certificate to be served upon the person by leaving it at his residence within a reasonable time after the inquest. And the fine so certified is estreated, levied and applied in like manner, and subject to the like powers, provisions and penalties in all respects as if part of the fines imposed at such General Sessions (5). If sufficient jurors attend the inquest, it is unusual to fine those who do not obey the summons.

SEC. 4.—*The Witnesses, and how Summoned.*

Who are competent witnesses has already been considered in the chapter on Evidence (6).

---

(1) See Form No. 10. (2) See Form No. 8; Jervis O. C. 322.

(3) Rev. Stat. 875; and Con. Stat. Can. ch. 88, s. 6. But see also Rev. Stat. 578, which empowers Coroners to fine defaulting jurors up to *twenty dollars*. As the two first mentioned Statutes are special Acts relating to inquests, and a fine up to four dollars is undoubtedly legal under any of the Acts, Coroners are recommended to adopt that sum as a limit.

(4) See Form No. 13. (5) Rev. Stat. 875, 578; and Con. Stat. Can. ch. 88, s. 6.

(6) See p. 97.

All persons competent to give evidence who are acquainted with the circumstances connected with the subject matter of inquiry, should offer their evidence to the Coroner, and if they do not, he has authority to issue a summons (1) to compel their attendance, and to commit them should they refuse to appear (2), or, after appearing, to give evidence upon the subject of inquiry (3); or he may fine them up to four dollars, which fine is enforced, &c., in the same manner as fines imposed upon jurors for non-attendance, as to which see the previous section (4).

The witnesses are summoned by giving a constable subpœnas (5) for them, which he must serve, and keep a memorandum of the service on each witness, in order to be able to prove it.

When the attendance of any person confined in the Penitentiary, or in any other prison or gaol in the Province, or upon the limits of any gaol, is required, the Coroner must make an order upon the warden of the Penitentiary, or upon the sheriff, gaoler, or other person having the custody of such prisoner, to deliver him to the person named in the order (6) to receive him.

On the appearance of each witness the Coroner should take down his name, abode and occupation, and then administer the oath that he shall speak the truth, &c. (7). The witnesses should be sworn in such manner as they think most binding upon their consciences. A Jew is sworn upon the Pentateuch, a Turk upon the Koran, &c. And Quakers, Mennonists, Tunkers and United Brethren or Moravians, are allowed by Rev. Stat. 778 to affirm or

---

(1) See Form No. 19. (2) See Form No. 22.

(3) See Form No. 25; 1 Chitty Cr. L. 164.

(4) Rev. Stat. 875, and Con. Stat. Can. ch. 88, s. 5; see also Rev. Stat. 578, and note 3, p. 117.

(5) See Form No. 19. (6) See Form No. 20, and 32-33 Vic. ch. 29, s. 60.

(7) See Form No. 28; Umf. 177.

declare (1). A witness or juror belonging to one of these sects must first affirm or declare as follows: "I, A. B., do solemnly, sincerely and truly declare and affirm that I am one of the Society called Quakers, Mennonists, Tunkers, or *Unitas Fratrum* or Moravians," as the case may be; and then he must make the further affirmation: "I, A. B., do solemnly, sincerely and truly declare and affirm," &c.

If any witness is a foreigner, unable to understand English, he must be examined through the medium of an interpreter, who must be sworn well and truly to interpret as well the oath to the witness, as the questions put to him by the court and jury, and his answers thereto (2).

The Coroner must hear evidence for and against the suspected person (3).

After each witness is sworn, and his evidence reduced into writing by the Coroner, it should be read over to him. Then ask him if it be the whole of the evidence he can give, and any additions or corrections he mentions may be noted. Request him to sign the depositions at the end and to the right hand of the paper. His doing so is not absolutely necessary (4), but to refuse is a contempt for which it is said the witness may be committed (5).

Each deposition should be certified and subscribed by the Coroner. He should do so to the left hand in the following words:

"I certify that the above information was taken and acknowledged the day, year and place above mentioned, before me, A. B., Coroner" (6).

If all the witnesses do not attend, or if there be any good reason, the Coroner may adjourn the inquest to another day

---

(1) See Form No. 29, and 32-33 Vic. ch. 29, s. 61.
(2) See Form No. 27.
(3) 2 Hale, 62, 157.
(4) L. C. L. 996.
(5) See Form No. 26; Chitty C. L. 164, s. 1; C. & K. 600.
(6) Powell's Ev. 307.

to the same or another place, first taking the jurors in a recognizance for their appearance at the adjourned time and place (1).

Sec. 5.—*Counsel.*

Counsel appear to be on the same footing as the general public with regard to having a right to attend the inquiry —the better opinion being that the Coroner can exclude them if he thinks proper. This power should be cautiously used, as few cases can occur in which its exercise can result in any good. Should the ends of justice or the feelings of the family of the deceased really require the inquest to be conducted privately, the Coroner may, in his discretion, exclude counsel for or against the suspected person (2), but the party accused must be given full opportunity to cross-examine the witnesses (3).

Sec. 6.—*Opening the Court.*

On the day appointed, the Coroner, constable, jurors and witnesses must all attend. The Coroner having received the return of the jurors and warrant from the constable, endorses a return on the back thereof, which is signed by the summoning constable, thus:

"The execution of this precept or warrant appears in the schedule annexed.

"The answer of A. B., constable."

Annex a schedule containing the names of the jurors summoned, and shewing when and where each juryman was served.

(1) See Form No. 32.

(2) The professional reader is referred to Jervis O. C. 264, *et seq.*, for arguments and cases for and against this power of exclusion.

(3) 32-33 Vic. ch. 30, s. 60.

The warrant must be carefully preserved by the Coroner, as the want of it may be fatal in cases of presentment or indictment (1).

A sufficient number of jurors being present (that is, not less than twelve), the Coroner now directs the constable to open the court by proclamation (2), and afterwards proceeds to call over the names of the jury, making a dash — against the name of each as he appears. They are not challengeable, but an objection properly made may be admitted (3). When the court is opened no other persons should be allowed to act as jurymen than those already selected or summoned (4).

The jury being brought in view of the body, are requested to choose their foreman. After the foreman is chosen he is called to the book and sworn, the Coroner first saying to the other jurors, "Gentlemen, hearken to your foreman's oath; for the oath he is to take on his part is the oath you are severally to observe and keep on your part."

After this the foreman is sworn (5), and then his fellows, by three or four at a time (6), in their order upon the panel, the body still being before them. The Coroner then takes down on his papers the names of the foreman and jurors, and proceeds to call them over one by one, first saying, "Gentlemen of the jury, you will answer to your names, and say 'sworn' if you are sworn." The Coroner now charges the jury, acquainting them with the purpose of the meeting (7). The jury should then view and examine the body, the Coroner drawing their attention to, and making observations upon, such appearances as call for notice.

---

(1) Impey's O. C. 513.
(2) See Form No. 11.
(3) Umf. 185.
(4) See Cox's Cr. Law Cases, Vol. IX., Part VI.
(5) See Form No. 15.
(6) See Form No. 16.
(7) See Form No. 17.

Sec. 7.—*Viewing the Body.*

This is an *indispensable* proceeding, as all inquests must be taken *super visum corporis*—that is, upon view of the body—the dead body itself being the first evidence offered to the jury. If, therefore, the body cannot be found, or is in such a state as to afford no evidence on inspection, an inquest is not to be held by the Coroner, unless under a special commission for the purpose (1).

The view must be taken at the first sitting of the inquest, and the Coroner *and* jury must be all present together. The jury are not to view the body one by one, or the Coroner at one time and the jury at another (2), but all must be present at one and the same time, in order that the observations of the Coroner may be heard by all (3).

The view, too, must be taken *after* the jury are sworn, otherwise a material part of the evidence will be given when the jury are not upon oath. When viewing the body, its position and appearance, its dress and marks of violence, blood spots and marks of mud thereon, and the appearance of the surrounding earth or objects, should all be most minutely noticed. The skill and intelligence of the Coroner and jury can here be shewn more than in the performance of any other part of their duties.

Before making some general remarks upon the appearances to be noticed, it will be proper to caution persons who may be required to take part in inquests not to permit sudden prejudice to influence their minds. If there is anything unusual in the death, nothing is more common than for a *suspicion* of murder to arise at once, which, from

---

(1) 2 Hawk. P. C. 9.

(2) In England, by Stat. 6 & 7 Vic. ch. 83, s. 2, the Coroner and the jury need not all view the body at the same time, but in Canada we must still go by the old law as stated in the text.

(3) 1 Chit. Rep. 745 s. c.; 3 B. & A. 260.

repetition, easily becomes a *belief* in many minds (1). Popular inclination of this kind should be guarded against by the jurymen in particular.

The general appearances to be noticed when viewing the body may be considered under the following heads: (2)

1. The Place where the Body is found.
2. The Position of the Body.
3. The Marks and Spots upon the Body and Clothing.
4. The surrounding Objects: their Position and Indications.
5. The Bearing and Conduct of the Parties in Attendance.

1. *The Place where the Body is found.*] When inspecting the place where the body is found, care should be taken to ascertain, if possible, whether or not the person *died* in that place, for most of the information to be obtained from an inspection depends entirely upon the death having taken place in the spot examined. A hasty conclusion, therefore, regarding the place of death being the same as the place where the body is found, is to be avoided. In cases of very severe wounds, particularly of the head, jurors and even medical men are too apt to think that the injured person must have been instantly deprived of the power of volition and locomotion, and have died immediately. This is not always the case, for persons have been known to live for days after the most severe wounds of important organs, and to have retained their power of willing and moving to the last. Instances of this kind have already been noticed in Chapter V., and others can readily be found in works on medical jurisprudence. Even when the wounded person is too much injured to walk, he may have sufficient power to turn upon his face or back, and thus change the relative positions of the murderer and the murdered, so as to render

(1) 2 Beck. p. 3.

(2) Much of the information given under these heads is taken from the *Upper Canada Law Journal* for February, 1856.

valueless any inference to be drawn therefrom. If a severe wound of an important organ is accompanied by great hemorrhage, *in general* there can be no *struggling or violent exertion* AFTER the wound is inflicted.

A careful examination of the place where the body is found and the place where the person died will often supply evidence to distinguish between homicidal, suicidal and accidental death, and the examination should be made bearing in mind these three kinds of death. Any peculiarity in the soil should be carefully noticed, and compared with any mud that may be found on the body or clothes of a suspected person. Foot-prints near the body should be guarded from obliteration. The method usually recommended for ascertaining if a foot-print was made with a particular boot is to make an impression with the boot *near* the one found, and compare the two. Placing the boot *into* the impression is not advisable, as doing so may destroy the print without giving any satisfactory evidence, and will not afford any means of comparing the nails, patches, &c., on the sole with the original impression. Some writers assert that the foot-print on the ground is generally smaller than the foot which made it, owing to the consistence of the soil, the shape of the foot, or the boot or shoe covering it, or the manner in which the foot was placed in walking. Sometimes it is said to be larger if on a light soil (1).

2. *The Position of the Body.*] The position of the body will sometimes indicate the mode of death, and will often afford evidence strongly corroborative of or adverse to its supposed or ascertained cause. For instance, a body found in an upright or sitting posture with a severe wound on the head, would lead to the supposition that it had been placed in that position after death. But murderers have been known to purposely place their victims in positions calcu-

(1) 2 Beck. 149.

lated to indicate accidental or suicidal death. And, on the other side, persons dying from accident or by their own hands have been found in positions strongly suggestive of murder. An extraordinary case of this kind is on record. A prisoner hung himself by means of his cravat tied to the bars of his window, which was so low that he was almost in a sitting posture, and when found *his hands were tied by a handkerchief.* This was undoubtedly a case of suicide. It was supposed that he had tied his hands with his teeth. In cases of death by hanging, the posture of the body may be of considerable importance in distinguishing suicidal from homicidal hanging, but in the former it is not necessary that the body should have been totally suspended. Cases frequently occur where the bodies are found with the feet on the ground, kneeling, sitting, or even in a recumbent posture (1). The reader will probably remember the case of the convict Greenwood, who hung himself in the Toronto Gaol. When found, he was hanging by a long towel from the bars of his cell window, and so close to the floor that he had to crouch in order to throw his weight on the towel.

A curious case connected with this subject occurred within the writer's own knowledge during the month of January, 1864. A woman of dissipated habits was found dead in her own house in a sitting posture. She appeared to have slipped from her chair while intoxicated, and in doing so caught the string of her cap over the back part of the chair, and being alone and unable to extricate herself, was strangled.

If possible, the body should be first viewed exactly in the position in which it was found.

3. *The Marks and Spots upon the Body and Clothing.*] These may be examined by the Coroner and jury, but a medical witness will be more competent to draw conclu-

(1) Taylor, 570.

sions from them, should the suspicious nature of the death render the production of such testimony proper. The body should be inspected for swellings, coloured spots, wounds, ulcers, contusions, fractures or luxations, and any fluid flowing from the nose, mouth, ears, sexual organs, &c., should be carefully noted. Before making this examination of the body, the clothes should be looked at, and mud or blood-stains thereon noticed. Also, any cuts or rents, their size, shape and direction, and whether they correspond with cuts or marks on the body. And, as the clothes are removed, notice what compresses or bandages, if any, are applied to particular parts.

It would be impossible to mention all the things to be noticed when examining the body and clothes. Indeed, little more can be done than suggest the sort of inquiries which should be made. Each case will present its own peculiar features, which the medical man must observe in such manner as his own judgment and foresight may prompt him. He should not, however, confine himself to mere inspection of what actually presents itself to his eyes. He should search for objects which are not obvious at the first glance, and conduct his search with great caution, if not scepticism, always remembering that hasty conclusions or thoughtless omissions may both endanger his own reputation and the lives of his fellow creatures.

4. *The Surrounding Objects.*] After concluding the examination of the body and clothes, the surrounding objects next demand attention. Ascertain the direction of footsteps near the body, and search for marks, &c., on the objects around. If blood is found, note whether it apparently fell with force, and in what direction; whether it is venous or arterial, fresh or old, &c. If the death has been a violent one, search for the instrument, and if found, see that its identity is preserved. In cases of suspected poisoning every vessel

in which food has recently been prepared should be examined, and the contents reserved for analysis.

The surrounding objects cannot be too carefully noticed, as the following cases will illustrate:—The perpetrators of the murder, in 1751, of Mr. Jeffries, by his niece and a servant, were discovered from the dew on the grass surrounding the house not having been disturbed on the morning of the murder. This led to the suspicion that the murderer was a domestic, and had not left the premises. The murder, in 1818, of Mr. Taylor, whose body was found in a river, was discovered from his hand being found clenched and containing grass, shewing he had struggled on the bank before he was thrown into the river.

5. *The Bearing and Conduct of the Parties in Attendance.*] Crime is rarely self-possessed; and when most on his guard, the culprit is apt to betray himself by an excess of caution, or by numerous and improbable suggestions as to the cause of death. An intelligent observation of the surrounding persons, then, may sometimes be of use.

Sec. 8.—*Continuing and Adjourning the Court.*

The body having been viewed, it may be removed, if necessary or proper, to some convenient place, and the Coroner and jury proceed with the inquiry. They need not sit in the same room with the body, nor at the place where it was found (1).

The Coroner first calls over the names of the jury, to see they are all present; and having ascertained they are satisfied with the view, he then adds to his former charge any observations suggested by viewing the body, and informs

(1) Jervis O. C. 323.

them briefly of the object of their inquiry—viz., the cause of death, adding:

"I shall proceed to hear and take down the evidence respecting the fact, to which I must crave your particular attention."

The officer in attendance now calls silence, and repeats after the Coroner the following proclamation for the attendance of witnesses:

"If any one can give evidence on behalf of our Sovereign Lady the Queen, when, how, and by what means A. B. came to *his* death, let him come forth and he shall be heard."

If the inquiry is to be conducted privately, the room must be cleared, and the witnesses called in one by one. When a witness comes forward to give evidence, the Coroner takes down his name, place of abode and occupation; swears him either in English (1) or through the medium of an interpreter, who must also be sworn (2), and then takes down his evidence, having previously prepared his examination papers or book by intituling the informations (3). So long as the fair and obvious meaning of the words of the witness is taken down (4) in presence of the party accused, if he can be apprehended, the requirements of the law will be fulfilled, but it is frequently desirable at trials following inquests that the exact words of the witness as uttered before the Coroner should be on record; and Coroners are strongly recommended to take down the depositions in the exact natural language and peculiar expressions used by the witnesses, following their language in the first person.

---

(1) See Form 128.

(2) See Form No. 27.

(3) See Form No. 30.

(4) In cases of manslaughter or murder, or of accessories to murder before the fact, Coroners are required by 32-33 Vic. ch. 30, s. 60, to put in writing the evidence, or so much thereof as shall be material, in presence of the party accused, if he can be apprehended.

The party accused, if present, must be allowed full opportunity of cross-examination (1).

Before the witness signs his examination, let it be read over to him, and ask him if it be the whole of the evidence he can give: he signs it to the right hand of the paper. Before he does so, ask the jurors if they have any further questions to be put to the witness. The Coroner then subscribes the examination himself to the left hand (2).

All the evidence offered, whether for or against the accused, must be received (3).

If, from all the witnesses not attending, or from a *post mortem* examination being necessary, or from other cause, it be thought advisable to adjourn, the Coroner may, in the exercise of a sound discretion, adjourn the inquest to a future day, to the same or another place, first taking the recognizances (4) of the jurors to attend at the time and place appointed, and notifying to the witnesses when and where the inquest will be proceeded in (5). The Coroner then dismisses them (6).

A warrant may now, in the discretion of the Coroner, be granted for burying the body (7), or the body may be kept unburied until the completion of the inquest, if no inconvenience is likely to arise. If it was found publicly exposed, and is unclaimed by any *bona fide* friend or relative, the Coroner must give notice thereof to the Inspector of Anatomy of the locality, if there be one, and deliver it to him. If there be no Inspector of Anatomy for the locality, the body must be interred as customary (8). And the body of any person found dead, who, immediately before

---

(1) 32-33 Vic. ch. 30, s. 60.
(2) See Form No. 31.
(3) 2 Hale, 157.
(4) See Form No. 32.
(5) In case a witness is too sick to attend the court, or if he is a prisoner, this power of adjournment may be used in order to take the court to the witness.
(6) See Form No. 33.
(7) See Forms Nos. 35, 36, 37.
(8) Rev. Stat. 1258, 1260.

death, had been supported in and by any public institution receiving pecuniary aid from the Provincial Government, is to be delivered to persons qualified to receive such bodies, unless the person so dying otherwise directs (when the body must be decently interred), or unless such body be claimed within the usual period for interment, by *bona fide* friends or relatives (when it must be delivered to them) (1).

The bodies of persons, being lunatics, dying in any Provincial Lunatic Asylum, however, are to be decently interred in all cases (2).

The persons qualified to receive unclaimed bodies are, public teachers of anatomy or surgery, or private medical practitioners having three or more pupils, for whose instruction the bodies are actually required; and if there be any public medical school in the locality, such school has a preferable claim to the body (3).

The Inspector of Anatomy is not mentioned as one of the persons qualified to receive these last-mentioned bodies, but from a perusal of the whole Act cited in the notes, the intention of the enactment seems to be that he should first receive all the bodies of such persons and deliver them over to the qualified persons for dissection.

The body of every convict who dies in the Penitentiary, if claimed, must be delivered over to the friends or relatives of the deceased; but if not claimed, it may be delivered to an Inspector of Anatomy, or to the Professor of Anatomy in any college wherein medical science is taught (4); and if not so delivered, it must be decently interred at the expense of the institution (5).

The adjournment of the court is done by the officer making proclamation (6).

---

(1) Rev. Stat. 1258.
(2) Rev. Stat. 1258.
(3) Rev. Stat. 1259.
(4) 31 Vic. ch. 75, s. 45.
(5) Con. Stat. Can. ch. 111, s. 63.
(6) See Form No. 34.

The Coroner should make an entry in his minutes of this adjournment, both of time and place. When settling the time for which to adjourn, he should consider for what purpose an adjournment is necessary. If for a *post mortem*, two or three days will likely be sufficient. If for a chemical analysis, a clear week or ten days should be given the chemist.

When the jury again meet at the adjourned time and place, the formalities of opening the court are gone through as at the commencement of the inquest.

The officer makes proclamation (1). The jurors' names are called over (2), and the Coroner recapitulates the state of the inquiry, and proceeds in the examination of witnesses. After the witnesses are examined the Coroner sums up the evidence to the jury, and directs them to consider of their verdict. No precise charge is necessary, but the law applicable to the facts of each particular case should be explained to them.

Formerly the jury had to inquire as to deodands, flight, forfeiture and escape, but now they need only consider the cause of death, except when the deceased came to his death by his own hands, when it is proper for the jury to find what goods he had at the time he committed the felony (3).

If the jury wish to consider their verdict, the officer is sworn to take care of them (4), and the Coroner withdraws; or, if more convenient, the officer takes the jury to another room, and attends at the outside of the door until they are agreed: when agreed, they return, and the Coroner calls over their names, and asks them if they have agreed upon their verdict. If they are unanimous, the verdict is delivered by the foreman; but if not, the Coroner collects their voices, beginning at the bottom of the panel, and according

---

(1) See Form No. 38.
(2) See Form No. 11.
(3) See p. 36.
(4) See Form No. 40.

to the opinion of the majority, the verdict is taken, provided twelve at least agree.

The jury must not now return a verdict from their own knowledge of the fact, without any evidence being adduced before them. If a juryman can give evidence, he should be sworn in the ordinary manner (1).

The Coroner records the verdict and draws up the inquisition, to which both he and the jury set their hands and seals. The names should be opposite the respective seals, and the Coroner adds to his name the office, as:

"A. B., Coroner, County of ———."

The inquisition thus being completed, the Coroner requests the jury to hearken to their verdict as recorded (2). The Coroner then makes out his warrant to bury the body, if not already done (3).

If it is a case that will come before the assizes, the witnesses must be bound over to appear at the trial (4), and the prosecutor to appear and prosecute (5). The jury are then discharged (6).

Having noticed the proceedings of the Coroner's court generally, it will now be proper to treat of some of its branches more particularly.

Sec. 9.—*The Medical Testimony.*

If the Coroner finds that the deceased was attended during his last illness or at his death by any legally qualified (7) medical practitioner, he may issue his order for the attend-

---

(1) 1 Salk. 405.

(2) See Form No. 41.

(3) See remarks at page 129.

(4) See Forms Nos. 45 and 46.

(5) See Form No 44.

(6) See Form No. 42.

(7) Legally qualified practitioners are persons duly licensed under the Ontario Medical Act, Rev. Stat. 1244. If there be any doubt whether a medical man is licensed or not, he should be asked at a convenient time to produce his license. Some Coroners adopt the plan of examining the medical witness upon oath as to his being licensed.

ance of such practitioner as a witness at such inquest (1). Or if the Coroner finds that the deceased was not so attended, he may issue his order for the attendance of any legally qualified (2) medical practitioner, being at the time in actual practice, in or near the place where the death happened; and the Coroner may, at any time before the termination of the inquest, direct a *post mortem* examination, with or without an analysis of the contents of the stomach or intestines, by the medical witness summoned to attend at such inquest.

It is usual, and Coroners are most strongly recommended to have the analysis made by an experienced chemist (3), but if any person states upon oath before the Coroner that in his belief the death was caused partly or entirely by the improper or negligent treatment of a medical practitioner or other person, such medical practitioner or other person must not assist at the *post mortem* examination (4).

Whenever it appears to the majority of the jurymen sitting at any Coroner's inquest that the cause of death has not been satisfactorily explained by the evidence of the medical practitioner, or other witnesses examined in the first instance, such majority may name to the Coroner in writing any other legally qualified medical practitioner or practitioners, and require the Coroner to issue his order (5) for the attendance of such medical practitioner or practitioners as a witness or witnesses, and for the performance of a *post mortem* examination as above mentioned, and whether before performed or not; and if the Coroner refuses to issue such order, he is guilty of a misdemeanor, and punishable by a fine not exceeding twenty dollars, or by imprisonment not exceeding one month, or by both fine and imprisonment (6).

---

(1) See Form No. 24, and Rev. Stat. 876. (2) See Form No. 24, and Rev. Stat. 876.
(3) See remarks as to analysis, *post*. (4) Rev. Stat. 876.
(5) See Form No. 24. (6) Con. Stat. U. C. ch. 125, s. 9; and Rev. Stat. 877.

When any such order for the attendance of a medical practitioner is personally served, or if not so served, but is received by him, or left at his residence in sufficient time for him to obey such order, and he does not obey the same, he forfeits the sum of forty dollars upon complaint by the Coroner who held the inquest, or by any two of the jurymen thereof, made before any two justices of the peace of the county where the inquest was held, or of the county where such medical practitioner resides. And if such medical practitioner does not shew a sufficient reason for not having obeyed such order, the justices must enforce the penalty by distress and sale of the offender's goods, in the same manner as they are empowered to do under their summary jurisdiction (1).

The practitioner chosen to make a *post mortem* examination should be the best qualified the neighbourhood affords; and when he is giving his evidence the Coroner should get as much information from him as possible, for he will generally prove the most important witness at the inquest (2). The medical witness had better be examined after the principal unprofessional witnesses, in order that he may have their testimony to aid his conclusions, and to avoid having to recall him for the purpose of asking additional questions suggested by the other evidence (3).

---

(1) Rev. Stat. 877. The Coroner alone is the proper person to say first of all whether medical testimony is called for or not; but when he does order such evidence to be procured, the jury have then the right above mentioned, to have more medical evidence if they think it requisite. When considering if they shall summon a medical man, Coroners should not be influenced by the jurymen desiring to find out the precise cause of death in cases where there can be no doubt of the deceased having died from natural causes. Juries very commonly think they ought to discover, in all cases, what occasioned the death; but this is a mistake, for if no one is to blame in the matter, no practical benefit can arise from finding the deceased died from any particular disease. The expense of medical testimony, therefore, in these cases should be avoided, and for this purpose the desire of the jury resisted.

(2) *U. C. Law Journal*, Vol. I. p. 85.

(3) *U. C. Law Journal*, Vol. I. p. 84.

The medical testimony should be as free from technical terms as possible, and be taken down in full.

Neither the Coroner nor jury should attempt to curtail the *post mortem* examination, or the testimony of the medical witness, but he should be allowed to make a thorough examination, and to give as full evidence as he may think proper. Indeed, the Coroner ought to insist upon his examining the separate viscera, as a little additional trouble taken at the inquest may save a vast amount of annoyance afterwards (1).

The remarks already made under section seven apply as much to medical men called to see a body as to Coroners and juries when viewing one; but in this place a few additional hints may be given for the guidance of medical witnesses in particular. Observe the dress, and compare it with the marks of violence on the body. The nature of dried spots of mud on the corpse or its clothing. The marks of blood on the person of the deceased, what shape they assume; if that of a hand or some fingers; of what hand, and whether the front or back; and could the deceased have made the marks himself. What appearances around the corpse deserve notice, and how have they been changed since the death. Do marks of blood found near the body indicate anything from their form, direction or colour. These and numerous other points will suggest themselves by a little consideration, and some, if not all, may lead to material results.

No one should be present at the *post mortem* examination except the medical man, Coroner and constable. The Coroner or a medical man, if more than one be present, should take down all the facts communicated by the dissector, from the commencement of the examination to its close, to prevent circumstances of importance escaping the memory.

---

(1) *U. C. Law Journal*, Vol. I., p. 86.

Before dissection is begun, an external examination of the body should be made. Dr. Beck says: "*If there be any external lesion present*, it should first be examined and its nature described: its length, breadth and depth; also whether it has been inflicted with a cutting, pointed or round instrument; whether it is accompanied with inflammation or gangrene; and whether any foreign bodies are found in it, such as balls or pieces of cloth. The scalpel should then be employed to trace its extent, but with judgment, so as not to render our researches useless, and prevent a comparison of the external wound with the internal injury. The nerves and blood-vessels, and particularly the arteries that are wounded, should be named, as should also the viscera, if any are in that state. *If there be a contusion without a solution of continuity*, the injury found in the internal parts should be particularly noticed, such as extravasation, rupture of vessels, &c. *If the cause of death is a burn*, its degree and extent should be examined, together with the state of the parts affected, whether inflamed merely or covered with blisters, the fluid contained in these blisters, and the condition of the neighbouring parts, whether sphacelated or gangrenous. *If a luxation or fracture be present*, notice the surrounding soft parts; the nature of the injury, whether simple or complicated, and the phenomena indicating the progress of disease or recovery (1).

After stating these circumstances, the dissection may be proceeded with, in a systematic manner, taking care not "*to make wounds while examining for them.*" The examination of the abdomen had better be left to the last, as putrefaction is there first developed, and the offensive odour by this means may be partly avoided. If chloride of lime or other disinfectant is used during the examination, it must not be sprinkled *on* the body, but merely around it or about the

(1) 2 Beck, pp. 6, 7.

room. The dissector should not desist because he supposes the cause of death is perfectly discovered in one or the other cavity; all of them should be inspected (1).

It is recommended to commence the dissection at the head. Remove the hair, and then lay bare the bones of the cranium, by making an incision from one ear to the other over the top of the head, and then another transverse to it, from the top of the nose to the occiput. Take care not to mistake irregular sutures for fractures: for this purpose, they should be rubbed over with ink. Notice the strength of the bones of the head, whether they are unusually thin or soft (2). Now remove the skull cap, taking care not to wound the dura mater, and inspect the membranes and substance of the brain. The base of the brain requires especial notice. View the vertebral column through its whole extent. In examining the neck, make an incision from the chin to the sternum; then from the upper point cut along the margin of the lower jaw to its angle, and from the lower point towards the clavicle. The great blood-vessels, the larynx, trachea, pharynx and œsophagus and their contents must be noticed. To inspect the thorax satisfactorily, an incision should be made through the integuments, from the top of the sternum to the pit of the stomach. Then dissect the flaps down to the ribs, and backwards about an inch and a half beyond the junction of the cartilages with the osseous substance of the ribs. Cut through these cartilages close to their joining, beginning with the second rib and ending with the seventh. Pull forward the lower part of the sternum a little, introduce a scalpel behind it and detach the diaphragm and mediastinum, then saw through it immediately below the connection of the first rib (3).

---

(1) 2 Beck, p. 7.
(2) 2 Beck, p. 8.
(3) 2 Beck, p. 10.

The viscera, the lungs, the pericardium and its contents, the heart and its great vessels, the thoracic duct, should be carefully examined. Remove the blood with a sponge, so as to ascertain the exact degree of colour that is present in the various parts, and notice the consistence or fluidity of the blood (1).

The abdominal cavity will now remain. It is examined by making a crucial incision, and, if necessary, by removing the pubal bone. Each part must be carefully examined: the intestines with a blunt-pointed bistoury, to avoid injuring them (2).

If there is any suspicion of poisoning, Dr. Beck says the whole of the alimentary canal, from the œsophagus to the rectum, should be carefully removed for further inspection; and he recommends Dr. Gordon's directions to be followed for this purpose. Apply a double ligature at the very commencement of the jejunum, and divide the intestine between the two threads; a similar ligature is then to be applied to the ileum, close to its termination in the colon, and the tube divided in the same manner. The root of the mesentery being now cut through, the whole jejunum and ileum are removed together. A double ligature is next to be applied to the rectum, as low down as possible, and being divided between the cords, it is to be removed with the whole of the colon. The œsophagus, stomach and duodenum are then to be extracted together, taking care previously to tie a ligature round the top of the œsophagus (3).

The examination being completed, the notes should be taken and reduced to order. The report or testimony should be as plain as possible, so that the court and jury may understand it. And the medical witness, in drawing up his report

(1) 2 Beck, p. 10.
(2) 2 Beck, p. 11.
(3) 2 Beck, p. 11.

or in giving his testimony, should remember that whatever he states before the Coroner's court will be seen by the prisoner's counsel, should a trial follow, who will cross-examine and sift him to the utmost of his ability.

A few practical remarks may now appropriately close this section.

Take particular notice during the dissection, of any peculiar odour on opening the body, brain or stomach; and if poisoning is suspected, mention the nature of the odour to the chemist who makes the analysis.

All vessels used in the examination should be thoroughly cleansed, and the whole examination should be conducted with a scrupulous regard to cleanliness. The necessity for this was once strongly illustrated. The stomach was negligently laid on some fine white sand, which gave rise to an idea of poisoning by means of powdered glass.

When an analysis is to follow, if it is thought advisable during the *post mortem* to examine the inner coats of the stomach, the contents of the stomach should be poured into a clean vessel, and after the examination (during which no water should be used for washing the stomach, or if used should be added to its contents) the stomach itself should be placed in the same vessel, and forwarded to the chemist. The stomach should be tied above and below; and a portion of the intestines, tied in the same way, should be sent. Also, a portion of the liver and a kidney. And if severe vomiting has attended the death, some of the vomited matter must be sent. Any suspected food—coffee, soup, &c.—should also be sent; and in cases of poisoning by arsenic, some of the urine.

Should the death have occurred within a few seconds or minutes of the administration of the suspected poison, the stomach, tied, should be put into a bottle with a tight cork or glass stopper, sealed all over, and sent off at once for immediate analysis.

The greatest care should be taken to preserve the identity of the vomited or other matter taken from the body, or the most correct analysis afterwards made will be inadmissible as evidence.

For packing the viscera to be sent for analysis, glass vessels should be used, or stoneware ; not common earthenware, as lead is used in its manufacture, and might interfere with the tests.

No extraneous substance should be introduced into or placed over the mouth of the vessel. Chloride of lime is sometimes introduced in this way to remove the smell ; but such a proceeding is highly objectionable, and may vitiate the whole analysis.

The vessel should be covered with bladder (tied) or cork, and sealed in several places with a seal having a peculiar crest or device. A wafer-stamp, coin, thimble, or other common article, of which a duplicate might be found, should not be used for this purpose. The sealing up should be done by the Coroner or examiner in presence of witnesses, and impressions of the seal used should be transmitted to the person who is to make the chemical analysis, together with an account of the symptoms attending the death.

If the vessel or vessels containing the viscera are packed in a box, they should be surrounded with plenty of hay or other soft substance, and the lid of the box *screwed*, not hammered down, otherwise the bottles are apt to be broken, and much if not all of the liquid lost, thus rendering the analysis useless, or at least unsatisfactory to the jury, on account of the small quantity of poison found. The package should never be out of the person's charge to whose care it is committed, until handed over to the chemist in person, who should be required to give a receipt for the same.

The time required to complete an analysis varies according to the occupation of the chemist. If he has nothing else to do, perhaps two or three days; but it is safer to allow him a clear week or ten days.

No respectable chemist will make an analysis for less than fifty dollars, and as no provision is made by law for defraying the expense, the Coroner should obtain the authority of the Attorney-General for incurring it.

Sec. 10.—*The Depositions.*

The depositions or evidence must be taken on oath and in presence of the party accused, if any such party there be and he can be apprehended, and must be certified and subscribed by the Coroner, and caused to be delivered without delay (1), together with the written information, if any, the recognizances, the statement of the accused, if any, and the inquisition, to the County Attorney for the county (2).

And when any person has been committed for trial by a Coroner, and he, his counsel, attorney or agent notifies the committing Coroner (3) that he will, so soon as counsel can be heard, move one of Her Majesty's courts of superior criminal jurisdiction, or one of the judges thereof, or the judge of the County Court in cases within his jurisdiction, for an order to the Coroner to admit such prisoner to bail, such committing Coroner must, with all convenient expedition, transmit to the office of the clerk of the crown, or the chief clerk of the court, or the clerk of the County Court (as the case may be), close under his hand and seal, a certified copy of all examinations and other evidences touching the offence wherewith such prisoner has been charged,

---

(1) Rev. Stat. 873, say "forthwith."
(2) 32-33 Vic. ch. 30. ss. 60, 61; and see Rev. Stat. 873.
(3) See Form No. 55.

together with a copy of the warrant of commitment and inquest; and the packet containing the same must be handed to the person applying therefor in order to such transmission; and it must be certified on the outside to contain the information touching the case in question. Any Coroner neglecting his duty in this respect may be fined such sum as the court to which the return ought to have been made thinks meet (1).

If a Coroner who has taken an inquest happens to die, having the record in his custody, it seems that a *certiorari* may be directed to his executors or administrators to certify it (2).

It seems doubtful whether the depositions taken before a Coroner when the prisoner is not present, can be used as evidence against him (3).

The depositions, if properly taken, will be sufficient evidence in case tho witnesses are dead, unable to travel, beyond sea, or kept out of the way by the contrivance of the party to whom their testimony is adverse (4). But they cannot be received, though the witnesses are dead, unless it is proved that they were signed by the Coroner (5). And before they can be received, evidence must be given that they are the identical papers taken before the Coroner without alteration (6).

Sec. 11.—*Obstructions—How Punished.*

It is a misdemeanor to interrupt or obstruct the Coroner or his jury in the view or inquiry (7). And the Coroner

(1) 32-33 Vic. ch. 30, ss. 61, 63.

(2) 2 Keb. 750; Dyer, 163; 2 Rol. Abr. 629; 2 Inst. 424; Hawk. b. 2, ch. 27, s. 39; Bro. Abr. Certiorari; 9 Bac. Abr. Certiorari.

(3) Wells Cr. Pr. 210; 2 Phill. 109; and see Roscoe's Cr. Evidence.

(4) 1 Kel. 55; 1 Lev. 180; Phil. Ev. 165.

(5) 2 Leach, 770, 771.

(6) Kel. 55; Fost. 337; Hawk. b. 2, ch. 46, s. 15; Phil. Ev. 162-5.

(7) Umf. 128.

has also authority forcibly to remove any person offering obstruction to the due administration of his duties, without being liable to an action (1); or he may commit any person for a contempt, the effects of which tend to obstruct and impede him in the performance of his office (2). It is better, however, for Coroners not to make use of this power, but to have the offending party punished for the misdemeanor.

Sec. 12.—*The Inquisition.*

The inquisition or written statement of the verdict or finding of the jury, when it contains the subject matter of accusation, is equivalent to the finding of a grand jury, and the parties charged may be tried and convicted upon it (3). Formerly it was required to be on parchment, but this is not now necessary (4).

The inquisition should be pleaded with the same strictness and legal precision as indictments (5).

It does not appear when this formal inquisition should be drawn up, but it had better in all cases be completed before the jury are dispersed (6).

The inquisition consists of three general parts: the caption or incipitur (7), being all that part which begins the inquisition, and immediately precedes what is called the verdict or finding of the jury; the verdict or finding of the jury (8) being that part which immediately follows the caption and precedes the attestation; and the attestation or conclusion (9).

The contents of each of these parts may be particularly noticed, a familiar knowledge of them being requisite in

---

(1) 6 B. & C. 611; 1 Ld. Raym. 454; 1 Mod. 184; 2 Mod. 218. (2) Jer. O. C. 268.
(3) Jer. O. C. 271; *Reg.* v. *Golding*, 39 Q. B. 259.
(4) *Reg.* v. *Golding*, 39 Q. B. 259; 32-33 Vic. ch. 29, s. 13. (5) Jer. O. C. 271.
(6) Impey O. C. 879. (7) See Form No. 59.
(8) See Forms Nos. 61 to 165. (9) See Form No. 60.

drawing up inquisitions, although many defects of a technical character, in inquisitions which formerly would have rendered them bad, may now be amended either by the Superior Courts or a judge thereof, or by a judge of assize or gaol delivery (1).

They are—

1. The Venue.
2. The Place where Holden.
3. The Time when Holden.
4. Before whom Holden.
5. The View.
6. The Description of the Deceased.
7. Where the Body lies.
8. The Jurors, and their Finding upon Oath.
9. The Charge to Inquire.
10. The Verdict.
11. The Party Charged.
12. The Addition.
13. The Allegation of Time and Place.
14. The Description of the Act.
15. The Attestation.

1. *The Venue*, or name of the county where the body lies dead and the inquisition is holden, should be inserted in the margin of the caption, thus:

"County of *Simcoe*, TO WIT: } An inquisition," &c.

The venue need not be stated in the *body* of an inquisition, except in case local description be required, when such local description must be given in the body thereof (2). The venue stated in the margin is the venue for all the facts stated in the body of the inquisition (3).

(1) Rev. Stat. 878.
(2) 32-33 Vic. ch. 29, s. 15.
(3) *Ibid.*

2. *The Place where Holden.*] The place at which the inquisition is holden must appear on the face of the inquisition (1). If no place is stated (2), or if the place stated is not shewn with sufficient certainty to be within the jurisdiction of the Coroner (3) it is insufficient (4).

3. *The Time when Holden.*] The inquisition must specify the day upon which it was holden, in order to show that the inquiry was recent, and was not held upon a Sunday, in which case it would be void (5). The day only need be stated without the hour. If the day stated be an impossible one, as the 30th of February for instance, the inquisition is bad (6).

The time should be stated in the present tense (7).

The year of the Queen's reign, without adding the year of our Lord, is sufficient; or the year of our Lord, without adding the year of the Queen's reign, will suffice. Numbers should not be expressed by figures, but by words at length (8), or at least by Roman numerals (9).

4. *Before whom Holden.*] The name and office of the Coroner must be stated, in order that it may appear that the inquisition was taken before a court of competent jurisdiction. Also the place for which he is Coroner (10).

5. *The View.*] The inquisition must state that the inquiry was taken on *view* of the body, or it will be bad (11).

6. *The Description of the Deceased.*] Both Christian and surname of the deceased, either his real name or that by which he was usually known, should be stated accurately, if known (12).

---

(1) 2 H. P. C. 166.
(2) Dyer, 69.
(3) Cro. Jac. 276, 277.
(4) 2 Hawk. P. C. ch. 25.
(5) 2 Saund. 291.
(6) 1 T. R. 316.
(7) 2 Hawk. P. C. ch. 25, s. 127.
(8) 2 Hawk. P. C. 170.
(9) 1 Str. 26.
(10) 22 Ed. IV. 13, 16; Sum. 207; S. P. C. 9.
(11) Jer. O. C. 277.
(12) 2 Hawk. P. C. ch. 25, ss. 71 72,

If the name be unknown, he may be described as a person to the jurors unknown; but such a description would it seems be bad if he were known (1).

No addition is necessary (2), nor need the deceased be distinguished from another person of the same name by the addition of "the younger" (3). A name of dignity, however, as baronet or knight, which is actually a part of the name and not merely an addition, should be stated. But an imperfect addition where none is necessary, would not render the inquisition defective (4).

The courts have certain powers of amending inquisitions at the trial, for which see Rev. Stat. 878.

7. *Where the Body lies.*] The place where the body lies must be stated to show the jurisdiction of the Coroner, and that he has power to take the view (5).

8. *The Jurors, and their Finding upon Oath.*] The inquisition must show that all the jurors took the oath, and who they are, by name; and therefore it is insufficient to allege that it was taken by the oaths of the several persons underwritten (6), or of so and so (naming one or two) and others (7). So it must expressly appear that the jurors are from the county or jurisdiction within which the inquisition is holden; that they are at least twelve in number, and present the inquisition upon their oaths (8). If their Christian names and surnames are given in the body of the inquisition, it is not necessary that the jurors should sign their names in full (9). Before attempting to insert the names of the jurors in the inquisition, it should be accurately ascertained what they are, and how spelt, in order that there may be no variance

(1) 3 Camp. 264; Holt. C. N. P. 595; 2 H. P. C. 281.
(2) 2 H. P. C. 182.
(3) 3 B. & A. 579.
(4) 2 C. & P. 230.
(5) Jer. O. C. 279.
(6) 6 B. & C. 247.
(7) 2 H. P. C. 168.
(8) 2 Hawk. P. C. ch. 25, s. 126.
(9) *Reg.* v. *Golding*, 39 Q. B. 259.

between the names in the caption and those in the attestation (1).

9. *The Charge to Inquire.*] It is usual to state in the inquisition that the jury were charged to inquire, but this is not in strictness necessary (2).

10. *The Verdict.*] The finding of the Coroner's jury being equivalent to an indictment, it must be stated with the same legal precision and certainty, and must not be repugnant or inconsistent, and the charge should be direct and positive (3).

If the jury in their verdict think proper to comment on the conduct of parties towards one under their subjection who has committed suicide, the superior courts will not alter the finding on that account (4).

Where a jury found the cause of death to have been disease, adding that it was accelerated by an overdose of certain drugs taken in excess, and improperly compounded, prescribed and administered by one F., as a cholera preventive, and that F. was deserving of severe censure for the gross carelessness displayed by him in such compounding and prescribing; the inquisition was brought up by certiorari by F., but the court refused to quash it, holding that the imputation which it contained, not amounting to any indictable offence, gave F. no right to have it quashed, and that under the circumstances public justice did not require the interference of the court (5).

The verdict of the jury does not prevent the accused being tried for a higher or lesser offence.

The principal parts requiring attention in the verdict will be treated of under the next three heads.

11. *The Party Charged.*] If the inquisition contain matter of accusation against a party, such party should, if known,

(1) 3 C. & P. 414. (2) Lord Raym. 710; 2 Hawk. P. C. ch. 25, s. 126.
(3) Jer. O. C. 281; 16 U. C. Q. B. 487. (4) 15 U. C. Q. B. 244.
(5) *Reg.* v. *Farley*, 24 Q. B. 384.

be described by his Christian and surname. The Christian name should be such as he acquired at his baptism or confirmation, or at both (1). A second Christian name cannot be added after an *alias dictus* (2); but a person may, if he has acquired two Christian names, be indicted by both; and if they are misplaced, it is as much a misnomer as if other and different names were stated (3). The surname should be the one usually given to or acknowledged by the party; and if there is a doubt which one of two names is his real surname, the second may be added after an *alias*, adding the Christian name to each (4).

When the party is unknown, he may be described as a "certain person to the jurors aforesaid unknown," adding, if possible, some description by which he may be designated, for no proceedings can be taken upon an inquisition charging a person unknown, without something by which to ascertain who the jury meant (5).

Any number of accessories to any felony may be charged with the substantive felony in the same inquisition, notwithstanding the principal felon be not included therein, or be not in custody, or amenable to justice (6).

An omission of the Christian or surname, or an error in either, can only be taken advantage of by a plea in abatement. By pleading over the objection is waived. If the name sounds the same it is no objection if it is misspelt (7). And the objection of one defendant, where several are named in the inquisition, will not abate the inquisition as to all, as it is several against each (8).

---

(1) Co. Lit. 3; 6 Mod. 115, 116; Jer. O. C. 281.
(2) Ld. Raym. 562; Willes, 554; 2 East. 111.
(3) 5 T. R. 195.
(4) Bro. Misn. 47: Jer. O. C. 282.
(5) R. & R. 409.
(6) Con. Stat. Can. ch. 97, s. 8; 31 Vic. ch. 72, ss. 1, 2.
(7) 10 East. 84; 16 East. 110.
(8) 2 H. P. C. 177; but see 32-33 Vic. ch. 29, s. 71, and Rev. Stat. 878, as to power of judge to amend.

12. *The Addition.*] The party charged should also be described by his addition or occupation; although the want of an addition or the stating a wrong one may be amended under 32-33 Vic. ch. 29.

13. *The Allegation of Time and Place.*] The time and place when and where the party is charged with having committed the offence should be stated accurately if possible. The hour of the day need not be stated. But defects in stating the time and place may be amended at the trial under 32-33 Vic. ch. 29. And it seems mention of the place is not absolutely necessary, where the venue is stated in the margin of the inquisition, except in cases where local description is required (1).

14. *The Description of the Act.*] The inquisition ought to contain a complete description of such facts and circumstances as constitute the crime without inconsistency or repugnancy (2). The charge must be distinct and substantive, and every fact and necessary ingredient must be stated, for it is not sufficient (in general) to charge the defendant generally with having committed the offence (3). There are, however, exceptions to this rule, amongst which are the principal crimes which come under the notice of Coroners. For instance, in the case of accessories before the fact (4), and aiders and abettors, it is not necessary to state the particulars of the incitement and solicitation, or of the aid and assistance. And in cases of murder or manslaughter, it is sufficient (if murder) to charge that the accused person "did feloniously, wilfully and of his malice aforethought, kill and murder;" and (if manslaughter) "did feloniously kill and slay" the deceased (5). Impertinent and unnecessary allegations and useless circumstances of aggravation ought to be avoided.

---

(1) 32-33 Vic. ch. 29.
(2) 16 U. C. Q. B. 487; 5 East. 244.
(3) Jer. O. C. 286.
(4) 2 East. 4.
(5) 32-33 Vic. ch. 29, s. 27.

The allegations must be made with certainty, and be stated *positively*, and not by way of recital (1), inference or argument (2), or the like. Statements should not be made in the *disjunctive*, or the inquisitions will be bad for uncertainty. For instance, "murdered *or* caused to be murdered," "wounded *or* murdered," "conveyed *or* caused to be conveyed," &c., would be bad (3). And the same if the party is charged in two different characters in the disjunctive (4).

The charge must also be single. For a party cannot in general be charged with two or more offences in the same inquisition. So neither can two persons be charged with different and distinct offences. Offences of different degrees, but dependent one upon the other, may be charged in the same inquisition as principals in the first and second degree and accessories before the fact (5).

If the jury find the cause of death was the act of any person, and there is something which excuses that person, the matter excusing him should be found also. For example, that the person was insane when he did the act.

In particular cases, certain words of a technical character must be used, or else the inquisition will be bad. These words are reduced to few in number by the present law. When drawing up an inquisition for any felony, the word "*feloniously*" must be inserted; for instance, in describing the offence of manslaughter, it is necessary to state "did *feloniously* kill and slay." Again, in charging a person with murder, in addition to the word feloniously, the actual word *murder* must be used (6). The word *kill*, or any other of the same meaning, will not suffice. Also, in this case and that of *felo de se*, the words *malice aforethought* must be inserted —"*feloniously* and of his *malice aforethought*." As the

(1) 2 Ld. Raym. 1363.
(2) 2 Hawk. P. C. ch. 25, s. 58.
(3) Jer. O. C. 289.
(4) 2 Ro. Rep. 263.
(5) Jer. O. C. 299.
(6) Fost. C. L. 424; 2 H. P. C. 184.

offence of *felo de se* admits of no degrees, it is not necessary to state the party *murdered* himself, but a word of similar meaning may be employed (1). Formerly there were several more words, and there were even sentences essential to the validity of Coroner's inquisitions, such as "with force and arms," "against the peace of our Lady the Queen," &c., &c.; but these have been got rid of, either by the express provisions of 32-33 Vic. ch. 29, or by the powers of amendment now vested in the courts.

15. *The Attestation.*] This is an essential part of the inquisition (2). Underneath it the Coroner and jurors sign their names opposite seals, and the Coroner adds his office, thus:

"A. B., Coroner, County of ——."

The Coroner and jurors should sign their names in full and not by initials (3), although if their names are stated in full in the caption this is not requisite (4). A person who cannot write his name should not be sworn as a juror.

It appears there is no express authority requiring the inquisition to be sealed, but the practice of sealing is universal, and had better not be departed from. Affix a separate seal for the Coroner and each of the jurymen.

Coroners should keep copies of all inquisitions, in order to be able to make their returns to the proper officers (5).

Sec. 13.—*Publication of Proceedings.*

Strictly speaking, it is unlawful to publish a statement of the evidence before a Coroner's jury, as long as the proceedings are pending at least (6); and one who is aggrieved by

(1) Plowd. 255; 1 Saund. 356; 1 Keb. 66; 1 Salk. 377; 7 Mod. 16.
(2) See Form No. 60.
(3) 6 B. C. 247.
(4) Jer. O. C. 297; *Reg.* v. *Golding*, 39 Q. B. 259.
(5) See p. 11.
(6) 1 B. & Ald. 37

the publication may obtain redress by civil action for the injury sustained (1), or the publishers may be punished by indictment or criminal information (2). But with the present "liberty of the press," a fair and honest publication of the proceedings, without being accompanied by unfounded or unjust comments, would hardly meet with much discountenance from the courts.

Sec. 14.—*Defraying Expenses.*

The expenses of an inquest are supposed to be paid by the Coroner, who afterwards can present his account to the County Treasurer for payment. In practice, however, each person having a claim for services rendered in connection with an inquest, makes out his own account, and after getting it certified as correct by the Coroner, leaves it with the County Treasurer in duplicate.

There is no provision for defraying the expense of an analysis when not made by a medical witness; and, as previously stated, it is necessary for the Coroner to obtain the sanction of the Attorney-General, in order to have the amount paid by Government. When, therefore, a Coroner finds an analysis will be necessary, he should at once apply to the Attorney-General for such sanction, and he should state that he has done so to the chemist, in order to prevent any delay on his part.

There is also no direct provision for defraying the expense of burying persons who have no friends or property available for the purpose, but if the Coroner issues his warrant to bury the body, all proper acts done in pursuance of that warrant ought to be paid by the Government, and if not so

(1) 3 B. & C. 556; 4 B. & A. 218; 5 D. & R. 447, s. c.
(2) Jer. O. C. 269

paid, the county authorities should sanction the amount being paid out of the county funds (1).

When a body has been exhumed under a Coroner's warrant, there is a sum of $2 allowed for re-burying the body, and it may be assumed that a like sum will be allowed for all interments ordered by the Coroner.

Each account must have attached thereto an information on oath that it had been made to appear to the Coroner that there was reason to believe that the deceased died from violence or unfair means, or by culpable or negligent conduct, either of himself or others, under such circumstances as required investigation, and not through mere accident or mischance; and also a certificate of the County Attorney that the inquisition and papers had been filed with him, and that he considered there were sufficient grounds to warrant the holding of an inquest within the meaning of the Act respecting Coroners, and there must be a statement of the verdict under the following heads: Murder, Manslaughter, Justifiable Homicide, Suicide, Accidental Death (specifying the cause), Injuries (cause unknown), Found Dead, Natural Death. And when mileage is claimed, the places from and to must be mentioned.

All accounts must have the proper dates placed opposite the respective charges, and must be verified by the oath of the party making the claim (2), and must be rendered in duplicate to the Treasurer of the County quarterly, corresponding as nearly as possible with the quarters ending with the months of March, June, September and December, care being taken that one quarter's account does not run into another, and such accounts should include all demands

---

(1) When the body of a deceased person has been found publicly exposed, the Coroner, if there is no Inspector of Anatomy for the locality, is required to cause it to be interred, as the Act says, "As has been customary" (See Rev. Stat. 1260).

(2) See Form No. 57.

of the party rendering the same up to the time of such rendering.

The constables' accounts in connection with inquests must be sent in separately from their claims for other services, and have the certificate of the Coroner attached that the services were performed (1).

Under the regulations issued from the Inspector General's office (2), Coroners are required to state in their accounts the verdict of the jury under the following heads, viz.:

Murder,
Manslaughter,
Justifiable Homicide,
Suicide,
Accidental Death (specifying the cause),
Injuries (cause unknown),
Found Dead,
Natural Death.

Unless this regulation is complied with, the accounts will not be passed.

By the same regulations, the constables' accounts for services on inquests should be rendered separate from their claims for other services.

Coroners, for services rendered by them in the execution and return of civil process, are allowed the same fees as would be allowed to a sheriff for the same services, except for summoning jurors, for which they are allowed one shilling for every juror, in lieu of any other fee (3).

For Schedule of Fees, see Chapter XIV.

(1) See Form No. 129.
(2) The circular is dated January 26th, 1864.
(3) See C. R. 164; and Co. C. R. 150.

CHAPTER XIII.

PROCEEDINGS SUBSEQUENT TO THE INQUISITION.

SEC. 1.—*With reference to the Trial* 155
" 2.—*Of Bail* 156
" 3.—*Of Amending and Taking New Inquisitions* 156
" 4.—*Of Traversing Inquisitions* 158
" 5.—*Of Quashing Inquisitions* 159
" 6.—*Of Pleading to Inquisitions* 160

SEC. 1.—*Proceedings with reference to the Trial.*

If the verdict be murder or manslaughter, or accessory to murder before the fact, the Coroner must bind by recognizance (1) all such persons as know or declare anything material touching the crime, to appear at the next Assizes for the county, then and there to prosecute or give evidence against the accused (2); and a warrant (3) must be issued to apprehend the accused party and to commit him to prison (4); or if he be already in prison, the Coroner must issue a detainer to the gaoler (5). The mode of taking the depositions and returning them to the proper officer has already been mentioned (6).

If a wife is a witness, and her husband is not present to enter into a recognizance, the wife is not to be bound in any penal sum, but *on pain of* imprisonment (7). If the husband is present, he must be bound for the appearance of

(1) See Form No. 45.
(2) Con. Stat. Can. ch. 102, s. 62; 32-33 Vic. ch. 30, s. 60.
(3) See Form No. 48. (4) See Form No. 49, and Chit. C. L. 164.
(5) See Form No. 50, and Jer. O. C. 298. (6) See Chapter XII., s. 10.
(7) See Form No. 45.

his wife (1). And if an apprentice or minor is a witness, the master or parent is bound for his appearance (2).

The Coroner should be present at the Assizes, when any case is tried on an inquisition taken before him; for if he is not present, the court may fine him (3).

Sec. 2.—*Of Bail.*

Coroners must not accept of bail, but if the party accused is advised that he is entitled to be bailed, his remedy is by application to one of the superior courts, or one of the judges thereof (4), who will, in their discretion, allow bail to be taken. In the exercise of this discretion, the court or judge is guided by the facts and circumstances of the case as disclosed upon the depositions (5). If the offence is manslaughter, the application will, in general, be granted (6), even when the inquisition is for murder (7). On the other hand, if the offence is really murder, bail will generally be refused, although the inquisition is for manslaughter only (8), or even a lower crime (9).

When the Coroner is notified (10) by the prisoner, his counsel, attorney or agent, that he will move for an order to admit such prisoner to bail, a certified copy of the informations, &c., must be returned as directed in Chapter XII. s. 10.

Sec. 3.—*Of Amending and Taking New Inquisitions.*

Criminal prosecutions do not come within the benefit of the Statute of Jeofails, yet in furtherance of justice the

(1) See Form No. 45, and Impey O. C. 265.
(2) See Form No. 45, and Impey O.C. 566.
(3) *In re Urwin*, O. B. 1827; Car. C. L. 17.
(4) Con. Stat. Can. ch. 102, s. 55.
(5) Cald. 295.
(6) 2 Str. 1242.
(7) 2 Str. 971.
(8) Comb. 111, 298.
(9) Comb. 298.
(10) See Form No. 55.

courts in their discretion have always allowed amendments in inquisitions which, though good in substance, were defective in form (1). And now ample powers of amendment are expressly given by legislative enactments (2). Under these either of the superior courts, or any judge thereof, or any judge of assize or gaol delivery, upon any inquisition being called in question before them or him, may order the same to be amended, if defective for want of the averment therein of any matter unnecessary to be proved, or for the omission of any technical words of mere form, or for any technicality.

If the inquisition is quashed, a new inquiry may, by leave of the court (3), be instituted by the Coroner (4), the body being disinterred by order of the court for that purpose, if it has not been a long time buried (5).

But if there is any imputation upon the Coroner, he will not be allowed again to make an inquiry, but a writ of *melius inquirendum* will be awarded to take a new inquisition by special commissioners, who proceed without viewing the body, by the testimony of witnesses only (6); or if the body can still be viewed, a new inquiry may be ordered to be taken by another Coroner, as was done in the case of the disaster on the Solent, arising from the Queen's yacht having run down the private yacht *Mistletoe*.

In the Balham inquiry as to the cause of Mr. Bravo's death, the first inquest not being considered satisfactory, the Attorney-General obtained an order from the Court of Queen's Bench, requiring the Coroner to shew cause why a fresh inquiry should not be made, upon which a final order was made quashing the first inquisition, and ordering the

(1) 1 Sid. 225, 259; 3 Mod. 101; 1 Saund. 356; 1 Keb. 907; 1 Hawk. P. C. ch. 27, s. 15; Jer. O C. 307.

(2) See 32-33 Vic. ch. 29, s. 32, and Rev. Stat. 878.

(3) Str. 167.

(4) 3 Mod. 80.

(5) Salk. 377; 1 Str. 22, 533.

(6) 2 Hawk. P. C. ch. 9, 556; 1 Salk. 190.

Coroner to hold a second inquiry before another jury, but on view of the body. This was not done from any defect on the face of the first inquisition, but because circumstances had arisen, subsequent to the first inquest, which caused a suspicion that Mr. Bravo had been poisoned, and had not committed suicide as was at first supposed. C. J. Cockburn, in giving judgment, stated that the court wished it to be distinctly understood that it is not in every case of an incomplete finding of the jury that the court will interfere to quash the inquisition and send the case to a fresh inquiry. It is only where the court sees that there has been a miscarriage, by evidence which might have thrown light upon the subject having been excluded, that they will interfere. The court must take care not uselessly to keep up the excitement in the public mind unless the way seems clear to some practical advantage (1).

But if the inquisition is quashed for a defect in form only, the Coroner may and ought to take a new inquisition, in like manner as if he had taken none before (2).

Sec. 4.—*Of Traversing Inquisitions.*

It seems that inquests of Coroners are in no case conclusive, but any one affected by them, either collaterally or otherwise, may deny their authority and put them in issue (3).

It has been doubted whether inquiries of flight and *felo de se* were traversable, but the law appears to be now settled that they are (4).

---

(1) *The Queen* v. *Carter*, Q. B. D. *Weekly Reporter*, July 8th, 1876.
(2) 2 Roll. Abr. 32; 2 H. P. C. 59; 2 Str. 69; Jer. O. C. 91.
(3) 3 Keb. 489; 6 B. & C. 247, 615, 627; Jer. O. C. 312.
(4) See Jer. O. C. 312, 313, 314; 2 Lev. 152.

An inquisition cannot be traversed to make a man *felo de se* who is found not to be so, unless the verdict be obtained by improper conduct of the Coroner, when a *melius inquirendum* may be obtained before special commissioners (1).

SEC. 5.—*Of Quashing Inquisitions.*

We have seen (2) that no inquisition found upon or by any Coroner's inquest, will be quashed for want of the averment therein of any matter unnecessary to be proved, nor for the omission of any technical words of mere form, nor for any technical defect; but if an inquisition is so defective that no judgment can be given upon it, it will in general be quashed; and where it contains the subject matter of accusation, this is done by the court before which the party is arraigned (3). If the application is made on behalf of the accused, it ought to be made before plea pleaded (4). An objection for any defect apparent on the face of the indictment must be taken by demurrer or motion to quash the indictment, before the defendant has pleaded, and not afterwards (5).

Inquisitions which do not contain the subject-matter of accusation, may also be quashed by application to one of the superior courts, the record being first removed there by *certiorari*. Inquisitions will be quashed if the facts are imperfectly stated, or, as stated, do not amount to a punishable offence, or if the inquisitions are uncertain in their

(1) 3 Mod. 80; 1 Salk. 190; Jer. O. C. 315; but see Impey O. C. 489.
(2) See p. 156; and Rev. Stat. 878.
(3) Jer. O. C. 315.
(4) Fost. C. L. 231; Holt, 684; 4 St. Tr. 677.
( ) 32-33 Vic. ch. 29, s. 32; *Reg.* v. *Golding*, 39 Q. B. 259.

language (1), or if the finding of the jury is not legally warranted by the facts set forth (2).

When an inquisition contains two or more substantial findings, it may be good in part, though void as to the residue (3).

Misconduct of the Coroner or jury will also be a good reason to quash the inquisition (4). For instance, if the Coroner wilfully misdirects the jury (5), or if he withdraw some of the jurymen in order to induce the others to find a particular verdict (6).

Also an inquisition will be quashed if taken without a view of the body, or if taken on view of a body which is so decomposed as to afford no information (7).

An inquisition taken before an unauthorized person, being a nullity, will not be quashed (8).

If an inquisition is quashed, a new inquiry may, by leave of the court, be instituted by the Coroner, unless he has been guilty of any corrupt practice, when the new inquiry will be taken by special commission, as stated above (9). The affidavits, in moving for a certiorari, should be entitled *The Queen* v. *A. B.* (naming the Coroner who held the inquest (10).

Sec. 6.—*Of Pleading to Inquisitions.*

When the inquisition contains the subject-matter of accusation of any person, it is equivalent to the finding of a grand jury, and such person may be tried and convicted

---

(1) 12 Mod. 112.

(2) 5 B. & Ad. 230; and see *Reg.* v. *Farley*, 24 Q. B. 384; *Reg.* v. *Golding*, 39 Q. B. 259.

(3) Jer. O. C. 318.

(4) 3 Mod. 80.

(5) 1 Str. 69.

(6) 12 Mod. 493.

(7) 1 Str. 22; 2 Hawk. P. C. ch. 9, s. 24.

(8) 8 A. & E. 936; 1 P. & D. 146.

(9) See p. 157.

(10) *The Queen* v. *Carter*, *Weekly Reporter*, July 8, 1876; *The Queen* v. *Farley*, 24 Q. B. 384.

upon it (1). And it seems if an indictment be found for the same offence, and the prisoner is acquitted on the one, he ought to be arraigned on the other, to which he may, however, plead his former acquittal (2). In practice, an indictment is always preferred to the grand jury, and the party *supposed* to be tried upon both proceedings at the same time so as to avoid a second trial.

When a prisoner is arraigned upon the inquisition it is done in the same form as upon an indictment, and the subsequent proceedings are in effect the same (3).

---

(1) 2 Hale, 61.
(2) 2 Hale, 61; 1 Salk. 382.
(3) Arch. Cr. Pl.

CHAPTER XIV.

SCHEDULE OF FEES.

Sec. 1.—*The Coroner's Fees in Inquests of Death* 162
" 2.—*The Coroner's Fees in Fire Inquests* 163
1. *In Cities, Towns and Villages* 163
2. *In Country Parts* 164
" 3.—*The Coroner's Fees for executing Civil Process* 164
" 4.—*The Fees of the Medical Witness* 166
" 5.—*The Chemist's Fees* 166
" 6.—*The Jurors and Witnesses* 166
" 7.—*The Constable's Fees* 167

Having referred to the Coroner's right to fees in Sec. 2, Chapter V., Part I., and having stated the manner in which the expenses of inquests are defrayed, and in what shape, and to whom the accounts are presented, in Sec. 14, Chapter XII., Part II., it will now, in connection with the subject of fees, only be necessary to give a list of them.

Sec. 1.—*The Coroner's Fees in Inquests of Death* (1).

Precept to summon jury	$0 50
Impanelling jury	1 00
Summons for witness, each (2)	0 25
Information or examination of each witness (3)	0 25

(1) These fees were established by the judges under and by virtue of 8 Vic. ch. 38; 32 Vic. ch. 10.

(2) If a witness is summoned and not examined, only 25c. can be charged, and if a witness is called from the persons present, without being summoned, the sum of 25c. for the examination can alone be charged. When a witness is both summoned and examined, then 50c. can be charged.

(3) See note No. 2.

Taking every recognizance (1) $0 50
Taking inquisition, and making return 4 00
Every warrant (2).. 1 00
Necessary travel to take an inquest, per mile (3) 0 20
Attending the Assizes, per diem (4)........................ 5 00

SEC. 2.—*The Coroner's Fees in Fire Inquests* (5).

1. *In Cities, Towns and Villages.*] For fire inquests in these places the Coroner is entitled, for the first day's inquiry, to ten dollars: should the inquiry extend beyond one day, then to ten dollars *per diem* for each of two days thereafter (6), and no more (7).

---

(1) When an inquest is adjourned, the charge of 50c. is for taking the recognizances of the whole jury, and not for each separate juryman; and where witnesses are bound over to appear and give evidence at the trial, all the witnesses should be entered in one recognizance, unless special circumstances prevent it.

(2) Where a warrant is issued to bury the body, the Government will not pay this fee, unless a certificate from the churchwardens or other proper authorities is obtained, stating they required a warrant to issue before they would permit the interment. If this certificate is not procured, however, the county will usually pay for the warrant. The purpose for which the warrant is issued must always be stated in the account.

(3) The mileage is only to be charged in going to the inquest, and not in returning also. If the Coroner holds more than one inquest during the same journey, he can only charge the mileage for the second or other inquests from the place of holding the previous inquest, and not from his residence. The allowance is for mileage *necessarily* travelled, and to hold the second inquest he only *necessarily* travels from the place where the last was held.

(4) Rev. Stat. 891.

(5) In all cases the party requiring an investigation into accidents by fire is alone responsible for the expenses of and attending such investigation; and no municipality can be made liable for any such expense, unless the investigation is required by an instrument under the hands and seals of the mayor or other head officer of the municipality, and of at least two other members of the council thereof. And such requisition is not to be given to charge any municipal corporation, unless there are strong special and public reasons for granting the same. Rev. Stat. 1991.

(6) No expenses of or for an adjournment of any fire inquest is chargeable against or payable by the party or municipal authorities requesting the investigation to be held, unless it is clearly shewn by the Coroner, and certified under his hand, why and for what purpose an adjournment took place, or became necessary in his opinion. Rev. Stat. 1991.

(7) Rev. Stat. 1991.

Mileage 20c – a/c must be made in duplicate

2. *In Country parts.*] For fire inquests in country parts the Coroner is entitled to five dollars for the first day; and should the inquiry extend beyond one day, then to four dollars for each of two days thereafter, and no more (1).

SEC. 3.—*The Coroner's Fees for executing Civil Process.*

The same fees are to be taxed and allowed to Coroners for services rendered by them in the execution and return of process in civil suits as would be allowed to a sheriff for the same service (2).

The following is a list of fees: the first list being for the Courts of Queen's Bench and Common Pleas, and the second for the County Court:

	Q.B. & C.P.	C.C.
Every warrant to execute any process, mesne or final, when given to a bailiff	$0 75	$0 50
Arrest—when amount endorsed does not exceed $200	2 00	2 00
Arrest—when amount endorsed is over $200 and under $400	4 00	4 00
Arrest—when amount endorsed is $400 and over	6 00	
Mileage, going to arrest, when arrest made, per mile	0 13	0 13
Mileage, conveying party arrested from place of arrest to gaol, per mile	0 13	0 13
Bail bond, or bond for the limits	2 00	1 00
Assignment of the same	1 00	25
For an undertaking to give a bail bond	1 00	
Service of process not bailable, *scire facias* or writ of revivor (including affidavit of service) each defendant.	1 50	1 00
Serving subpœna, declaration, notices, or other papers (besides mileage for each party served)	0 75	0 40
Receiving, filing, entering and endorsing all writs, declarations, rules, notices or other papers to be served, each	0 25	0 10
Return of all process and writs (except supœnas)	0 50	0 25

(1) Rev. Stat. 1091; and see note No. 6, p. 163.

(2) R. C. No. 164; and R. Co. Ct. No. 150.

	Q.B. & C.P.	C.C.
Every search, not being by a party to a cause or his attorney	$0 30	$0 30
Certificate of result of search, when required	0 75	0 75
Serving each juror	0 20	0 20
Poundage on executions, and on attachments in the nature of executions, where the sum made shall not exceed $1,000, six per cent.		
Where it exceeds $1,000, and is less than $4,000, three per cent.		
When the sum is $4,000 and over, 1½ per cent., in addition to the poundage, allowed up to $1,000.		
Schedule of goods taken in execution, including copy to defendant, if not exceeding five folios	1 00	0 50
Each folio above five	0 10	0 10
The sum actually disbursed for advertisements required by law to be inserted in the official *Gazette* or other newspaper.		
Drawing up advertisements required by law to be published in the official *Gazette* or other newspaper, and transmitting the same in each suit	1 50	0 75
Every notice of sale of goods in each suit	0 75	0 40
Every notice of postponement of sale on execution, in each suit	0 25	0 20
Service of writ of possession or restitution, besides mileage	6 00	2 00
Bringing up prisoner on attachment or *habeas corpus*, besides travel at 20c. per mile	1 50	1 00
Actual mileage from the court house to the place where the service of any process, paper or proceeding is made, per mile	0 13	0 13
Seizing estate and effects on attachment against an absconding debtor	3 00	1 50
Every inventory, not exceeding five folios	1 00	0 50
Each folio above five	0 10	0 10
Removing or retaining property, reasonable and necessary disbursements and allowances, to be made by the Master, or by order of the court or a judge, or by the clerk in county court matters.		
Bond to secure goods taken under an attachment, if prepared by Coroner	1 50	1 50

IN REPLEVIN.	Q.B. & C.P.	C.C.
Precept to a bailiff	$0 75	$0 40
Notice for service on defendant	0 75	0 40
Delivering goods to party obtaining the writ	3 00	1 50
For writ, &c., *de retorno habendo*	1 00	0 50
Replevin bond	2 00	1 00

SEC. 4.—*The Fees of the Medical Witness* (1).

Attendance without a *post mortem* (2)	$5 00
Attendance with a *post mortem*, but without an analysis	10 00
Attendance with a *post mortem* and an analysis	20 00
Travel both to and from the inquest, per mile (3)	0 20

SEC. 5.—*The Chemist's Fees.*

There is no provision for paying a chemist for an analysis any particular sum; but when a Coroner represents to the Attorney-General the necessity for such analysis, he will, in all proper cases, authorize the payment of a reasonable fee (4).

SEC. 6.—*The Jurors and Witnesses.*

There is no provision for paying either jurymen or witnesses at inquests, and consequently they are not entitled to any remuneration. The recent Act under which crown witnesses are paid does not apply to Coroners' courts.

---

(1) See Rev. Stat. 877.

(2) The medical witness is only entitled to $5 for each day's attendance, and not $5 for each body where there are several dead. 13 U. C. Q. B. 498.

(3) The mileage must be proved by the oath of the medical witness administered by the Coroner, who then makes an order on the treasurer of the county (see Form No. 43) in favour of such medical practitioner for the payment of his mileage and fees, and the treasurer must pay the amount out of any funds he may then have in the county treasury. See Rev. Stat. 877.

(4) See remarks on this subject at p. 141.

Sec. 7.—*The Constable's Fees* (1).

Attending on the inquest the first day, including summoning jury and witnesses, but not including mileage	$2 00
Attending inquest each day other than the first, if not engaged over four hours	1 00
Attending inquest each day other than the first, if engaged more than four hours....................................	1 50
Serving summons or subpœna to attend before Coroner if inquest not held the same day as service	0 25
Mileage serving same, one way	0 10
Exhuming body under Coroner's warrant..................	2 00
Arrest of each individual upon a warrant..................	1 50
Mileage to serve warrant (2) and to take prisoners to gaol or attend assizes	0 10
Attending assizes each day	1 50
Taking prisoners to gaol, exclusive of disbursements necessarily expended on their conveyance per mile	0 10
Burying the body	2 00

All other special services, a reasonable amount.

(1) Constables' accounts for services on inquests should be rendered separate from their other claims. Assistant constables must render their own accounts, certified by the Coroner as correct, and that assistance was necessary. See Form No. 131. If the inquest is adjourned, in addition to the fee for each other day, the constable is allowed for serving witnesses served after the first day, together with mileage.

(2) If no service effected, mileage is still allowed on proof of due diligence in trying to effect service. No extra charge can be made for a conveyance, unless one is necessary to convey the prisoner.

APPENDIX.

FORMS.

Any form required can be readily found by ascertaining its number or page from the following list.

No.		Page.
1.	Coroner's Commission	172
2.	Oath of Allegiance	173
3.	Oath of Office	173
4.	Indictment for not taking an Inquest	174
5.	Writ *De Coronatore Exonerando*	174
6.	Sheriff's Return thereon	175
7.	Warrant to Constable to summon Jury	175
8.	Warrant to Gaoler to summon Jury	175
9.	Summons to Jury	176
10.	Return of Coroner's Warrant	176
11.	Proclamation before calling Jury	176
12.	Proclamation for default of Jurors	177
13.	Certificate of fine of Juror or Witness	177
14.	Address to Jury before swearing the Foreman	177
15.	Foreman's Oath	177
16.	Oath of Jurymen	178
17.	Coroner's Charge to Jurymen after they are sworn	178
18.	Coroner's Charge to Jury after viewing the Body	178
19.	Summons to a Witness	178
20.	Order for the attendance of a Prisoner	179
21.	Proclamation for the attendance of Witnesses	179
22.	Warrant against Witness for contempt of Summons	179
23.	Oath on the *voir dire*	180
24.	Summons for a Medical Witness	180
25.	Commitment of Witness for refusing to give Evidence	180
26.	Commitment of Witness for refusing to sign his Information	181
27.	Oath of Interpreter	182
28.	Oath of Witness	182
29.	Declaration or Affirmation of Witness	183
30.	Information of Witnesses	183

No. PAGE.
31. Coroner's Certificate to each separate Information........ 183
32. Recognizance of Jurors upon an Adjournment 183
33. Coroner's Address on Adjournment 184
34. Proclamation of Adjournment 184
35. Warrant to bury the Body 184
36. Warrant to bury a *felo de se* 184
37. Return thereto 185
38. Proclamation at adjourned meeting 185
39. Caution to, and Statement of, Accused 185
40. Oath of Officer in charge of Jury 186
41. Coroner's Address to Jury after recording their Verdict .. 186
42. Proclamation at close of Inquest 186
43. Order for payment of a Medical Witness................ 186
44. Recognizance to prosecute 187
45. Recognizance to give Evidence 188
46. Commitment of Witness for refusing to enter into recognizance 189
47. Warrant to take up a Body 190
48. Warrant to apprehend Accused......................... 190
49. Warrant of Commitment of Accused 191
50. Warrant of Detainer to Gaoler 191
51. *Certiorari* to the Coroner.............................. 192
52. Return thereon 192
53. *Habeas Corpus* 192
54. Return thereon 193
55. Notice of Bail.. 193
56. *Venire facias* to Coroner to amend his Inquisition........ 194
57. Declaration of correctness of account 194
58. Oath of Mileage....................................... 194

INQUISITIONS.

59. The Caption 195
60. The Attestation.. 195
61. By an Infant drowning himself 195
62. By poisoning the deceased 196
63. By striking an Infant with a hammer 196
64. By shooting himself, being a lunatic.................. 197
65. By cutting his throat, being a lunatic 197
66. By stabbing himself, where the cause and the death are in different counties.................................... 198
67. By hanging himself, being a lunatic 198
68. By poisoning himself, being a lunatic 198

No. PAGE.

69. By drowning himself, being a lunatic 199
70. By throwing himself out of a window, being a lunatic.... 199
71. By throwing the deceased out of a window 200
72. By shooting himself in a fit of delirium 200
73. Murder, stating aid and abetment specially............. 201
74. Murder, charging accessories with the principal.......... 201
75. Murder, charging the accessory alone, principal unknown. 201
76. By hanging himself 202
77. By stabbing himself 202
78. By shooting himself 203
79. By drowning himself.................................. 203
80. By poisoning himself.................................. 204
81. By strangling himself 204
82. By cutting his own throat 205
83. Finding of goods 205
84. Murder 205
85. Manslaughter 206
86. Homicide, by correction 206
87. Homicide by shooting at butts 206
88. Homicide by a knife.................................. 207
89. Homicide in defence of person 207
90. Homicide against a street robber 208
91. Death by a cart...................................... 209
92. Death by falling from a cart in sport 210
93. Death by falling from a coach box. 210
94. Death by the overturning of a chaise 210
95. Drowned by the overturning of a boat................. 211
96. Killed by the fright of a horse 211
97. Killed by the kick of a horse........................ 212
98. Killed by falling into an area 212
99. Killed by falling from the leads of a house............ 213
100. Killed by a fall from a hayloft, being in liquor 213
101. Drowned whilst in a fit 213
102. Drowned 214
103. Drowned by bathing................................. 214
104. Drowned by falling out of a boat 215
105. Found drowned...................................... 215
106. By a fire 215
107. By the explosion of gunpowder during a fire 216
108. By being burnt 216
109. By being suffocated 216

No. Page.
110. Killed by the fall of a house 217
111. Suffocated in the mud 217
112. Killed by being shut up in a turn-up bed 217
113. Death of a child by sudden delivery 218
114. Death by a difficult birth and hard labour 218
115. Still born 219
116. Starved 219
117. Another form 219
118. Natural death 219
119. Found dead 220
120. Found dead, cause of death unknown 220
121. Sudden death by fits 220
122. By excessive drinking 220
123. Death in prison 221
124. Killed by explosion of boiler of steam engine 221
125. Killed by collision on a railway 221

126. Caption of a Fire Inquest 222
127. Requisition to hold a Fire Inquest 223
128. Return to Division Registrar 224
129. Certificate of Coroner to Constable's account 225
130. Information to hold Inquest 225
131. Declaration of Coroner to be attached to his account 225

No. 1.

COMMISSION.

Province of Canada.

[Great Seal] Elgin and Kincardine.

VICTORIA, by the grace of God, of the United Kingdom of Great Britain and Ireland, Queen, Defender of the Faith, &c. &c. &c.

To —— Greeting.

Know you, that having special trust and confidence in your loyalty, integrity and ability, We have constituted and appointed, and by these presents do constitute and appoint you the said —— —— to be Coroner within the District of —— of our Province of Canada, in addition to those persons who have been heretofore appointed by our Royal Commission, to execute the said office in the said district. To have, hold and enjoy the said office of Coroner, and to execute the duties thereof according to the laws of that part of our said Province, formerly called Upper Canada, together with all and singular the rights, fees, profits and privileges thereunto belonging and appertaining, unto you the said —— —— for and during our pleasure, and your residence within our said Province.

In testimony whereof, we have caused these our letters to be made patent, and the Great Seal of our said Province to be hereunto affixed. Witness, our right trusty and right well-beloved cousin, James, Earl of Elgin and Kincardine, Knight of the most ancient and most noble Order of the Thistle, Governor General of British North America, and Captain General and Governor in Chief in and over our Province of Canada, Nova Scotia, New Brunswick and the Island of Prince Edward and Vice-Admiral of the same, &c. &c. &c., at Montreal, this 17th day of August, in the year of our Lord one thousand eight hundred and forty-eight, and in the twelfth year of our reign.

ROBERT BALDWIN, *Attorney-General.*

By Command, W. B. SULLIVAN, *Secretary.*

No. 2.

OATH OF ALLEGIANCE.

CANADA,
Province of Ontario,
County of ——
To wit:

I, A. B., do sincerely promise and swear, that I will be faithful and bear true allegiance to Her Majesty Queen Victoria, as lawful Sovereign of the United Kingdom of Great Britain and Ireland, and of this Province, dependent on, and belonging to the said Kingdom; and that I will defend her to the utmost of my power against all traitorous conspiracies or attempts whatever which shall be made against her person, crown and dignity, and that I will do my utmost endeavour to disclose and make known to Her Majesty, her heirs and successors, all treasons and traitorous conspiracies and attempts which I shall know to be against her, or any of them. All this I do swear without any equivocation, mental evasion or secret reservation. So help me God. (See Rev. Stat. 203.)

No. 3.

OATH OF OFFICE.

You shall swear that you will well and truly serve our Sovereign Lady Queen Victoria and her liege people in the office of Coroner, and as one of Her Majesty's Coroners of this County of ——. And therein you shall diligently and truly do and accomplish all and every thing and things appertaining to your office, after the best of your cunning, wit and power, both for the Queen's profit, and for the good of the inhabitants within the said county; taking such fees as you ought to take by the laws and statutes of this Province, and not otherwise. So help you God.

No. 4.

INDICTMENT FOR NOT TAKING AN INQUEST.

CANADA, Province of Ontario, County of —— To wit: } The Jurors of our Lady the Queen upon their oath present, that on, &c., one A. B., *was drowned and suffocated in a certain pond, and of that drowning and suffocation he, the said A. B., then instantly died;* and that the body of the said A. B., at, &c., lay dead, of which C. D., Esquire, afterwards, to wit, on the —— day of —— in the year aforesaid, then being one of the Coroners of our said Lady the Queen for the county aforesaid, had notice; nevertheless the said C. D., not regarding the duty of his office in that behalf, afterwards to wit, on, &c., to execute his office of and concerning the premises, and to take inquisition of our said Lady the Queen, according to the laws and customs of this Province, concerning the death of the said A. B., unlawfully, obstinately and contemptuously did neglect and refuse; and that the said C. D. no inquisition in that behalf hath as yet taken against the peace, &c.

No. 5.

WRIT DE CORONATORE EXONERANDO.

CANADA, Province of Ontario, County of —— [L. S.] } VICTORIA, by the grace of God, of the United Kingdom of Great Britain and Ireland, Queen, Defender of the Faith, &c. To the Sheriff of the County of —— greeting. Forasmuch as we have for certain understood that C. D., one of our Coroners of your county, was appointed Coroner for your county in the year one thousand eight hundred and —— that *he is about to quit the county and to reside at a distance therefrom, and, therefore, cannot perform the duty of a Coroner in your county;* we command you, that without delay you remove the said C. D. from the office of Coroner in your county. Witness, &c. (1).

Or thus,

CANADA, Province of Ontario, County of —— [L. S.] } VICTORIA, &c.—To the Sheriff of —— greeting. Forasmuch as we have for certain understood that C. D., of —— in your county, Esquire, one of our Coroners of your county, was appointed a Coroner for your county in the year ——: *That in Trinity Term last a certain information was exhibited against him, for certain misdemeanors alleged to have been committed by him in his office of one of the Coroners of your county, on which he was tried at the last —— Assizes, when a verdict was found for the Crown, the jury at the same time stating that there was no proof* before them of his having received any bribe, and that he is also subject to severe rheumatic attacks; and from the above circumstances, he considers himself incapable any longer to perform the duty of Coroner as he ought to do: we command you, that without delay you remove the said C. D. from the office of a Coroner in your county. Witness, &c.

---

(1) See the grounds of removal, *ante* p. 26.

No. 6.

SHERIFF'S RETURN THEREON.

By virtue of the within writ to me directed, I have removed the within named C. D. from the office of a Coroner of and in my county, as within I am commanded. Dated this —— day of —— 18—.

The answer of A. B., Sheriff, County of ——

No. 7.

WARRANT TO CONSTABLE TO SUMMON JURY.

CANADA,
Province of Ontario,
County of ——
To wit:

To the Constables of the Township of —— in the County of ——, and all other Her Majesty's officers of the peace in and for the said county. By virtue of my office, these are in Her Majesty's name to charge and command you, that on sight hereof you summon and warn twenty-four (1) able and sufficient men of your several *townships* personally to be and appear before me on —— the —— day of —— instant, at —— of the clock, in the —— at the house of —— called or known by the sign of the —— in the said *township* of —— in the said county of —— then and there to do and execute all such things as shall be given them in charge, on behalf of our Sovereign Lady the Queen, touching the death of R. F. And for your so doing this is your warrant. And that you also attend at the time and place above mentioned, to make a return to those you shall so summon; and further to do and execute such other matters as shall be then and there enjoined you. And have you then and there this warrant. Given under my hand and seal this —— day of —— one thousand eight hundred and ——

C. D., Coroner, County of —— [L. S.]

No. 8.

WARRANT TO GAOLER TO SUMMON JURY.

CANADA,
Province of Ontario,
County of ——
To wit:

To the Keeper of the Common Gaol of the County of —— or his deputy there or other proper officer. By virtue of my office, these are in Her Majesty's name to authorize and require you, upon receipt hereof, to summon or cause to be summoned twelve (2) good and lawful men, prisoners within the walls of your prison, to be and appear before me at the —— room of the said prison, on —— the —— day of —— at —— of the clock, in the —— of the same day, to inquire into the cause of the death of ——

---

(1) Any number not less than twelve can be summoned.

(2) Or such number as will constitute half the jury.

late a prisoner within the said prison, and to do and execute all such things as in Her Majesty's behalf shall be given them in charge, and have then and there the names of the persons so summoned, together with my precept. And hereof you are not to fail, as you will answer the contrary at your peril. Given under my hand and seal this —— day of —— in the year of our Lord one thousand eight hundred and ——

C. D., Coroner, County of —— [L. S.]

No. 9.

SUMMONS FOR JURY (1).

CANADA,
Province of Ontario,
County of ——
To wit:

To the Constables of the Township of —— in the County of —— and all other Her Majesty's officers of the peace in and for the said county. By virtue of a warrant under the hand and seal of C. D., gentleman, one of Her Majesty's Coroners for this county, you are hereby summoned personally to be and appear before him as a juryman, on the —— day of —— instant, at —— of the clock, in the —— precisely, at the house of —— known by the sign of —— in the township of —— in the county of —— then and there to inquire on Her Majesty's behalf, touching the death of R. F., and further to do and execute such other matters and things as shall be then and there given you in charge, and not depart without leave. Hereof fail not at your peril. Dated the —— day of —— one thousand eight hundred and ——

Yours, &c.,
H. S., Constable of the said County of ——

To Mr. E. B., of the Township of —— in the County of —— carpenter.

No. 10.

RETURN OF CORONER'S WARRANT.

The execution of this warrant appears by the schedule thereto annexed.

The answer of —— Constable.

No. 11.

PROCLAMATION BEFORE CALLING JURY.

Oyez! Oyez! Oyez! You good men of this county, summoned to appear here this day, to inquire for our Sovereign Lady the Queen, when, how and by what means R. F. came to his death, answer to your names as you shall be called, every man at the first call, upon the pain and peril that shall fall thereon.

---

(1) The Coroner should furnish these summonses to the constable.

No. 12.

PROCLAMATION FOR DEFAULT OF JURORS.

Oyez! Oyez! Oyez! You good men who have been already severally called, and have made default, answer to your names and save your peril.

No. 13.

CERTIFICATE OF FINE OF JUROR OR WITNESS.

CANADA, Province of Ontario, County of —— To wit:	I, A. B., Coroner of and for the County of —— do certify, that C. D., of the —— of —— in the County of —— yeoman (*or as the case may be*) after being duly summoned

as a juror (*or as a witness*) and after being openly called three times, was fined by me on this —— day of —— A. D. 18— the sum of —— (1) for not appearing at an inquest holden before me this —— day of —— A.D. 18— upon the body of —— about the age of —— who was found dead at —— (*or other particulars or description*) to serve as a juror (*or as a witness to give evidence*) upon such inquest (2).

A. B., Coroner, County of ——

No. 14.

ADDRESS TO JURY BEFORE SWEARING FOREMAN.

Gentlemen, hearken to your foreman's oath; for the oath he is to take on his part is the oath you are severally to observe and keep on your part.

No. 15.

FOREMAN'S OATH.

You shall diligently inquire and true presentment make of all such matters and things as shall be here given you in charge, on behalf of our Sovereign Lady the Queen, touching the death of R. F., now lying dead, of whose body you shall have the view; you shall present no man for hatred, malice or ill-will, nor spare any through fear, favour or affection; but a true verdict give according to the evidence, and the best of your skill and knowledge. So help you God (3).

---

(1) The sum must not exceed four dollars. See note 3, p. 117.

(2) This certificate should be made out at the time the juror or witness makes default, and be transmitted to the Clerk of the Peace of the county in which the delinquent resides, on or before the first day of the next General Sessions. And a copy of the certificate must be served upon the person by leaving it at his residence within a reasonable time after the inquest. Rev. Stat. 875, and Rev. Stat. 578; and see Rev. Stat. 1990, as to fires.

(3) The oath should be adminstered in view of the body.

No. 16.

OATH OF JURYMEN.

The same oath which A. B., your foreman upon this inquest, hath now taken before you on his part, you and each of you are severally well and truly to observe and keep on your parts. So help you God (1).

No. 17.

THE CORONER'S CHARGE TO JURY AFTER THEY ARE SWORN.

Gentlemen, you are sworn to consider on behalf of the Queen, how and by what means H. H. came to *his* death. Your first duty is to take a view of the body of the deceased, wherein you will be careful to observe if there be any and what marks of violence thereon; from which and a proper examination of the witnesses intended to be produced before you, you will endeavour to discover the cause of *his* death, so as to be able to return a true and just verdict on this occasion.

No. 18.

CORONER'S CHARGE AFTER VIEW OF THE BODY.

After the view is taken, and the Jury called over, the Coroner should add to his former charge any necessary observations he may have made on view of the body, and add: "I shall now proceed to hear and take down the evidence respecting the fact, to which I must crave particular attention."

No. 19.

SUMMONS TO A WITNESS.

CANADA,
Province of Ontario,
County of ——
To wit:

To A. P., of the Township of —— in the County of —— *yeoman*. Whereas, I am credibly informed that you can give evidence on behalf of our Sovereign Lady the Queen, touching the death of A. P., now lying dead, in the township of —— in the said county of ——. These are, therefore, by virtue of my office, in Her Majesty's name, to charge and command you personally to be and appear before me at the dwelling house of J. R., known as the sign of —— situate at —— in the said township at —— o'clock, in the —— on the —— day of —— instant, then and there to give evidence and be examined, on Her Majesty's behalf, before me and my inquest touching the premises. Herein fail not,

---

(1) See note 3, p. 177.

as you will answer the contrary at your peril. Given under my hand and seal this —— day of —— one thousand eight hundred and ——.

C. D., Coroner, County of —— [L. S.]

No. 20.

ORDER FOR THE ATTENDANCE OF A PRISONER (1).

CANADA, Province of Ontario, County of —— To wit: } By virtue of section sixty of chapter twenty-nine of 32–33 Victoria, you are ordered to deliver C. D., now a prisoner in your custody, to E. F., who is hereby authorized to receive such prisoner for the purpose of conveying *him* before me and the jury, now on this —— day of —— one thousand eight hundred and —— holding an inquest upon the body of —— about the age of —— who was found dead at —— (*or other particulars or description*). Hereof fail not, as you will answer the contrary at your peril. Dated this —— day of —— one thousand eight hundred and ——

By the Court, A. B., Coroner.

To the Warden (*or Sheriff or Gaoler, as the case may be*) of the Provincial Penitentiary (*or of the County of* ——).

No. 21.

PROCLAMATION FOR THE ATTENDANCE OF WITNESSES.

If any one can give evidence on behalf of our Sovereign Lady the Queen, when, how, and by what means A. B. came to *his* death, let him come forth and he shall be heard.

No. 22.

WARRANT AGAINST A WITNESS FOR CONTEMPT OF SUMMONS.

CANADA, Province of Ontario, County of —— To wit: } To A. B., Constable of the —— of —— in the County of —— and to all other Her Majesty's officers of the peace in and for the said county. Whereas, I have received credible information that C. D., of the —— of —— in the said county, can give evidence on behalf of our Sovereign Lady the Queen, touching the death of E. F., now lying dead in the said —— of ——; and whereas the said C. D. having been duly summoned to appear and

(1) Formerly no prisoner confined for any debt or damages in a civil suit could be removed out of the district or county where he was confined; but now any prisoner can be taken anywhere as a witness. See 32–33 Vic. ch. 29, s. 60.

give evidence before me and my inquest touching the premises, at the time and place in the said summons specified, of which oath hath been duly made before me, hath refused and neglected so to do, to the great hindrance and delay of justice. These are, therefore, by virtue of my office in Her Majesty's name, to charge and command you, or one of you, without delay to apprehend and bring before me, one of Her Majesty's Coroners for the said —— now sitting at the —— aforesaid, by virtue of my said office, the body of the said C. D., that he may be dealt with according to law: and for so doing this is your warrant. Given under my hand and seal the —— day of —— one thousand eight hundred and ——

G. H., Coroner, County of —— [L. S.]

No. 23.

OATH TO BE ADMINISTERED ON THE VOIR DIRE.

You shall true answer make to all such questions as the court shall demand of you. So help you God.

No. 24.

SUMMONS FOR THE ATTENDANCE OF A MEDICAL WITNESS.

Coroner's Inquest at —— upon the body of ——

By virtue of this my order as Coroner for —— you are required to appear before me and the jury at —— on the —— day of —— one thousand eight hundred and —— at —— o'clock, to give evidence touching the cause of the death of —— (*and when the witness is required to make or assist at a post mortem examination, add*) and make or assist in making a *post mortem* examination of the body, with (*or without*) an analysis (*as the case may be*) and report thereon at the said inquest.

(Signed), A. B., Coroner.

To C. D., Surgeon (*or M.D., as the case may be*).

No. 25.

COMMITMENT OF A WITNESS FOR REFUSING TO GIVE EVIDENCE.

CANADA,
Province of Ontario,
County of ——
To wit:

To the Constables of the Township of —— in the County of —— and all other Her Majesty's officers of the peace in and for the county aforesaid, and also to the Keeper of the Gaol in the said county. Whereas, I heretofore issued my summons under my hand directed to C. D., of, &c., requiring his personal appearance before me, then and now one of Her Majesty's Coroners for the said county of —— at the time and place therein mentioned, to give evidence and be examined, on Her Majesty's behalf, touching and concerning the death of E. F., then and there lying dead, of the personal service of which said summons oath hath been duly made before me; and whereas the said C. D. having neglected and refused to appear, pursuant to the contents of the said summons, I thereupon afterwards issued my warrant under my hand and seal, in order that the said C. D., by virtue thereof, might be apprehended and brought before me to answer the premises. And whereas the said C. D., in pursuance thereof, hath been apprehended and brought before me, now duly sitting by virtue of my office, and hath been duly required to give evidence, and to be examined before me and my inquest, on her said Majesty's behalf, touching the death of the said E. F., yet the said C. D., notwithstanding, hath absolutely and wilfully refused, and still doth wilfully and absolutely refuse to give evidence and be examined touching the premises, or to give sufficient reason for his refusal, in wilful and open violation and delay of justice: these are, therefore, by virtue of my office, in Her Majesty's name, to charge and command you or one of you, the said constables and officers of the peace in and for the said township and county, forthwith to convey the body of the said C. D. to the gaol of the said county at the —— of —— in the said county, and him safely to deliver to the keeper of the said gaol; and these are, likewise, by virtue of my said office, in Her Majesty's name, to will and require you, the said keeper, to receive the body of the said C. D. into your custody, and him safely to keep in the gaol, until he shall consent to give his evidence and be examined before me and my inquest, on Her Majesty's behalf, touching the death of the said E. F., or until he shall from thence be discharged by due course of law; and for so doing this is your warrant. Given under my hand and seal the —— day of —— in the year of our Lord one thousand eight hundred and ——

A. B., Coroner, County of —— [L.S.]

No. 26.

COMMITMENT OF A WITNESS FOR REFUSING TO SIGN HIS INFORMATION.

CANADA,
Province of Ontario,
County of ——
To wit:

To M. N., one of the constables of the Township of —— in the County of —— and all other Her Majesty's officers of the peace in and for the said county, and also to the Keeper of the Gaol of the said county. Whereas C. D., of the —— of —— in the said county of —— *yeoman*, is a material witness on behalf of our Sovereign Lady the Queen, against G. H., late of the —— of —— in the county aforesaid, labourer, now charged before me, one of Her Majesty's Coroners for the said county, and my inquest, with the wilful murder of E. F., there now lying dead; and whereas the said C. D., at this time of my inquiry, on view of the body of the said E. F., how and by what means *he*, the said E. F., came by *his* death, hath personally appeared before me, and my said inquest, and, on Her Majesty's behalf, hath given evidence and information on oath touching the premises, which said evidence and information having by me been reduced into writing, and the contents thereof by me, in the presence of my said inquest, openly and truly read to *him*, the said C. D., who doth acknowledge the same to be true, and that the same doth contain the full substance and effect of the evidence by *him* given before me to my said inquest, and the said C. D. having by me been requested and desired to sign and set *his* hand to *his* said testimony and information, and to acknowledge the same as by law is required, yet notwithstanding, the said C. D. hath wilfully and absolutely refused, and still doth wilfully and absolutely refuse so to do, in open defiance of law, and to the great hindrance of public justice. These are, therefore, by virtue of my office, in Her Majesty's name, to charge and command you, or one of you, the said constables and other Her Majesty's officers of the peace in and for the said county of —— forthwith to convey the body of the said C. D. to the gaol of the said county at —— in the said county, and *him* safely to deliver to the keeper of the said gaol; and these are, likewise, by virtue of my said office, in Her Majesty's name, to will and require you, the said keeper, to receive the body of the said C. D. into your custody, and *him* safely to keep in prison until *he* shall duly sign and acknowledge *his* said information, or shall be from thence otherwise discharged by due course of law: and for so doing this is your warrant, Given under my hand and seal this —— day of —— in the year of our Lord one thousand eight hundred and ——

A. B., Coroner, County of —— [L. S.]

No. 27.

OATH OF INTERPRETER.

You shall well and truly interpret unto the several witnesses here produced on the behalf of our Sovereign Lady the Queen, touching the death of E. F., the oath that shall be administered unto them, and also the questions and demands which shall be made to the witnesses by the court or the jury concerning the matters of this inquiry; and you shall well and truly interpret the answers which the witnesses shall thereunto give, according to the best of your skill and ability. So help you God.

No. 28.

OATH OF WITNESS.

The evidence which you shall give to this inquest on behalf of our Sovereign Lady the Queen, touching the death of E. F., shall be the truth, the whole truth, and nothing but the truth. So help you God.

No. 29.

DECLARATION OR AFFIRMATION OF WITNESS.

I, A. B., do solemnly, sincerely and truly declare and affirm, that I am one of the Society called Quakers (*Mennonists, Tunkers or Unitas Fratrum or Moravians, as the case may be*).

Then let the witness add—I, A. B., do solemnly, sincerely and truly declare and affirm that the evidence I shall give to this inquest on behalf of our Sovereign Lady the Queen, touching the death of —— shall be the truth, the whole truth, and nothing but the truth. So help me God.

No. 30.

INFORMATION OF WITNESSES.

CANADA,
Province of Ontario,
County of ——
To wit: } Informations of witnesses severally taken and acknowledged on behalf of our Sovereign Lady the Queen, touching the death of E. F., at the dwelling-house of J. B., known by the name or sign of —— in the —— of —— in the county of —— on the —— day of —— in the —— year of our Lord one thousand eight hundred and —— before me, A. B., *Esquire*, one of Her Majesty's Coroners for the said county, on an inquisition then and there taken on view of the body of the said E. F., then and there lying dead, as follows, to wit:

C. D., of the —— of —— in the said county of —— *yeoman*, being sworn, saith, &c. (*stating the evidence in the first person*). C. D.

At the end of each separate information the Coroner adds the following certificate.

No. 31.

CORONER'S CERTIFICATE TO EACH SEPARATE INFORMATION.

Taken upon oath and acknowledged this —— day of —— in the year of our Lord one thousand eight hundred and —— before me.

A. B., Coroner, County of ——

No. 32.

RECOGNIZANCE OF JURORS UPON AN ADJOURNMENT.

Gentlemen, you acknowledge yourselves severally to owe to our Sovereign Lady the Queen the sum of one hundred dollars, to be levied upon your goods and chattels, lands and tenements, for Her Majesty's use, upon condition that if you and each of you do personally appear here again (*or at an adjourned place*) on —— next, being the —— day of —— instant, at —— of the clock in the —— precisely, then and there to make further inquiry, on behalf of our Sovereign Lady the Queen, touching the death of the said E. F., of whose body you have had the view; then this recognizance to be void, or else to remain in full force. Are you content?

No. 33.

THE CORONER'S ADDRESS ON ADJOURNMENT.

Gentlemen, the court doth dismiss you for this time; but requires you severally to appear here again (*or at the adjourned place*) on —— the —— day of —— instant, at —— of the clock in the —— precisely, upon pain of $100 a man, on the condition contained in your recognizance entered into.

No. 34.

PROCLAMATION OF ADJOURNMENT.

Oyez! Oyez! Oyez! All manner of persons who have anything more to do at this court before the Queen's Coroner for this county, may depart home at this time, and give their attendance here again (*or at the adjourned place*) on —— next, being the —— day of —— instant, at —— of the clock in the —— precisely. God save the Queen.

No. 35.

WARRANT TO BURY AFTER A VIEW.

CANADA,
Province of Ontario,
County of ——
To wit:

To the Minister and Churchwardens of —— (*or to the proper authorities having charge of the intended place of burial*) and to all others whom it may concern. Whereas an inquisition hath this day been held upon view of the body of R. F., who, not being of sound mind, memory and understanding, but lunatic and distracted, shot himself, and now lies dead in your township; these are therefore to certify that you may lawfully permit the body of the said R. F. to be buried; and for your so doing this is your warrant. Given under my hand and seal this —— day of —— one thousand eight hundred and ——

A. B., Coroner, County of —— [L. S.]

No. 36.

WARRANT TO BURY A FELO DE SE AFTER INQUISITION FOUND (1).

CANADA,
Province of Ontario,
County of ——
To wit:

To the Churchwardens of —— (*or to the proper authorities having charge of the intended place of burial*) and Constables in the Township of —— in the County of ——. Whereas, by an inquisition taken before me, one of Her Majesty's Coroners for

(1) The interment must take place within twenty-four hours after the finding of the inquisition (see p. 36). and the warrant to bury a *felo de se* is not to be directed to the minister, for no service is to be said (see p. 35); it may be directed to the constables only.

the said county of —— this —— day of —— in the —— year of Her present Majesty Queen Victoria, at the —— of —— in the said county of —— on view of the body of J. D., then and there lying dead, the jurors in the said inquisition named have found that the said J. D. feloniously, wilfully, and of his malice aforethought did kill and murder himself; these are, therefore, by virtue of my office, to will and require you forthwith to cause the body of the said J. D. to be buried according to law; and for your so doing this is your warrant. Given under my hand and seal this —— day of —— in the year of our Lord one thousand eight hundred and ——

A. B., Coroner, County of —— [L. S.]

No. 37.

THE RETURN THERETO.

By virtue of the within warrant to us directed, we have caused the body within named to be buried according to law.

C. D., } Churchwardens.
E. F., }
J. D., Constable.

No. 38.

PROCLAMATION AT ADJOURNED MEETING.

Oyez! Oyez! Oyez! All manner of persons who have anything more to do at this court before the Queen's Coroner for this county, on this inquest now to be taken, and adjourned over to this time and place, draw near, and give your attendance; and you gentlemen of the jury who have been impanelled and sworn upon this inquest to inquire touching the death of R. F., severally answer to your names and save your recognizances.

No. 39.

CAUTION TO AND STATEMENT OF THE ACCUSED.

CANADA,
Province of Ontario,
County of ——
To wit:

A. B. stands charged before me the undersigned, one of Her Majesty's Coroners in and for the county of —— this —— day of —— in the year of our Lord one thousand eight hundred and —— by an inquisition taken before me, this —— day of —— in the year of our Lord one thousand eight hundred and —— at the —— of —— in the said county of —— on view of the body of R. F., then and there lying dead; for that the said A. B., on the —— day of —— in the year of our Lord one thousand eight hundred and —— at the —— of —— in the county of —— did wilfully murder the said R. F. *(or as the finding may be)*, and the said charge being read to the said A. B., and the witnesses for the prosecution, C. D., E. F., &c., being severally examined in his presence, the said A. B. is now addressed by me as follows:—"Having heard the evidence, do you wish to say anything in answer to the charge? You are not obliged to say anything, unless you desire to do so; but whatever you say will be taken down in writing, and may be given in evidence against you at your trial." Whereupon the said A. B. saith as follows: [*Here state whatever the prisoner may say, and in his very words as nearly as possible. Get him to sign it, if he will, at the end thus: A. B.*]

Taken before me at —— the day and year first above mentioned.

J. S., Coroner, County of ——

No. 40.

OATH OF OFFICER TO KEEP THE JURY UNTIL THEY ARE AGREED IN THEIR VERDICT.

You shall well and truly keep the jury upon this inquiry without meat, drink or fire; you shall not suffer any person to speak to them, nor shall you speak to them yourself, unless it be to ask them if they have agreed on their verdict, until they shall be agreed. So help you God (1).

No. 41.

CORONER'S ADDRESS TO THE JURY AFTER RECORDING THEIR VERDICT.

Gentlemen, hearken to your verdict as delivered by you, and as I have recorded it. You find, &c. [*Here repeat the substance of the verdict, and then add*] So say you all.

No. 42.

PROCLAMATION AT THE CLOSE OF INQUEST.

Oyez! oyez! oyez! You good men of this township who have been impanelled and sworn of the jury to inquire for our Sovereign Lady the Queen, touching the death of R. F., and who have returned your verdict, may now depart hence and take your ease. God save the Queen.

No. 43.

ORDER FOR PAYMENT OF MEDICAL WITNESS.

By virtue of section nine of chapter seventy-nine of the Revised Statutes of Ontario, I, A. B., one of the Coroners of and for the

(1) See p. 116, note 2.

county of —— do order you the treasurer of the said county of —— to pay to —— the sum of —— being the fees due to him for having attended as a medical witness at an inquest holden before me this —— day of —— upon the body of —— about the age of —— who was found dead at —— *(or other particulars or description)* and at which said inquest the jury returned a verdict of ——. [*State the verdict concisely*].

A. B., Coroner, County of ——

Witnessed by me C. D., of the Township of —— in the County of ——

To the Treasurer of the County of ——

No. 44.

RECOGNIZANCE TO PROSECUTE, &c.

CANADA,
Province of Ontario,
County of ——
To wit:

Be it remembered, that on the —— day of —— in the year of the reign of our Sovereign Lady Victoria (1) of the United Kingdom of Great Britain and Ireland, Queen, Defender of the Faith, A. B., of the township of —— in the county of —— *baker; C. G., of the same place, victualler;* E. F., *of the same place, labourer (and so insert the names of all bound over)* do severally acknowledge to owe to our Sovereign Lady the Queen, the sum of two hundred dollars of lawful money of Canada, to be levied on their several goods and chattels, lands and tenements, by way of recognizance, to Her Majesty's use, in case default shall be made in the conditions following:

The condition of this recognizance is such, that if the above bounden —— do severally personally appear at the Assizes to be holden at —— in and for the county of —— and the said A. B. shall then and there prefer or cause to be preferred to the grand jury a bill of indictment against G. H., and now in custody for the wilful murder of R. F., late the wife of the said E. F. *(or as the finding may be);* and that the said A. B., C. G. and E. F. do then and there severally personally appear to give evidence on such bill of indictment to the said grand jury, and in case the said bill of indictment shall be returned by the grand jury a true bill, that then they the said A. B., C. G. and E. F., do severally personally appear at the next Assizes to be holden for the said county of —— and the said A. B. shall then and there prosecute or cause to be prosecuted the said G. H. on such indictment; and the said A. B., C. G., and E. F. do then and there severally give evidence to the jury, that shall pass on the trial of the said G. H. touching the premises; and in case the said bill of indictment shall be returned by the grand jury not found, that then they do severally personally appear at the

---

(1) The years of the reign of Queen Victoria are reckoned from the 20th of June, 1837, consequently up to but not including the 20th of June, 1878, will be the 41st year of her reign.

said Assizes to be then and there holden for the said county, and then and there prosecute and give evidence to the jury that shall pass on the trial of the said G. H., upon an inquisition taken before me, one of Her Majesty's Coroners for the said county of —— on view of the body of the said R. F., late the wife of the said E. F., and not depart the court without leave; then this recognizance to be void, otherwise to remain in full force (1).

Taken and acknowledged this —— day of —— one thousand eight hundred and —— before me

C. D., Coroner, County of ——

No. 45.

RECOGNIZANCE TO GIVE EVIDENCE.

CANADA,
Province of Ontario,
County of ——
To wit:

Be it remembered (*as in the last precedent*), J. P., of the township of —— in the county of —— *blacksmith;* T. P., *of the same place, victualler;* J. R., *of the same place, whitesmith,* the husband of S. R.; J. B. *of the same place, haberdasher,* the mainpernor of J. J., his apprentice, an infant; J. S., *of the same place, sword cutler,* the mainpernor of G. S., his son, an infant, do severally acknowledge to owe to our Sovereign Lady the Queen, the sum of two hundred dollars of lawful money of Canada, to be levied on their several goods and chattels, lands and tenements, by way of recognizance to Her Majesty's use, in case default shall be made in the condition following; and *Susan,* the wife of J. P., *of the same place, labourer,* on pain of imprisonment in case she shall make default in such condition: The condition of this recognizance is such, that, if the above bounden J. P., T. P., S. R., the wife of the said J. R., J. J., G. S., and S. P., do severally personally appear at the next Assizes, to be holden at ——, in and for the county of ——, and then and there give evidence on a bill of indictment to be preferred to the grand jury against C. D., now at large, for the wilful murder of *Sarah,* his wife (*or as the finding may be*); and in case the said bill of indictment shall be returned by the grand jury a true bill, then that they do severally personally appear at the Session of Gaol Delivery, to be holden for the said county of ——, next after the

(1) If a wife be to give evidence, and the husband be not present to enter into the recognizance, the wife is to be bound, not in any penal sum, but upon pain of imprisonment, thus:—"*Sarah, the wife of John Rogers of the same place; hatter,* on pain of imprisonment in case she shall make default in such condition." If the husband be present he is to be bound for the appearance of his wife (not as mainpernor, for they are but one flesh) and the wife's name only is inserted throughout the condition. If an infant or an apprentice be to give evidence, the parent or master is to be bound in recognizance, thus:—"*John Styles, of the same place, sword-cutler,* the mainpernor of *George Adams,* his apprentice," *or* "the mainpernor of *George Styles,* his son, an infant *(as the fact may be)* do severally owe," &c. *(as before)*, and the child's or apprentice's name is to be inserted throughout the condition.

When the parties are to enter into recognizance call them over by their names, and state the recognizances in the second person. The record is usually made out afterwards, and need not be signed by the conusors.

apprehending or surrender of the said C. D., and then and there severally give evidence to the jury that shall pass on the trial of the said C. D., touching the premises; and in case the said bill of indictment shall be returned by the grand jury "not found," that then they do severally personally appear at such Session of Gaol Delivery to be then and there holden for the said county, and then and there give evidence to the jury that shall pass on the trial of the said C. D. upon an inquisition taken before me, one of Her Majesty's Coroners for the said county of ——, on view of the body of the said S. D., and not depart the court without leave, then this recognizance will be void, otherwise to be and remain in full force.

Taken and acknowledged, this —— day of ——, one thousand eight hundred and ——, before me (1).

F. E., Coroner, County of ——

No. 46.

COMMITMENT OF A WITNESS FOR REFUSING TO ENTER INTO RECOGNIZANCE TO APPEAR TO GIVE EVIDENCE.

CANADA,
Province of Ontario,
County of ——
To wit:

To the Constables of the Township of —— in the County of —— and all other Her Majesty's officers of the peace in and for the said county, and also, to the Keeper of the Gaol of the said county. Whereas, upon an inquisition this day taken before me, one of Her Majesty's Coroners for the county aforesaid, at —— in the said county, on view of the body of C. D., then and there lying dead, one J. U., of the township aforesaid, in the county aforesaid, labourer, was by my inquest, then and there sitting, found guilty of the wilful murder of the said C. D.; and whereas one U. B., of the township and county aforesaid, yeoman, was then and there examined, and gave information in writing before me and my inquest touching the premises, and which said information he, the said U. B., then and there before me and my inquest duly signed and acknowledged, and by which said information it appears that the said U. B. is a material witness on Her Majesty's behalf against the said J. U., now in custody, and charged by my said inquest with the said murder, and the said U. B. having wilfully and absolutely refused to enter into the usual recognizance for his personal appearance at the next General Gaol Delivery to be holden in and for the county of —— aforesaid, and then and there to give evidence on Her Majesty's behalf against the said J. U. touching the premises, to the great hindrance and delay of justice. These are, therefore, by virtue of my office, in Her Majesty's name to charge and command you, or one of you, the said constables and other Her Majesty's officers of the peace in and for the said county, forthwith to convey the body of the said U. B. to the gaol of the said county, and safely to deliver the same to the keeper of the said gaol there; and these are likewise by virtue

(1) See note, p. 188.

of my said office, in her Majesty's name to will and require you, the said keeper, to receive the body of the said U. B. into your custody, and him to safely keep in the said gaol until he shall enter into such recognizance before me, or before one of Her Majesty's justices of the peace for the said county, for the purposes aforesaid, or in default thereof, until he shall be from thence otherwise discharged by due course of law: and for your so doing this is your warrant.

Given under my hand and seal, this —— day of —— one thousand eight hundred and ——

G. H., Coroner, County of —— [L. S.]

No. 47.

WARRANT TO TAKE UP A BODY INTERRED.

CANADA,
Province of Ontario,
County of ——
To wit:

To the Minister and Churchwardens of —— (*or to the proper authorities having charge of the place of burial*). Whereas, complaint hath been made unto me, one of Her Majesty's Coroners for the said county, on the —— day of ——, that the body of one G. R. was privately and secretly buried in your township, and that the said G. R. died, not of a natural but violent death; and whereas no notice of the violent death of the said G. R. hath been given to any of her Majesty's Coroners for the said county, whereby, on Her Majesty's behalf, an inquisition might have been taken on view of the body of the said G. R. before his interment, as by law is required. These are, therefore, by virtue of my office, in Her Majesty's name, to charge and command you that you forthwith cause the body of the said G. R. to be taken up and safely conveyed to —— in the said township, that I with my inquest may have a view thereof, and proceed therein according to law. Herein fail not, as you will answer the contrary at your peril. Given under my hand and seal this —— day of —— one thousand eight hundred and ——

G. H., Coroner, County of —— [L. S.]

No. 48.

WARRANT TO APPREHEND THE ACCUSED.

CANADA,
Province of Ontario,
County of ——
To wit:

To the Constables of the Township of —— in the County of —— and all other Her Majesty's peace officers in the said county. Whereas, by an inquisition taken before me, G. H., one of Her Majesty's Coroners for the said county, this —— day of —— at —— in the said county, on view of the body of G.R., then and there lying dead, one C. D., late of —— in the said county, *labourer*, stands charged with the wilful murder of the said G. R. These are, therefore, by virtue of my office, in Her Majesty's name, to charge and command you and every of you, that you or some or one of you, without delay, do apprehend and bring before me, G. H., the said Coroner, or one of Her Majesty's justices of the peace of the said county, the body of the said C. D., of whom you shall have notice, that he may be dealt with according to law; and for your so doing this is your warrant. Given under my hand and seal this —— day of —— one thousand eight hundred and ——

G. H., Coroner, County of —— [L. S.]

No. 49.

WARRANT OF COMMITMENT.

CANADA, Province of Ontario, County of —— To wit: } To the Constables of the Township of —— in the County of —— and all other Her Majesty's officers of the peace for the said county, and to the Keeper of her Majesty's Gaol at —— in the said county. Whereas, by an inquisition taken before me, one of Her Majesty's Coroners for the said county of —— the day and year hereunder mentioned, on view of the body of R. L., lying dead in the said —— of —— in the county of —— aforesaid, J. K., late of the —— of —— in the said county, *labourer*, stands charged [*here insert the crime charged, for instance*, the wilful murder of the said R. L.] These are, therefore, by virtue of my office, in Her Majesty's name, to charge and command you, the said constables and others aforesaid or any of you, forthwith safely to convey the body of the said J. K. to Her Majesty's gaol at —— aforesaid, and safely to deliver the same to the keeper of the said gaol. And these are, likewise, by virtue of my said office, in Her Majesty's name, to will and require you the said keeper to receive the body of the said J. K. into your custody, and him safely to keep in the said gaol, until he shall thence be discharged by due course of law; and for your so doing this shall be your warrant. Given under my hand and seal this —— day of —— one thousand eight hundred and ——.

G. H., Coroner, County of —— [L. S.]

No. 50.

WARRANT OF DETAINER.

CANADA, Province of Ontario, County of —— To wit: } To the Keeper of Her Majesty's Gaol at —— of the County of —— Whereas you have in your custody the body of J. K.; and whereas by an inquisition taken before me, one of Her Majesty's Coroners for the said county of —— the day and year hereunder written, at the —— of —— in the said county, on view of the body of R. L. then and there lying dead, he, the said J. K., stands charged with [*here insert the crime charged, for instance*, the wilful murder of the said R. L.] These are, therefore in Her Majesty's name, by virtue of my office, to charge and command you to detain and keep in your custody the body of the said J. K., until he shall thence be discharged by due course of law; and for your so doing this is your warrant. Given under my hand and seal this —— day of —— one thousand eight hundred and ——.

G. H., Coroner, County of —— [L. S.]

No. 51.

CERTIORARI TO THE CORONER.

[L. S.] Victoria, &c. To G. H., Coroner for our County of —— greeting. We being willing, for certain reasons, that all and singular the inquisition, examinations, informations, and depositions taken by or before you, touching the commitment of C. D. to the custody of the keeper of our gaol at —— in and for our county of —— for murder [*or manslaughter*] as is said, be sent by you before the Honourable —— Chief Justice of our Court of Queen's Bench, at Toronto, do command you that you send under your seal before our said Chief Justice, in our court before us at Toronto, immediately after the receipt of this our writ, all and singular the said inquisition, examinations, informations and depositions, with all things touching the same, as fully and perfectly as they have been taken by and before you, and now remain in your custody or power, together with this our writ, that we may cause further to be done thereon what of right, and according to the law and custom of this Province we shall see fit to be done. Witness, &c.

By the Court.

No. 52.

RETURN THEREON.

The execution of this writ appears by the schedule hereunto annexed. The answer of G. H., one of the Coroners of our Lady the Queen for the County of —— within named, with the seal affixed.

No. 53.

HABEAS CORPUS.

[L. S.] Victoria, &c. To the Sheriff of —— and also to the Keeper of our Gaol at —— in and for our County of —— or his deputy, greeting. We command you that you have before the Honourable —— Chief Justice of our Court of Queen's Bench, at Toronto, immediately after the receipt of this our writ, the body of —— being committed and detained in our prison under your custody (as is said) together with the day and cause of *his* taking and detainer, by whatsoever name the said —— may be called therein, to undergo and receive all and singular such things as our said Chief Justice shall then and there consider of concerning him in that behalf; and have you then there this writ. Witness, &c.

By the Court.

[*Endorsed on the back of the writ*]. The execution of this writ appears in the schedule hereto annexed. The answer of —— Sheriff, County of ——.

No. 54.

RETURN THEREON (1).

I, —— of the county of —— do humbly certify and return to the Honourable Chief Justice in the writ to this schedule annexed named, that before the said writ came to me, that is to say, on the —— day of —— in the —— year of the reign of her present Majesty Queen Victoria, C. D., in the said writ named, was taken and in Her Majesty's gaol for the said county under my custody is detained, by virtue of a warrant under the hand and seal of G. H., Esquire, one of Her Majesty's Coroners for the said county, the said C. D., by an inquisition taken before the said Coroner, on view of the body of R. F., lying dead at the —— of —— in the said county, standing charged with the killing and slaying of the said R. F., and this is the cause of the taking and detaining of the said C. D., which writ, together with his body, I have ready, as by the said writ I am commanded.

No. 55.

NOTICE OF BAIL.

In the Queen's Bench.

The Queen v. *C. D.*

Take notice that an application will be made in Her Majesty's Court of Queen's Bench, at Toronto, on —— next, or so soon after as counsel can be heard, that the above-named defendant, then brought into court by virtue of a writ of *habeas corpus*, may be admitted to bail for his personal appearance at the next Sessions of Oyer and Terminer and General Gaol Delivery, to be holden in and for the county of —— to answer all such matters and things as in Her Majesty's behalf shall then and there be objected against him, and so from day to day, and not depart the court without leave; and the names and descriptions of the bail are, A. B., of, &c.; E. F. of, &c. Dated, &c.

To G. H., Esquire, Coroner for the County of —— and to L. M. (*the prosecutor*).

---

(1) On a separate piece of paper and annexed to the writ.

No. 56.

VENIRE FACIAS TO THE CORONER TO AMEND HIS INQUISITION.

VICTORIA, &c. To the Sheriff of —— greeting. We command you that you do not forbear by reason of any liberty in your balliwick, but that you cause to come before us on —— wheresoever, &c., G. H., gentleman, one of the Coroners of your county, to answer to us touching several defects in a certain inquisition lately taken before him, upon view of the body of one R. F., there lying dead. Witness, &c.

No. 57.

OATH OF CORRECTNESS OF ACCOUNT.

ONTARIO,
County of ——
To wit: } I, A. B., of the —— of —— in the county of —— Coroner (*or Constable*) make oath and say:

1. That the above (*or within*) amount for services performed by me is just and true in every particular.

2. That I have not been paid any portion of the charges, nor has any other person received payment for me or on my behalf, nor has any other person or persons to my knowledge rendered a similar account for the same services. [*If there is any charge in the account for mileage, add the following clause:*]

3. That to perform such services, I necessarily travelled from —— to —— being —— miles.

Sworn before me at the ——
of —— in the county of ——
this —— day of —— 18 ——
J. P. }

A. B.,
Coroner (*or Constable.*)

No. 58.

OATH OF MILEAGE (1).

I, A. B., Constable (*or as the case may be*) make oath and say, that I did on the —— day of —— in the matter of the inquest held at —— on the body of —— necessarily travel from —— to —— being —— miles in order to [*here state the nature of the service*].

Sworn before me at —— this
— day of —— A.D. 18—.
C. D., J. P. }

A. B.

---

(1) This affidavit must be sworn before a justice of the peace.

INQUISITIONS.

No. 59.

THE CAPTION OR INCIPITUR OR BEGINNING OF EVERY INQUISITION OF DEATH.

CANADA,
Province of Ontario,
County of ——
To wit:

An Inquisition indented taken for our Sovereign Lady the Queen, at the house of A. B., known by the sign of —— situate in the —— of —— in the county of —— on the —— day of —— in the —— year of the reign of our Sovereign Lady Victoria (1). before C. D., *Esquire*, one of the Coroners of our said Lady the Queen for the *said county*, on view of the body of E. F., then and there lying dead, upon the oath (*or oath and affirmation*) of —— [*naming all the jurors sworn*] good and lawful men of the said county, duly chosen, and who being then and there duly sworn, and charged to inquire for our said Lady the Queen, when, where, how and by what means the said E. F. came to *his* death, do upon their oath say—That, &c. [*Then follows the verdict or finding of the jury, and after that the attestation or closing part of the Inquisition. See the next form*].

No. 60.

THE ATTESTATION OR CLOSING PART OF EVERY INQUISITION.

[*After the caption and verdict should follow the attestation in these words:*] In witness whereof, as well the said Coroners as the jurors aforesaid, have hereunto set and subscribed their hands and seals the day and year first above written. [*Under the attestation the Coroner signs his name, adding his office, thus:* "Coroner of the county of ——," *and the jury sign their names in rotation under the Coroner's. A seal should be affixed for the Coroner and for each of the jurymen*].

HOMICIDE BY INFANTS UNDER DISCRETION.

No. 61.

By drowning himself.

Copy caption as above (*No.* 59) *and then proceed,*] that the said R. F., then being an infant under the age of discretion, to wit, of the of —— years, not having discernment between good and evil, on the —— day of —— in the year aforesaid, into a certain river of water commonly called the —— did cast and throw himself, by means of which said casting and throwing the said R. F., then being such infant under the age of discretion as aforesaid, in the waters of the said river was then there suffocated and drowned; of which said drowning and suffocation he, the said R. F., then there instantly died: and so the jurors aforesaid upon their oath aforesaid, do say,

(1) See note, p. 187.

that the said R. F., so being such infant under the age of discretion as aforesaid, in the manner and by the means aforesaid, did kill himself. In witness, &c. [*finish with the attestation as at p.* 195].

No. 62.

By poisoning the deceased.

Copy caption as at p. 195,] that one C. D., then being an infant and under the age of discretion, to wit, of the age of —— years, not having discernment between good and evil, on the —— day of —— in the year aforesaid, a large quantity of a certain deadly poison called white arsenic, to wit, two drachms of the said white arsenic, which the said C. D., so being such infant as aforesaid, then accidentally found, into and with a certain quantity of beer did put, mix and mingle, the said C. D. not knowing that the said white arsenic so as aforesaid by him put, mixed and mingled into and with the said beer was a deadly poison; and that the said R. F. afterwards, to wit, on the day and year aforesaid, did take, drink and swallow down a certain large quantity to wit, half a pint of the said beer, with which the said white arsenic was so mixed and mingled by the said C. D. as aforesaid, the said R. F. at the time he so took, drank and swallowed down the said beer, not knowing that there was any white arsenic or any other poisonous or hurtful ingredient mixed or mingled therewith; by means whereof he, the said R. F., then became sick and greatly distempered in his body; and the said R. F. of the poison aforesaid, so by him taken, drunk and swallowed down as aforesaid and of the sickness occasioned thereby, from the said —— day of —— in the year aforesaid, until the —— day of the same month in the year aforesaid, did languish, and languishing did live; on which said last mentioned day in the year aforesaid he, the said R. F., of the poison aforesaid and of the sickness and distemper occasioned thereby, did die: and so the jurors aforesaid, upon their oath aforesaid, do say that the said C. D., so being such infant under the age of discretion as aforesaid, him, the said R. F., in the manner and by the means aforesaid, did kill and slay, but not feloniously nor of his malice aforethought; and so the said R. F. came to his death. In witness, &c. [*finish with the attestation as at p.* 195.]

No. 63.

By striking an infant with a hammer.

Copy caption as at p. 195,] that one C. D., then being an infant under the age of discretion, to wit, of the age of —— years, not having discernment between good and evil, on the —— day of —— in the year aforesaid, with a certain hammer the said R. F., an infant of tender age, to wit, of the age of —— years, in and upon the head of him the said R. F. did strike, thereby then giving to the said R. F. with the hammer aforesaid, in and upon the head of him the said R. F., one mortal bruise, of which said mortal bruise the said R. F., from the day and year last aforesaid, until the —— day of —— in the same year, did languish, and languishing did live, on which said last-mentioned day in the year aforesaid, the said R. F., of the said mortal bruise, did die: and so the jurors aforesaid, upon their oath aforesaid, do say, that the said C. D., so being such infant under the age of discretion as aforesaid, him, the said R. F., in the manner and by the means aforesaid, did kill and slay, but not feloniously nor of his malice aforethought; and so the said R. F. came to his death. In witness, &c. [*finish with the attestation as at p.* 195].

HOMICIDE BY MADMEN, LUNATICS AND IDIOTS.

No. 64.

By shooting himself.

Copy caption as at p. 195,] that the said R. F. not being of sound mind, memory and understanding, but lunatic and distracted, on the —— day of —— in the year aforesaid, a certain pistol loaded and charged with gunpowder and one leaden bullet, which pistol he, the said R. F., in his right hand then held, to and against the head of him the said R. F., did shoot off and discharge, by means whereof the said R. F. did then give unto himself, with the leaden bullet aforesaid, so discharged and shot out of the pistol aforesaid, by force of the gunpowder aforesaid, in and upon the head of him the said R. F. one mortal wound, of which said mortal wound he the said R. F. then and there instantly died: and so the jurors aforesaid, upon their oath aforesaid, do say, that the said R. F., not being of sound mind, memory and understanding, but lunatic and distracted, in the manner and by the means aforesaid did kill himself. In witness, &c. [*finish with the attestation as at p.* 195].

No. 65.

By cutting his throat.

Copy caption as at p. 195,] that the said R. F. not being of sound mind, memory and understanding, but lunatic and distracted, on the —— day of —— in the year aforesaid, with a certain razor, which he, the said R. F., in his right hand then held, the throat of him the said R. F. did strike, stab and penetrate, thereby then giving unto himself, the said R. F., with the razor aforesaid, in and upon the throat of him the said R. F. one mortal wound, of which said mortal wound he the said R. F. then instantly died: and so the jurors aforesaid, upon their oath aforesaid, do say, that the said R. F., not being of sound mind, memory and understanding, but lunatic and distracted, in the manner and by the means aforesaid, did kill himself. In witness, &c. [*finish with the attestation as at p.* 195].

No. 66.

By stabbing himself, where the cause and death are in different counties.

Copy caption as at p. 195,] that the said R. F. not being of sound mind, memory and understanding, but lunatic and distracted, on the —— day of —— in the year aforesaid, at the —— of —— in the county of —— with a certain penknife, which he, the said R. F., in his right hand then held, in and upon the left side of the belly of him the said R. F., near the abdomen, did strike, stab and penetrate, thereby then giving unto himself, the said R. F.; with the penknife aforesaid, in and upon the left side of the belly of him the said R. F., near the abdomen aforesaid, one mortal wound, of which said mortal wound he the said R. F., from the said —— day of —— in the year aforesaid, at the —— last aforesaid, in the county last aforesaid, and also in the —— of —— in the county of —— aforesaid, did languish, and languishing did live, on which said last-mentioned day, in the year aforesaid, he the said R. F. at the —— last aforesaid, in the county of —— aforesaid, of the said mortal wound did die; and so the jurors aforesaid, upon their oath aforesaid, do say, that the said R. F., not being of sound mind, memory and understanding, but lunatic and distracted, in the manner and by the means aforesaid, did kill himself. In witness, &c. [*finish with the attestation as at p.* 195].

No. 67.

By hanging himself.

Copy caption as at p. 195,] that the said R. F. not being of sound mind, memory and understanding, but lunatic and distracted, on the —— day of —— in the year aforesaid, one end of a certain piece of small cord unto an iron staple then fastened into the ceiling of a certain room of him the said R. F. in the dwelling-house of one —— situate at the —— of —— in the county of —— and the other end thereof about his own neck did fix, tie and fasten, and therewith then did hang, suffocate and strangle himself, of which said hanging, suffocation and strangling he the said R. F. then instantly died: and so the jurors aforesaid, upon their oath aforesaid, do say, that the said R. F., not being of sound mind, memory and understanding, but lunatic and distracted, in the manner and by the means aforesaid, did kill himself. In witness, &c. [*finish with the attestation as at p.* 195].

No. 68.

By poisoning himself.

Copy caption as at p. 195,] that the said R. F. not being of sound mind, memory and understanding, but lunatic and distracted, on the —— day of —— in the year aforesaid, a certain large quantity of a certain deadly poison called white arsenic, to wit, two drachms of the said white arsenic, into a certain quantity of tea steeped and infused in hot water, did put, mix and mingle, and a large quantity of the said tea, to wit, half a pint of the said tea, with which the said white arsenic was so then put, mixed and mingled as aforesaid, the said R. F. not being of sound mind, memory and understanding, but lunatic and distracted as aforesaid, did then take, drink and swallow down, by means whereof the said R. F. then became sick and distempered in his body, and of the poison aforesaid so by him taken, drunk and swallowed down as aforesaid, and of the sickness and distemper occasioned thereby, from the said —— day of —— in the year aforesaid, until the —— day of the same month of —— in the year aforesaid, did languish, and languishing did live, on which said last mentioned day in the year aforesaid, he the said R. F. of the poison aforesaid, and of the sickness and distemper occasioned thereby, did die: and so the jurors aforesaid, on their oath aforesaid, do say, that the said R. F., not being of sound mind, memory and understanding, but lunatic and distracted, in the manner and by the means aforesaid, did kill himself. In witness, &c. [*finish with the attestation as at p.* 195].

No. 69.

By drowning himself.

Copy caption as at p. 195,] that the said R. F. not being of sound mind, memory and understanding, but lunatic and distracted, on the —— day of —— in the year aforesaid, into a certain pond of water, situate in the —— of —— in the county of —— did cast and throw himself, by means of which said casting and throwing he the said R. F., not being of sound mind, memory and understanding, but lunatic and distracted, in the waters of the said pond was then suffocated and drowned, of which said drowning and suffocation he the said R. F. then instantly died: and so the jurors aforesaid, upon their oath aforesaid, do say, that the said R. F. not being of sound mind, memory and understanding, but lunatic and distracted, in the manner and by the means aforesaid, did kill himself. In witness, &c. [*finish with the attestation as at p.* 195].

No. 70.

By throwing himself out of a window.

Copy caption as at p. 195,] that the said R. F. not being of sound mind, memory and understanding, but lunatic and distracted, on the —— day of —— in the year aforesaid, from and out of a certain window in the dwelling-house of him the said R. F., situate at the —— of —— in the county of —— did violently cast and throw himself to the ground, to and against a certain stone pavement then there being, by means of which said casting and throwing to and against the said stone pavement, he the said R. F. did then receive one mortal wound on the upper part of the head of him the said R. F., of which said mortal wound he the said R. F. then instantly died: and so the jurors aforesaid, upon their oath aforesaid, do say, that the said R. F. in the manner and by the means aforesaid, not being of sound mind, memory and understanding, but lunatic and distracted, did kill himself, In witness, &c. [*finish with the attestation as at p.* 195].

No. 71.

By throwing the deceased out of a window.

Copy caption as at p. 195,] that one C. D. not being of sound mind, memory and understanding, but lunatic and distracted, on the —— day of —— in the year aforesaid, him the said R. F. through and out of a certain window of a certain dwelling-house, situate at the —— of —— in the county of —— to and against the ground then did violently cast and throw, thereby giving to the said R. F., by the casting and throwing aforesaid, to and against the ground as aforesaid, a violent concussion of the brain, of which said violent concussion the said R. F. then instantly died: and so the jurors aforesaid, upon their oath aforesaid, do say, that the said C. D., not being of sound mind, memory and understanding, but lunatic and distracted, him the said R. F., in manner and by the means aforesaid, did kill and slay, but not feloniously nor of his malice aforethought, and so the said R. F. came to his death. In witness, &c. [*finish with the attestation as at p.* 195].

HOMICIDE IN A FIT OF DELIRIUM.

No. 72.

By shooting himself.

Copy caption as at p. 195,] that the said R. F. then labouring under a grievous disease of the body, to wit, a fever (*or as the case may be*), and by reason of the violence of the said grievous disease, then being delirious and out of his mind, on the —— day of —— in the year aforesaid, a certain pistol loaded with gunpowder and one leaden bullet, which said pistol the said R. F. in his right hand then held to and against the head of him the said R. F., he the said R. F. being so delirious and out of his mind as aforesaid, did shoot off and discharge, thereby then giving unto himself in and upon the head of him the said R. F., with the leaden bullet aforesaid out of the pistol aforesaid, then by force of the gunpowder aforesaid shot off and discharged as aforesaid, one mortal wound, of which said mortal wound he the said R. F. then instantly died: and so the jurors aforesaid, upon their oath aforesaid, do say, that the said R. F. so being delirious and out of his mind as aforesaid, in the manner and by the means aforesaid, did kill himself. In witness, &c. [*finish with the attestation as at p.* 195].

AIDERS AND ABETTORS (1).

No. 73.

Murder, stating the aid and abetment specially.

Copy caption as at p. 195], that one C. D. not having the fear of God before his eyes, but being moved and seduced by the instigation of the devil, on the —— day of —— in the year aforesaid, the said R. F. feloniously, wilfully, and of his malice aforethought, did kill and murder [and the jurors aforesaid, upon their oath aforesaid, further say that E. F. and G. H. at the time of the felony and murder aforesaid, to wit, on the day and year aforesaid, were feloniously present comforting, aiding, abetting and assisting the said C. D. the felony and murder aforesaid to do and commit]: and so the jurors aforesaid, upon their oath aforesaid, do say, that the said C. D., E. F. and G. H. him the said R. F., in manner aforesaid, feloniously, wilfully, and of their malice aforethought, did kill and murder, against the peace of our said Lady the Queen, her crown and dignity. In witness, &c. [*finish with the attestation as at p.* 195].

ACCESSORIES BEFORE THE FACT.

No. 74.

Murder, charging the accessories jointly with the principal.

Copy caption as at p. 195, *and continue as in the last precedent, omitting the charge within brackets, and then proceed,*] and the jurors aforesaid, upon their oath aforesaid, further say, that E. F. before the said felony and murder was committed, to wit, on the —— day of —— in the year aforesaid, feloniously and maliciously did incite, move, procure, aid, counsel, hire and command the said C. D. the said felony and murder to do and commit, against the peace of our said Lady the Queen, her crown and dignity. In witness, &c. [*copy attestation as at p.* 195].

No. 75.

Murder, charging the accessory alone, where the principal is unknown.

Copy caption as at p. 195,] that certain persons to the jurors aforesaid unknown, on the —— day of —— in the year aforesaid, feloniously, wilfully and of their malice aforethought, the said R. F. did kill and murder, against the peace of our said Lady the Queen, her crown and dignity : and the jurors aforesaid, upon their oath aforesaid, do further say, that C. D., before the said felony and murder was committed, to wit, on the —— day of —— in the year

---

(1) When several are present aiding and abetting, the inquisition may lay it generally as done by all, or, according to the fact, as done by one and abetted by the rest. 2 Hawk. P. C. ch. 23.

aforesaid, did feloniously and maliciously counsel, hire, procure and command the said persons to the said jurors aforesaid unknown as aforesaid, the said felony and murder to do and commit against the peace of our said Lady the Queen, her crown and dignity. In witness, &c. [*copy attestation as at p.* 195].

FELO DE SE.

No. 76.

By hanging himself.

Copy caption as at p. 195,] that the said R. F., not having the fear of God before his eyes, but being moved and seduced by the instigation of the devil, on the —— day of —— in the year aforesaid, in and upon himself, in the peace of God and of our said Lady the Queen then being, feloniously, wilfully and of his malice aforethought, did make an assault; and that the said R. F. one end of a certain piece of small cord unto a certain iron bar then fixed in the ceiling of Her Majesty's gaol for the county of —— (wherein the said R. F. was then a prisoner in custody charged with felony) and the other end thereof about his own neck did then fix, tie and fasten, and therewith did then hang, suffocate and strangle himself, of which said hanging, suffocation and strangling he the said R. F. then (1) instantly died: and so the jurors aforesaid, upon their oath aforesaid, do say, that the said R. F., in the manner and by the means aforesaid, feloniously, wilfully and of his malice aforethought, did kill and murder himself, against the peace of our said Lady the Queen, her crown and dignity; and that the said R. F. at the time of committing the felony and murder aforesaid had no goods or chattels, lands or tenements, within the said county or elsewhere, to the knowledge of the said jurors. In witness, &c. [*finish with the attestation as at p.* 195].

No. 77.

By stabbing himself.

Copy caption as at p. 195, *and then continue as in the preceding form,*] did make an assault; and that the said R. F. with a certain drawn sword, which he the said R. F. in his right hand then had and held, did then give unto himself one mortal wound (2) upon the belly of him the said R. F., under his left breast, (3), of the breadth

---

(1) The respective times of the wound and death must be shewn. The death must appear to be within a year and a day after the cause of death.

(2) The wound must be set forth, and it must be alleged that it was mortal, and that the party died of it. 1 Salk. 177; 7 Mod. 16.

(3) It has been considered necessary to state in what part of the body the wound was given, and also the length and depth of the wound. 2 H. P. C. 185, 186; 2 Hawk. P. C. ch. 23, ss. 80, 81; Trem. Ent. 10; St. P. C. 78 *b*, 79 *a*; 4 Rep. 40, *b*, 41; 5 Ld. 120, 121, 122; Cro. Jac. 95.

of one inch, and of the depth of six inches (1), of which said mortal wound he the said R. F. then instantly died (2): and so the jurors aforesaid, upon their oath aforesaid, do say, that the said R. F., in the manner and by the means aforesaid, feloniously, wilfully and of his malice aforethought, did kill and murder himself, against the peace of our said Sovereign Lady the Queen, her crown and dignity; and that the said R. F., at the time of the said felony and murder, so as aforesaid done and committed, had no goods or chattels, lands or tenements, within the said county or elsewhere, to the knowledge of the said jurors. In witness, &c. [*finish with the attestation as at p.* 195].

No. 78.

By shooting himself.

Copy caption as at p. 195, *and then continue as in the* 76*th form,*] did make an assault; and that the said R. F. a certain pistol charged with gunpowder and one leaden bullet, which he the said R. F. in his right hand then had and held, feloniously, wilfully and of his malice aforethought, to and against the head of him the said R. F. did then shoot off and discharge; and that the said R. F. with the leaden bullet aforesaid, out of the pistol aforesaid, then by force of the gunpowder aforesaid shot and sent forth as aforesaid, in and upon the head of him the said R. F., feloniously, wilfully and of his malice aforethought, did strike, wound and penetrate, then giving unto himself with the leaden bullet aforesaid, so as aforesaid discharged and shot out of the pistol aforesaid by the force of the gunpowder aforesaid, in and upon the head of him the said R. F., one mortal wound, of the breadth of one inch and depth of three inches, of which said mortal wound he the said R. F. then instantly died: and so the jurors, &c. [*conclude as in preceding form*].

No. 79.

By drowning himself.

Commence as in Form No. 76,] did make an assault, and that the said R. F. in a certain pond there situate, wherein there was a great quantity of water, then and there feloniously, wilfully and of his malice aforethought, did cast and throw himself; by means of which said casting and throwing into the pond aforesaid, he the said R. F. in the pond aforesaid with the water aforesaid was then and there choked, suffocated and drowned; of which said choking, suffocation

---

(1) See note, p. 202.
(2) See note, p. 202.

and drowning he the said R. F. then and there instantly died. And so the jurors, &c. [*conclude as in Form No.* 77].

No. 80.

By poisoning himself.

Copy caption as at p. 195,] that the said R. F. not having the fear of God before his eyes, but being moved and seduced by the instigation of the devil, and of his malice aforethought, wickedly contriving and intending with poison wickedly, feloniously and of his malice aforethought to kill and murder himself, on the —— day of —— in the year aforesaid, feloniously, wilfully and of his malice aforethought a large quantity of a certain deadly poison called white arsenic (1), to wit, two drachms of the said white arsenic, into and with a certain quantity of tea infused in warm water, feloniously, wilfully and of his malice aforethought, did put, mix and mingle, the said R. F. then well knowing the said white arsenic so as aforesaid by him put, mixed and mingled with the said tea so infused in warm water as aforesaid, to be deadly poison; and the said R. F. a large quantity, to wit, half-a-pint of the said tea, in which the said white arsenic was so put, mixed and mingled by the said R. F. as aforesaid, afterwards, to wit, on the day and year aforesaid, feloniously, wilfully and of his malice aforethought, did take, drink and swallow down, by means whereof he the said R. F. then became sick and greatly distempered in his body, and of the poison aforesaid, and of the sickness and distemper occasioned thereby, from the said —— day of —— in the year aforesaid until the —— day of the same month in the same year, did languish, and languishing did live, on which said last mentioned day, in the year aforesaid, he the said R. F. of the poison, sickness and distemper aforesaid did die. And so the jurors, &c. [*conclude as in Form No.* 76].

No. 81.

By strangling himself.

Copy caption as at p. 195, *and continue as in Form No.* 76, *and then proceed thus,*] did make an assault; and that the said R. F. a certain silk handkerchief about the neck of him the said R. F. then and there feloniously, wilfully and of his malice aforethought, did fix, tie and fasten; and that the said R. F. with the silk handkerchief aforesaid, then feloniously, wilfully, and of his malice aforethought, did choke, suffocate and strangle himself, of which said choking, suffocation and strangling he the said R. F. then instantly died. And so the jurors, &c. [*finish as in Form No.* 76].

---

(1) The precise nature of the poison is immaterial.—2 H. P. C. 185, 186; 2 Hawk. P. C. ch. 23, s. 84.

No. 82.

By cutting his throat.

Copy captain as at p. 195, *and continue as in Form No.* 76, *and then proceed thus,*] did make an assault; and that the said R. F., with a certain razor, which he the said R. F. in his right hand then had and held, the throat of him the said R. F. did then strike and cut, thereby then giving unto himself with the razor aforesaid, in and upon the throat of him the said R. F. one mortal wound of the length of three inches, and of the depth of one inch, of which said mortal wound he the said R. F. then instantly died: and so the jurors aforesaid, upon their oath aforesaid, do say that the said R. F., in manner and by the means aforesaid, feloniously, wilfully and of his malice aforethought, did kill and murder himself, against the peace of our said Lady the Queen, her crown and dignity. In witness whereof, &c. [*finish with attestation, as at p.* 195].

No. 83.

Finding of goods.

Copy caption as at p. 195; *commencement as in the former precedents,*] her crown and dignity: and the jurors aforesaid, upon their oath aforesaid, do say, that the said R. F., at the time of the doing and committing of the felony and murder aforesaid, had the goods and chattels specified in the inventory to this inquisition annexed, which remain in the custody of C. D. In witness, &c. [*finish with attestation, as at p.* 195].

An inventory of the goods and chattels of R. F., in the inquisition annexed named, who feloniously, wilfully and of his malice aforethought, did kill and murder himself.

First—In the hall, &c. &c. (*specifying every article, as well out of doors as in*). All which said goods and chattels are appraised and valued at the sum of $—— (*as the value is*). (1)

MURDER (2).

No. 84.

Copy caption as at p. 195,] that C. D., otherwise called E. F. (*or, that a certain person to the jurors aforesaid unknown*) on the —— day of —— in the year aforesaid, at —— in the county of —— did feloniously, wilfully and of his malice aforethought, kill and murder one

(1) The schedule should be signed and sealed by the Coroner and jury, and annexed to the inquisition, with which it should be returned.

(2) Inquisitions against principals in the second degree in murder should state distinctly that they were present when the mortal stroke was given. 1 Russ. 29

R. F., against the peace of our Lady the Queen, her crown and dignity. In witness, &c. [*finish with attestation, as at p.* 195].

MANSLAUGHTER.

No. 85.

Copy caption as at p. 195,] that C. D., on the —— day of —— in the year aforesaid, at —— in the county of —— did feloniously and unlawfully kill and slay one R. F., against the peace of our Lady the Queen, her crown and dignity. In witness, &c. [*finish with attestation as at p.* 195].

EXCUSABLE HOMICIDE.

No. 86.

By correction.

Copy caption as at p. 195,] that C. D., on the —— day of —— in the year aforesaid, with a certain cane, which he the said C. D. in his right hand then held, the said R. F. then being an apprentice to him the said C. D., moderately and by way of chastisement did beat and strike; and that the said C. D. him the said R. F. with the cane aforesaid, in and upon the right side of him the said R. F. casually, by misfortune, and against the will of him the said C. D., did then beat and strike, thereby then giving unto him the said R. F., with the cane aforesaid, casually, by misfortune, and against the will of the said C. D., in and upon the right side of him the said R. F., one mortal bruise, of which said mortal bruise the said R. F., from the said —— day of —— in the year aforesaid, did languish, and languishing did live; on which said last mentioned day, in the year aforesaid, the said R. F. of the said mortal bruise did die: and so the jurors aforesaid, upon their oath aforesaid, do say that the said C. D. him the said R. F., in the manner and by the means aforesaid, casually and by misfortune, and against the will of him the said C. D., did kill and slay. In witness, &c. [*finish with attestation as at p.* 195].

No. 87.

By shooting at butts.

Copy caption as at p. 195,] that C. D., on the —— day of —— in the year aforesaid, a certain gun charged with gunpowder and a leaden bullet, which he the said C. D. then had and held in both his hands, casually and by misfortune, and against the will of him the said C. D., was discharged and shot off; and that the said C. D., with the leaden bullet aforesaid, then discharged and shot out of the said gun by the force of the gunpowder aforesaid, him the said R. F., in and upon the left breast of him the said R. F., casually, by misfortune, and against the will of him the said C. D., did then strike and penetrate, thereby then giving unto him the said R. F., with the bullet aforesaid, out of the gun aforesaid, so shot off and discharged as aforesaid, in and upon the said left breast of him the said R. F., one mortal wound, of which said mortal wound he the said R. F. then instantly died: and so the jurors, &c. [*conclude as in the above precedent, and with the attestation at p.* 195].

No. 88.

By a knife.

Copy caption as at p. 195,] that the said R. F. and one C. D., on the —— day of —— in the year aforesaid, being infants under the age of twelve years, in the peace of God and of our said Lady the Queen, then being in friendship, and wantonly and in play struggling together, and then and there both falling to the ground, it so happened that, casually and by misfortune, and against the will of him the said C. D., the said R. F. then fell upon the point of a certain open clasp-knife, which he the said C. D. then had and held in his right hand; by means of which said falling he the said R. F. did then, casually, by misfortune, and against the will of him the said C. D., receive one mortal wound in and upon the right breast of him the said R. F., of the breadth of one inch and depth of three inches; of which said mortal wound the said R. F., from the said —— day of —— in the year aforesaid, until the —— day of —— in the same year, did languish, and languishing did live; on which said —— day of —— in the year aforesaid, the said R. F, of the mortal wound aforesaid did die: and so the jurors, &c. [*conclude as in Form No.* 86].

No. 89.

In defence of person.

Copy caption as at p. 195,] that on the —— day of —— in the year aforesaid, the said R. F. being in a certain common drinking-room belonging to a public house, known by the sign of ——, in which said common drinking-room one C. D. and divers other persons were then present, the said R. F., without any cause or provocation whatsoever given by the said C. D., did then menace and threaten the said C. D. to turn him the said C. D. out of the said common drinking-room, and for that purpose did then lay hold of the person of him the said C. D., and on him the said C. D. violently did make an assault, and him the said C. D. without any cause or provocation whatsoever did then beat, abuse and ill-treat: whereupon the said C. D., for the preservation and safety of his person, and of inevitable necessity, did then, with the hands of him the said C. D., defend himself against such the violent assault of him the said R. F., as it was lawful for him to do; and the said R. F. did then receive, against the will of him the said C. D., by the falls and blows which he the said R. F. then sustained by his the said C. D.'s so defending himself as aforesaid, divers mortal bruises in and upon the head, back and loins of him the said R. F.; of which said mortal bruises he the said R. F., from the said —— day of —— in the year aforesaid, until the —— day of the same month in the same year did languish, and languishing did live; on which said —— day of —— in the year aforesaid, the said R. F. of the mortal bruises aforesaid did die: and so the jurors aforesaid, upon their oath aforesaid, do say that the said C. D. him the said R. F., in the defence of himself the said C. D. in manner and by the means aforesaid, did kill and slay. In witness, &c. [*finish with attestation as at p.* 195].

JUSTIFIABLE HOMICIDE.

No. 90.

Against a street robber.

Copy caption as at p. 195,] that the said R. F., with certain other persons to the jurors aforesaid unknown, on the —— day of —— in the year aforesaid, in and upon C. D., in the Queen's highway then being, feloniously did make an assault, and him the said C. D. in bodily fear and danger of his life did then put, and one gold watch of the goods and chattels of him the said C. D., from the person and against the will of him the said C. D. in the Queen's highway aforesaid, then feloniously did steal, take and carry away, against the peace of our said Lady the Queen, her crown and dignity. And the jurors aforesaid, upon their oath aforesaid, do say that after the said R. F. and the said persons to the jurors aforesaid unknown, had done and committed the felony and robbery aforesaid, they the said R. F. and the said persons to the jurors aforesaid unknown, did then endeavour to fly and escape for the same; whereupon the said C. D., together with E. H. and E. F., and certain other persons to the jurors aforesaid unknown, called in and taken to their assistance, did then pursue and endeavour to take and apprehend the said R. F. and the said persons to the jurors aforesaid unknown, for the doing and the committing of the said felony and robbery; and that the said R. F. in such pursuit was overtaken by them the said C. D., E. H., and E. F. and the said persons to the jurors aforesaid unknown: whereupon the said C. D., E. H., E. F. and the said persons to the jurors aforesaid unknown, did then lawfully and peaceably endeavour to take and apprehend the said R. F., who was then peaceably required to surrender himself, in order to be brought to justice for the felony and robbery aforesaid; and that the said R. F., to prevent his being taken and apprehended, did then with a pistol loaded with gunpowder and a leaden bullet which he the said R. F. then had and held in his right hand, menace and threaten to shoot the first man that should attempt to seize him the said R. F.; and that the said R. F. did then refuse to surrender himself, and did obstinately and unlawfully stand upon his defence, in open defiance of the laws of this province; and that upon such endeavour to take and apprehend the said R. F., he the said R. F. did then discharge and shoot off the said pistol so loaded with gunpowder and a leaden bullet as aforesaid, at and against him the said C. D.; and that on the said R. F. so continuing obstinately and unlawfully to resist and refuse to surrender himself to public justice, they the said C. D., E. H. and E. F., in order to apprehend and take the said R. F., to be brought to justice for the said felony and robbery, and in order to oblige the said R. F. to surrender himself for the purposes aforesaid, did then, justifiably and of inevitable necessity, attack and assault the said R. F., by means whereof the said R. F. did then receive in such his obstinate and unlawful defence, and before he could be taken and apprehended, divers mortal wounds and bruises, of which said mortal wounds and bruises the said R. F. did languish, and languishing did live; and that after the said R. F. was so wounded and bruised as aforesaid, he the said R. F. was then taken and apprehended, and on the day and year last mentioned was lawfully committed to the common gaol for the county of ——, and of such mortal wounds and bruises did then and there languish, and languishing did live; on which said day of —— in the year aforesaid, within the gaol aforesaid, the said R. F. of the mortal wounds and bruises aforesaid did die: and so the jurors aforesaid, upon their oath aforesaid, do say that the said C. D., E. H. and E. F., him the said R. F., in manner and by means aforesaid, in the pursuit of justice, of inevitable necessity and justifiably, did kill and slay. In witness [*finish with attestation as at p.* 195].

CASUAL DEATH.

No. 91.

By a cart.

Copy caption as at p. 195,] that C. D. on the —— day of —— in the year aforesaid, in a certain public highway in the —— of —— in the county aforesaid, being driving a certain cart drawn by three horses, and laden with twelve sacks of coal, it so happened that the said R. F. being in the said highway, was then there accidentally, casually and by misfortune, forced to the ground by the foremost horse of the said three horses so drawing the said cart, and the said cart so laden as aforesaid, was then there by the said horses violently and forcibly drawn to and against the said R. F., and the off-wheel of the said cart, so drawn and laden as aforesaid, did then there accidentally, casually and by misfortune, violently go upon and pass over the breast and body of the said R. F., by means whereof the said R. F., from the weight and pressure of the said cart, so laden and drawn as aforesaid, did then receive one mortal bruise in and upon his said breast and body, of which said mortal bruise the said R. F. then instantly died: and so the jurors aforesaid, upon their oath aforesaid, do say, that the said R. F., in manner and by the means aforesaid, accidentally, casually and by misfortune, came to his death, and not otherwise. In witness, &c. [*finish with attestation as at p.* 195].

No. 92.

By falling from a cart.

Copy caption as at p. 195,] that the said R. F., on the —— day of —— in the year aforesaid, being in company with certain boys to the jurors aforesaid unknown, and a scavenger's empty cart then standing on the top of a hill, they agreed together to get into the said empty cart, and afterwards to run and force the same down the said hill, and that in the forcing and running of the said cart down the said hill, and the said R. F. then being in the said cart, it so happened that accidentally, casually and by misfortune, the said cart, by reason of the violence of its being forced down the said hill, overturned, and the said R. F. was then thrown out of the said cart to and upon the ground, under the head-board of the said cart, by means whereof the pulmonary vessels of him the said R. F. were then broken, and the said R. F. then also received divers mortal bruises in and upon the breast of him the said R. F., of which said mortal bruises, and also by the breaking of the pulmonary vessels aforesaid, the said R. F. then and there instantly died: and so the jurors aforesaid, upon their oath aforesaid, do say, that the said R. F., in the manner and by the means aforesaid, accidentally, casually and by misfortune, came to his death, and not otherwise. In witness, &c. [*finish with attestation as at p.* 195].

No. 93.

By falling from a coach box.

Copy caption as at p. 195,] that the said R. F. on the —— day of —— in the year aforesaid, then driving two horses drawing a hackney coach, it so happened that the said R. F. then accidentally, casually and by misfortune, fell from the coach-box belonging to the same coach, to and against the ground, and by means thereof the said R. F. did then receive one mortal concussion in and upon the brain of him the said R. F., of which said mortal concussion the said R. F., from the said —— day of —— in the year aforesaid, until the —— day of the same month in the same year, did languish, and languishing did live; on which said —— day of —— in the year aforesaid, the said R. F. of the mortal concussion aforesaid did die: and so the jurors aforesaid, upon their oath aforesaid, do say, that he the said R. F., in the manner and by the means aforesaid, accidentally, casually and by misfortune, came to his death, and not otherwise. In witness, &c. [*finish with attestation as at p.* 195].

No. 94.

By the overturning of a chaise.

Copy caption as at p. 195] that the said R. F. on the —— day of —— in the year aforesaid, then being in a certain chaise, driving a certain gelding then drawing the same, it so happened that the said R. F. was then and there casually, accidentally and by misfortune, overturned and violently thrown out of the said chaise to and against the ground, by means whereof the said R. F. did then receive one mortal fracture in and upon the hinder part of the head of him the said R. F., of which said mortal fracture the said R. F., from the said —— day of —— in the year aforesaid, until the —— day of —— in the same year, did languish, and languishing did live; on which said —— day of —— in the year aforesaid, the said R. F. of the mortal fracture aforesaid did die: and so the jurors aforesaid, upon their oath aforesaid, do say, that the said R. F., in the manner and by the means aforesaid, accidentally, casually and by misfortune, came to his death, and not otherwise. In witness, &c. [*finish with attestation as at v.* 195].

No. 95.

Drowned by the overturning of a boat.

Copy caption as at p. 195] that the said R. F. on the —— day of —— in the year aforesaid, being ordered by one C. D., his master, to fasten the boat of the said C. D. to her moorings or road in the river —— instead thereof did then pin the same to a pile, under one of the arches of —— and in the said boat the said R. F. did then lay himself down to sleep, and it so happened that by the flowing in of the tide the said boat (the said R. F. being then asleep in the same) was then forced athwart the said arch, and pinned down and overset, by means whereof the said R. F. was then accidentally, casually and by misfortune, thrown out of the said boat into the said river —— and in the waters thereof was then suffocated and drowned, of which said suffocation and drowning the said R. F. then instantly died: and so the jurors aforesaid, upon their oath aforesaid, do say, that the said R. F., in the manner and by the means aforesaid, come to his death, and not otherwise. In witness, &c. [*finish with the attestation as at v.* 195].

No. 96.

By the fright of a horse.

Copy caption as at p. 195,] that the said R. F. on the —— day of —— in the year aforesaid, then riding and galloping on a certain gelding, on a certain highway in the —— of —— in the county aforesaid, it so happened that the said gelding took fright at a certain cow which then suddenly appeared and crossed the said highway wherein the said R. F. was then riding the said gelding, and that the said gelding fell over the said cow, and accidentally, casually and by misfortune, then flung the said R. F. with great violence to and against the ground there, by means whereof the said R. F. then received one mortal fracture on the upper part of the head of him the said R. F., of which said mortal fracture the said R. F. then instantly died: and so the jurors aforesaid, upon their oath aforesaid, do say, that the said R. F., in manner and by the means aforesaid, accidentally, casually and by misfortune, came to his death, and not otherwise. In witness, &c. [*finish with attestation as at p.* 195].

No. 97.

By the kick of a horse.

Copy caption as at page 195,] that the said R. F. on the —— day of —— in the year aforesaid, was riding upon a certain horse of J. K., Esquire, and the said R. F. from the back of the said horse then casually fell to the ground, and the horse aforesaid then struck the said R. F. with one of his hinder feet, and thereby then gave to the said R. F. upon the head of the said R. F. one mortal wound, of which the said R. F. did languish, and languishing did live, from the said —— day of —— in the year aforesaid, until the —— day of —— in the year aforesaid, on which said —— day of —— in the year aforesaid, the said R. F., of the mortal wound aforesaid, died: and so the jurors aforesaid, upon their oath aforesaid, do say, that the said R. F., in manner and form aforesaid, and not otherwise, came to his death. In witness, &c. [*finish with attestation as at p.* 195.]

No. 98.

By falling into an area.

Copy caption as at p. 195,] that the said R. F. on the —— day of —— in the year aforesaid, being at work in a certain yard belonging to a house in the township of —— in the county aforesaid, at the height of one story from the area of a cellar thereto belonging, and the said R. F. then stepping upon a stone then hanging over the brickwork of the said house, it so happened that the said stone accidentally, casually and by misfortune, gave way and fell to the ground; by means whereof the said R. F. did then accidentally, casually and by misfortune, fall from the said yard upon the stone pavement of the said area, and by means thereof did then receive by the fall aforesaid one mortal bruise and contusion on the crown of his head, of which said mortal bruise and contusion the said R. F. then instantly died: and so the jurors aforesaid, upon their oath aforesaid, do say, that the said R. F., in manner and by the means aforesaid, accidentally, casually and by misfortune, came to his death, and not otherwise. In witness, &c. [*finish with attestation as at p.* 195].

No. 99.

By falling from the leads of a house.

Copy caption as at p. 195,] that the said R. F., on the —— day of —— in the year aforesaid, being upon certain garret leads belonging to the dwelling house of C. D., situate in the township of ——, in the county aforesaid, it so happened that, accidentally, casually and by misfortune, the said R. F. then fell from the said leads to and against the ground; by means whereof the said R. F. then received one mortal wound on the crown of the head of him the said R. F.; of which said mortal wound the said R. F. then and there instantly died: and so the jurors aforesaid, upon their oath aforesaid, do say that the said R. F., in manner and by the means aforesaid, accidentally, casually and by misfortune, came to his death, and not otherwise. In witness, &c. [*finish with attestation as at p.* 195].

No. 100.

By falling from a hay-loft, being in liquor.

Copy caption as at p. 195,] that the said R. F., on the —— day of —— in the year aforesaid, being in a certain hay-loft, in the stable yard of J. B., situate in the township of ——, in the county aforesaid, and then being greatly intoxicated and in liquor, it so happened that, accidentally, casually and by misfortune, the said R. F. fell out of the said hay-loft to and against the ground there (which said ground was then paved with bricks); by means of which said fall the said R. F. then received a violent concussion of the brain; of which said violent concussion the said R. F., from the said —— day of —— in the year aforesaid, until the —— day of the same month, in the same year, did languish, and languishing did live; on which said —— day of —— in the year aforesaid, the said R. F., of the violent concussion aforesaid, did die: and so the jurors aforesaid, upon their oath aforesaid, do say that the said R. F., in manner and by the means aforesaid, accidentally, casually and by misfortune, came to his death, and not otherwise. In witness, &c. [*finish with attestation as at p.* 195].

No. 101.

Drowned whilst in a fit.

Copy caption as at p. 195,] that the said R. F., on the —— day of —— in the year aforesaid, being an in-patient in a certain hospital, called the ——, situate in —— of —— in the county of ——, and under cure there for falling fits, under which the said R. F. then laboured and languished; and the said R. F., by the advice and direction of the physicians to the said infirmary, being to dip and wash himself in the bath then belonging to the said hospital, it so happened that the said R. F., after such dipping and washing of himself as aforesaid, and as the said R. F. was then wiping himself dry, near the side of the said bath, was then suddenly seized with a violent falling fit, and by reason thereof then accidentally, casually and by misfortune, fell into the said bath, and in the waters thereof was then suffocated and drowned; of which said suffocation and drowning the said R. F. then instantly died: and so the jurors aforesaid, upon their oath aforesaid, do say that the said R. F., in manner and by the means aforesaid, accidentally, casually and by misfortune, came to his death, and not otherwise. In witness, &c. [*finish with attestation as at p.* 195].

No. 102.

Drowned.

Copy caption as at p. 195,] that the said R. F., on the —— day of —— in the year aforesaid, being employed by C. D. to carry and wheel gravel in a certain wheel-barrow, over a certain long and narrow plank of wood, braced with cords unto two long wooden poles, lying over a certain deep pond of water, situate at the —— of —— in the county aforesaid, it so happened that the said R. F., in wheeling the said wheel-barrow, so filled with the said gravel, over the said plank, accidentally, casually and by misfortune, fell from the said plank into the said pond, and in the waters thereof was then suffocated and drowned; of which said suffocation and drowning the said R. F. then instantly died: and so the jurors aforesaid, upon their oath aforesaid, do say that the said R. F., in manner and by the means aforesaid, accidentally, casually and by misfortune, came to his death, and not otherwise. In witness, &c. [*finish with attestation as at p.* 195].

No. 103.

Drowned by bathing.

Copy caption as at p. 195,] that the said R. F., on the —— day of —— in the year aforesaid, going into a certain pond situate in the —— of —— in the county aforesaid, to bathe, it so happened that accidentally, casually and by misfortune, the said R. F. was in the waters of the said pond then suffocated and drowned, of which said suffocation and drowning the said R. F. then instantly died: and so the jurors aforesaid, upon their oath aforesaid, do say that the said R. F., in manner and by the means aforesaid, accidentally, casually and by misfortune, came to his death, and not otherwise. In witness, &c. [*finish with attestation as at p.* 195].

No. 104.

Drowned by falling out of a boat.

Copy caption as at p. 195,] that the said R. F., on the —— day of —— in the year aforesaid, being with other children in a certain lighter commonly called a ballast-lighter, then floating in a certain deep pond of water, situate at the —— of —— in the county aforesaid, it so happened that the said R. F. accidentally, casually and by misfortune, fell from the said lighter into the said pond, and in the waters thereof was then suffocated and drowned, of which said suffocation and drowning the said R. F. then instantly died: and so the jurors aforesaid, upon their oath aforesaid, do say that the said R. F., in manner and by the means aforesaid, accidentally, casually and by misfortune, came to his death, and not otherwise. In witness, &c. [*finish with attestation as at p.* 195].

No. 105.

Found drowned.

Copy caption as at p. 195,] that the said man, to the jurors aforesaid unknown, on the —— day of —— in the year aforesaid, was found drowned and suffocated in a certain pond situated at the —— of —— in the county aforesaid, and that the said man, to the jurors aforesaid unknown, had no marks of violence appearing on his body, but how or by what means the said man became drowned and suffocated, no evidence doth appear to the jurors. In witness, &c. [*finish with attestation as at p.* 195].

No. 106.

By a fire.

Copy caption as at p. 195,] that on the —— day of —— in the year aforesaid, the warehouse of C. D., situate at the —— of —— in the county aforesaid, casually took fire, and the said R. F., being then present and aiding and assisting to extinguish the said fire, it so happened that a piece of timber, by the force and violence of the said fire, accidentally, casually and by misfortune, fell from the top of the said warehouse upon the head of him the said R. F., by means whereof the said R. F. then received one mortal fracture on the head of him the said R. F., of which said mortal fracture the said R. F. from the —— day of —— in the year aforesaid, until the —— day of the same month in the same year, did languish, and languishing did live; on which said —— day of —— in the year aforesaid, the said R. F. of the said mortal fracture did die: and so the jurors aforesaid, upon their oath aforesaid, do say that the said R. F., in manner and by the means aforesaid, accidentally, casually and by misfortune, came to his death, and not otherwise. In witness, &c. [*finish with attestation as at p.* 195].

No. 107.

By the explosion of gunpowder during a fire.

Copy caption as at p. 195,] that on the —— day of —— in the year aforesaid, the warehouse of C. D., situate at the —— of —— in the county aforesaid, casually and by misfortune took fire, and the said R. F. being then present, and aiding and assisting to extinguish the same, it so happened that by the explosion of a great quantity of gunpowder then there deposited, the roof of said warehouse blew up, by means whereof a piece of timber accidentally, casually and by misfortune, fell from the said roof in and upon the left side of the head of him the said R. F., by means whereof the said R. F. then received one mortal fracture on the said left side of the head of him the said R. F., of which said mortal fracture the said R. F. then instantly died: and so the jurors aforesaid, upon their oath aforesaid, do say that the said R. F., in manner and by the means aforesaid, accidentally, casually and by misfortune, came to his death, and not otherwise. In witness, &c. [*finish with attestation as at p.* 195].

No. 108.

By being burnt.

Copy caption as at p. 195,] that the said R. F., on the —— day of —— in the year aforesaid, being alone in her room or apartment, in a certain almshouse, situate at the —— of —— in the county aforesaid, it so happened as she the said R. F. was then there sitting by her fireside, that the woollen petticoat of her the said R. F., which she the said R. F. then had on her body, accidentally, casually and by misfortune, took fire, by means whereof, and from the smoke and flame arising from the said fire, the said R. F. was then suffocated and burnt, of which said suffocation and burning the said R. F. then instantly died: and so the jurors aforesaid, upon their oath aforesaid, do say that the said R. F., in manner and by the means aforesaid, accidentally, casually and by misfortune, came to her death, and not otherwise. In witness, &c. [*finish with attestation as at p.* 195].

No. 109.

By being suffocated.

Copy caption as at p. 195,] that the said R. F., on the —— day of —— in the year aforesaid, being intoxicated with liquor, and laying himself down to sleep near unto a certain tile kiln then burning in a certain field, commonly called the brick field, situate at the —— of —— in the county aforesaid, it so happened that accidentally, casually and by misfortune, the said R. F., by the smoke and sulphurous smell arising from the fire in the said tile kiln, was there and then choked, suffocated and stifled, of which said choking, suffocation and stifling the said R. F. then instantly died: and so the jurors aforesaid, upon their oath aforesaid, do say that the said R. F., in manner and by the means aforesaid, accidentally, casually and by misfortune, came to his death, and not otherwise. In witness, &c. [*finish with attestation as at p.* 195].

No. 110.

By the fall of a house.

Copy caption as at p. 195,] that the said R. F., then being a lodger in a certain decayed building, situate at the —— of —— in the county aforesaid, it happened that on the —— day of —— in the year aforesaid, the said building in which the said R. F. then was, accidentally, casually and by misfortune, sunk and fell in, by means whereof the said R. F. was then, under the ruin and materials thereof, suffocated and smothered, of which said suffocation and smothering the said R. F. then instantly died: and so the jurors aforesaid, upon their oath aforesaid, do say that the said R. F., in the manner and by the means aforesaid, accidentally, casually and by misfortune, came to his death, and not otherwise. In witness, &c. [*finish with attestation as at p.* 195].

No. 111.

Suffocated in the mud.

Copy caption as at p. 195,] that the said R. F., on the —— day of —— in the year aforesaid, being on board a certain ship or vessel, called the *Fortune*, of Leith, then lying at her moorings near the Hermitage, in the River Thames, in the —— of —— in the county aforesaid, it so happened that the said R. F. accidentally, casually and by misfortune, fell from the side of the said ship or vessel into the mud or soil then being in the said river, by means whereof the said R. F. in the mud or soil of the said river was then suffocated and smothered, of which said suffocation and smothering the said R. F. then instantly died: and so the jurors aforesaid, upon their oath aforesaid, do say, that the said R. F., in manner and by the means aforesaid, accidentally, casually and by misfortune, came to his death, and not otherwise. In witness, &c. [*finish with attestation as at p.* 195].

No. 112.

By being shut up in a turn-up bed.

Copy caption as at p. 195,] that the said R. F., on the —— day of —— in the year aforesaid, being laid to sleep in a certain turn-up bed, then being in the room of the dwelling-house of one G. F., the father of the said R. F., it so happened that one B. M., the servant of the said G. F., not knowing that the said R. F. was then lying in the said bed, accidentally, casually and by misfortune, then innocently turned up the said bed in which the said R. F. was so laid as aforesaid, by means whereof the said R F. in the clothes of the said bed was then suffocated and smothered, of which said suffocation and smothering the said R. F. then instantly died: and so the jurors aforesaid, upon their oath aforesaid, do say, that the said R. F., in manner and by the means aforesaid, accidentally, casually and by misfortune, came to his death, and not otherwise. In witness, &c. [*finish with attestation as at p.* 195].

No. 113.

Of a child by sudden delivery.

Copy caption as at p. 195,] that C. D., the mother of the said new-born male child, on the —— day of —— in the year aforesaid, the said male child did bring forth of her body alive suddenly and by surprise, and that the said new-born male child then died soon after its birth, in a natural way, and not from any violence, hurt or injury received from the said C. D., its mother, or any other person, to the knowledge of the said jurors; nor had the said new-born male child any marks of violence appearing on his body. In witness, &c. [*finish with attestation as at p.* 195].

No. 114.

By a difficult birth and hard labour.

Copy caption as at p. 195,] that the said R. F., on the —— day of —— in the year aforesaid, being big with a certain female child, afterwards, to wit, on the same day and year, after a violent and lingering pain and hard labour, with great difficulty did bring forth the said female child alive; and that the said R. F., from the said —— day of —— in the year aforesaid, until the —— day of the same month, in the same year, of the weakness and disorder occasioned by such violent and lingering pain, difficult birth and hard labour aforesaid, did languish, and languishing did live; on which said —— day of —— in the year aforesaid, the said R. F. of the weakness and disorder aforesaid, occasioned by the hard labour and difficult birth aforesaid, did die: and so the jurors aforesaid, upon their oath aforesaid, do say, that the said R. F., in manner and by the means aforesaid, came to her death, and not otherwise. In witness, &c. [*finish with attestation as at p.* 195].

No. 115.

Still-born.

Copy caption as at p. 195,] that the said new-born female still-born. In witness, &c. [*finish with attestation as at p.* 1

No. 116.

Starved.

Copy caption as at p. 195,] that the said R. F., on the —— day of —— in the year aforesaid, through the inclemency of the weather and the want of the common necessaries of life, and by no violent ways or means whatsoever, to the knowledge of the said jurors, did die. In witness, &c. [*finish with attestation as at p.* 195].

No. 117.

Another form.

Copy caption as at p. 195,] that the said man, to the jurors aforesaid unknown, on the —— day of —— in the year aforesaid, was found dead in a ditch, in a certain lane, situate at the —— of ——, in the county aforesaid, and that the said man, to the jurors aforesaid unknown, had no marks of violence appearing on his body, but through want and the inclemency of the weather, and by no violent ways or means whatsoever, to the knowledge of the said jurors, did then die. In witness, &c. [*finish with attestation as at p.* 195].

No. 118.

Natural death.

Copy caption as at p. 195,] that the said R. F., on the —— day of —— in the year aforesaid, and for a long time before, did labour and languish under a grievous disease of the body, to wit, an asthma, and on the said —— day of —— in the year aforesaid, the said R. F., by the visitation of God, in a natural way, of the disease and distemper aforesaid, and not by any violent means whatsoever, to the knowledge of the said jurors, did die. In witness, &c. [*finish with attestation as at p.* 195].

No. 119.

Found dead.

Copy caption as at p. 195,] that the said R. F., on the —— day of —— in the year aforesaid, in a certain field, situate at the —— of —— in the county aforesaid, was found dead; and that the said R. F. had no marks of violence appearing on his body, but, by the visitation of God, in a natural way, and not by any violent means whatsoever, to the knowledge of the said jurors, did die. In witness, &c. [*finish with attestation as at p.* 195].

No. 120.

Found dead; cause of death unknown.

Copy caption as at p. 195,] that the said man, to the jurors aforesaid unknown, on the —— day of —— in the year aforesaid, in a certain wood called —— situate at the —— of —— in the county aforesaid, was found dead; and that the said man, to the jurors aforesaid unknown, had no marks of violence appearing on his body, but how or by what means he came to his death, no evidence thereof doth appear to the said jurors. In witness, &c. [*finish with attestation as at p.* 195].

No. 121.

Sudden death by fits.

Copy caption as at p. 195,] that the said R. F., on the —— day of —— in the year aforesaid, being a person liable and subject to violent fits, was, for the benefit of his health, gently riding on a certain gelding, in the Queen's common highway, called —— in the —— of —— in the county aforesaid; and being so riding as aforesaid, it so happened that the said R. F. was then suddenly seized with a fit, and by reason of the violence thereof the said R. F. then fell from the back of the said gelding to and against the ground in the said highway, and then instantly died; but had no marks of violence or bruises appearing on his body: and so the jurors aforesaid, upon their oath aforesaid, do say that the said R. F., by the violence of the fit aforesaid, and in the manner and by the means aforesaid, came by his death and not otherwise. In witness, &c. [*finish with attestation as at p.* 195].

No. 122.

By excessive drinking.

Copy caption as at p. 195,] that the said R. F., on the —— day of —— in the year aforesaid, by excessive drinking, and not from any hurt, injury or violence done or committed to the said R. F. to the knowledge of the said jurors, did die. In witness, &c. [*finish with attestation as at p.* 195].

No. 123.

Death in Prison.

Copy caption as at p. 195,] that the said R. F., being a prisoner in the prison aforesaid, on the —— day of —— in the year aforesaid, at the prison aforesaid, by the visitation of God, in a natural way, to wit, of a fever, and not otherwise, did die. In witness &c., [*finish with attestation as at p.* 195].

No. 124.

Killed by explosion of boiler of steam engine.

Copy caption as at p. 195,] that on the —— day of —— in the year aforesaid, the said R. F. being on board of a certain steamboat called the —— then floating and being navigated on the water of the River —— it so happened that accidentally, casually and by misfortune, a certain boiler containing water, and then forming part of a certain steam engine in and on board of the said steamboat and attached thereto, and which said boiler was then used and employed in the working of the said steam engine, for the purpose of propelling the said steamboat along the said river, and was then heated by means of a fire, then also forming part of the said steam engine in the said steamboat, burst and exploded, by means whereof a large quantity, to wit, ten gallons of the boiling and scalding water and steam then being within the cavity of the said boiler, and a large quantity, to wit, one bushel of hot and burning cinders and coals forming part of the said fire, accidentally, casually and by misfortune, were cast, thrown and came from and out of the said boiler and steam engine with great force and violence upon and against the head, face and neck of him the said R. F., whereby he the said R. F. then received in and upon his head, face and neck divers mortal burns and scalds, of which said mortal burns and scalds he the said R. F. then instantly died: and so the jurors aforesaid, upon their oath aforesaid, do say that the said R. F., in manner and by the means aforesaid, accidentally, casually and by misfortune, came to his death, and not otherwise. In witness, &c. [*finish with attestation as at p.* 195].

No. 125.

Killed by collision on a railway.

Copy caption as at p. 195,] that on the —— day of —— in the year aforesaid, a certain locomotive steam engine, numbered ——, with a certain tender attached thereto and worked therewith, and also with divers, to wit, ten carriages used for the conveyance of passengers for hire, on a certain railway called the —— Railway, and which said carriages respectively were then attached and fastened together and to the said tender, and were then propelled by the said locomotive steam engine, were moving and travelling along the said railway towards the town of ——: and the jurors aforesaid, upon their oaths aforesaid, do further say that whilst and during the time the said locomotive steam engine, tender and carriages, were so moving and travelling along the said railway as aforesaid, a certain other locomotive steam engine, numbered ——, with a certain other tender attached thereto and worked therewith, and also with divers, to wit, five other carriages used for the conveyance of passengers for hire, on the said railway, and which said last mentioned carriages respectively were then attached and fastened together and to the said last mentioned tender, and were then propelled by the said last mentioned locomotive steam engine, and in one of which said last mentioned carriages the said R. F. was then a passenger, and was then riding and being carried and conveyed therein, were then also moving and travelling along the said railway in a direction from the said town of ——, and towards the said first mentioned locomotive steam engine, tender and carriages; and that the said first mentioned locomotive steam engine, tender and carriages, and the said secondly mentioned locomotive steam engine, tender and carriages, being then so respectively moving and travelling upon the said railway in different and opposite directions as aforesaid, then accidentally, casually and by misfortune, came into sudden, violent and forcible contact and collision; by means whereof the said R. F. then received divers mortal wounds, bruises and concussions; of which said mortal wounds, bruises and concussions, he the said R. F. then instantly died: and so the jurors aforesaid, upon their oath aforesaid, do say that the said R. F., in manner and by the means aforesaid, accidentally, casually and by misfortune, came to his death, and not otherwise. In witness, &c. [*finish with attestation as at p.* 195].

No. 126.

THE CAPTION, OR INCIPITUR OF A FIRE INQUISITION.

CANADA, Province of Ontario, County of —— To wit:	An inquisition taken for our Sovereign Lady the Queen, at the house of A. B., known by the sign of —— situate in the —— of —— in the county of —— on the —— day of ——

in the —— year of the reign of our Sovereign Lady Victoria (1) before C. D., Esquire, one of the Coroners of our said Lady the Queen for the said county, to inquire into the cause or origin of a certain fire which occurred in the said —— of —— on the ——

(1) See note, p. 187.

day of —— A.D. 18— in the said —— year of the reign of our Sovereign Lady Victoria, at or about the hour of —— o'clock *noon (or in the forenoon or afternoon as the case may be)*, whereby the house *(or other building)* of A. B., &c., situate upon Lot No. —— on the —— side of —— street in the said —— of —— *(or upon Lot No.* —— *in the* —— *concession of the township of* —— *in the said county of* —— *as the case may be)* was wholly *(or in part)* consumed, upon the oath (*or* oath and affirmation) of —— *(naming all the jurors sworn)*, good and lawful men of the said —— duly chosen from among the householders resident in the vicinity of the said fire; and who, being then and there duly sworn and charged to inquire, for our said Lady the Queen, into the cause or origin of said fire, and whether it was kindled by design or was the result of negligence or accident, do upon their oaths say that, &c. [*then follows the verdict or finding of the jury, and after that the attestation or closing part of the inquisition. See Form No. 60, p.* 195].

No. 127.

REQUISITION TO HOLD A FIRE INQUEST.

To A. B., Esquire, one of the Coroners of the County of ——.

I, the undersigned C. D., of the —— of —— in the county of —— *(occupation)* hereby require you to institute an inquiry into the cause or origin of the fire which wholly (*or* partly *as the case may be*) consumed the shop (*or* dwelling *or other buildings*) situated upon Lot No. —— on the —— side of —— street in the —— of —— in the county of —— (*or as the case may be*) on the —— day of —— A.D. 18—. And to ascertain whether the said fire was kindled by design, or was the result of negligence or accident * ; and I undertake and agree to pay the expenses of and attending such investigation (1).

Dated at —— this —— day of —— A.D. 18—.

C. D.

---

(1) If a jury is required, the requisition must be from an agent of an insurance company, or three householders in the vicinity of the fire, and a clause must be added to the above form where marked with an * as follows: "And you are required to proceed in the said investigation with the assistance of a jury."

And if the requisition is intended to charge a municipality with the expense of the investigation, it must be under the hands and seals of the Mayor or other head officer of the municipality, and of at least two other members of the council thereof.

On the back of the requisition, a short affidavit should in all cases be endorsed, stating that the deponent has reason to believe that the fire referred to was the result of culpable or negligent conduct or design, or occurred under such circumstances as in the interests of justice, and for the due protection of property, require an investigation, as the case may be.

No. 128.

RETURN OR CERTIFICATE OF DEATH FOR DIVISION REGISTRAR.

County of ______ Division of (1) ______

Name and Surname of Deceased.	Sex.	Residence.	Rank or Profession.	Duration of Illness.	Cause of Death.

I hereby Certify the foregoing to be a true and correct certificate of the cause of the death of the person (*or persons*) therein named.

Given under my hand this —— day of —— A. D. 18—.

______

Coroner, County of ——

(1) Each city, town, incorporated village, township or union of townships, is a Registration Division, and the Clerks of such Municipalities are the Division Registrars, except in the Districts of Algoma, Nipissing and Thunder Bay. For these latter places Division Registrars are appointed by the Lieutenant-Governor in Council.

No. 129.

CERTIFICATE OF CORONER TO CONSTABLE'S ACCOUNT.

I hereby Certify that the above (*or within*) services were performed by Constable A. B. under my directions (*if the account is an assistant Constable's, add* and that assistance was necessary) (1).

C. D., Coroner.

No. 130.

INFORMATION TO HOLD INQUEST.

Province of Ontario, County of —— To wit: } I, A. B., of the —— of —— in the County of —— (*occupation*) make oath and say:

1. That the body of a man (woman *or* child, *as the case may be*) now lies dead at —— in the county of ——.

2. That the said body is the body of —— [*or, if unknown, say,* is the body of a man (*woman or child, as the case may be*), to me, this deponent, unknown].

3. That I have reason to believe the said deceased person came to his (*or* her) death from violent (*or* unfair) means (*or by culpable or negligent conduct of himself or of others, under such circumstances as require investigation, and not through mere accident or mischance, or that the deceased was a prisoner or lunatic confined in a penitentiary, gaol, house of correction, lock-up house, or house of industry, or private lunatic asylum*).

4. And my reason for so believing is [*here state any reasons, if any there be that can be stated*].

Sworn before me, at the —— of —— in the county of —— this —— day of —— A.D. 18—.
C. D., Coroner, County of ——. }

A. B.

No. 131.

DECLARATION OF CORONER TO BE ATTACHED TO HIS ACCOUNT (2).

I, A. B., of the —— of —— in the county of —— one of the Coroners for the said county, hereby declare that it was made to appear to me by the information of C. D., hereto annexed, that

---

(1) All accounts must have the proper date placed opposite the respective charges, and must be verified by the oath of the party making the charge. See Form No 57.

(2) The information, evidence, inquisition and all the papers are to be attached together and delivered to the County Attorney, who will give a certificate that they have been filed with him, and that it appears from the information and papers there was sufficient grounds to warrant the holding of an inquest within the meaning of the statute. This certificate, and the declaration above given, must be attached to the Coroner's accounts.

there was reason to believe E. F., late of —— (*or* a person unknown, whose body lay dead at ——) had come to his (*or* her) death from violent (*or* unfair) means (*or state whatever reason for holding the inquest was given in the information*); and I thereupon proceeded to hold an inquest upon the said body, which inquest resulted in a verdict of the jury finding the deceased came to his (*or* her) death by [*here state the verdict under one of the following heads:* Murder, Manslaughter, Justifiable Homicide, Suicide, Accidental Death, (specifying the cause), Injuries (cause unknown), Found Dead, or Natural Death].

Dated at —— the —— day of —— A.D. 18—.

A. B., Coroner, County of ——

INDEX.

A

ABATEMENT,
pleas in, 148.

ABETTORS AND AIDERS,
definition of, 31, 201.

ACCESSORY,
inquisitions against, 201.
may be charged in same inquisition as principal, 148.
before the fact, 32.
can be none to manslaughter, 33.
cannot be guilty of higher crime than principal, 33.
and principal, 31.

ACCIDENTALIA DEMENTIA,
definition of, 29.

ACCIDENTS.
deaths from, 42, 47.

ACCOMPLICE,
evidence of, 99.

ACCOUNTS,
how to be rendered, 153.
certificate to constable's, 225.

ACCUSED,
statement of, 185.

ACONITUM NAPELLUS,
symptoms of, 76.

ACQUIRED MADNESS,
definition of, 29.

ACTION,
liability of Coroner to, 111.

ADDITION,
the, 149.

ADDRESS,
to jury, 177, 186.

ADJOURNMENT,
address on, 184.
proclamation on, 184.
of inquiry, 119, 127.
recognizance on, 183,

ADVENTITIOUS INSANITY,
definition of, 29.

ÆTHUSA CYNAPIUM,
symptoms of, 76.

AFFECTATA DEMENTIA,
definition of, 29.

AFFIRMATION,
of witnesses, 183.

AGED PERSONS,
death of, from want or neglect, 46.

AIDERS AND ABETTORS,
definition of, 32.
inquisitions against, 201.

ALCOHOL,
symptoms of, 74.

ALFRED,
Coroners were known in time of, 1.

ALKALIES,
symptoms of, 67.
antidotes, 78.

ALIEN,
may not be killed, 38.
enemy may be killed in time of war, 38.

ALLEGIANCE,
oath of, 173.

AMENDING,
inquisitions and taking new ones, 156.

AMMONIA,
symptoms of, 67.

ANALYSIS,
who should perform, 133.
time required to perform, 141.
cost of, 141, 152.

ANATOMY,
inspector of, 130.

ANTIDOTES,
general remarks upon, 77.
for sulphuric acid, 77.
for nitric acid, 77.
for oxalic acid, 77.
for phosphorus, 78.
for alkalies, 78.
for arsenic—arsenious acid, 78.
for corrosive sublimate, 78.
for lead, 78.
for copper, 79.
for antimony, 79.
for zinc, 79.
for cantharides, 79.
for tin, 79.
for nitrobenzole, 79.
for essence of mirbane, 79.
for aniline, 79.
for carbolic acid, 79.
for prussic acid, 79.
for strychnine, 79.

ANTIMONY,
symptoms of, 70.
antidotes, 79.

ANTIQUITY,
of office of Coroner, 1.

APOTHECARIES AND CHEMISTS,
how liable, 45.

APPEAL,
of felony, 17.

APPOINTMENT,
of Coroners, 3.

APPRENTICE,
death of, from want or neglect, 46.
how bound over to give evidence, 156.

ARRAIGNMENT,
of prisoner on inquisition, 161.

ARREST,
Coroner's privilege from, 22.

ARSENIC,
symptoms of, 67.
antidotes, 78.

ASSAULT,
provocation by, 58.

ASSOCIATE,
Coroners, 3.

ATHEISTS,
incompetent to give evidence, 99.

ATHELSTAN,
charter of, 1.

ATTACHMENT,
of Coroners, 16.
writ of, should be personally delivered, 16.

ATTESTATION,
the, 151.
form of, 195.

AUTHORITY,
of Coroners, 5.

B.

BALHAM,
inquiry, 157.

BAIL,
of, 156
notice of, 156, 193.

BARRISTERS,
right of, to attend inquests, 120.

BASTARD,
death of, by exposure, 46.
and see under INFANTICIDE.

BEARING,
and conduct of parties at inquests, 127.

BEAVER POISON,
symptoms of, 76.

BEVERLY,
charter to, 1.

BLOOD,
tests of, 92.

BODY,
power of Coroner to take up, 110.
disposal of, 129.

BOUNDARIES,
felonies committed near, 19.

BOXING,
deaths from, 41.

BRAVO,
inquest on Mr., 157.

BRUISES,
remarks on, 80.

BURIAL,
of *felo de se*, 35.
of body, when proper, 129.
expenses of, how paid, 153.

C.

CANTHARIDES,
symptoms of, 72.

CAPABILITY,
of committing crimes, 27.

CAPTAIN,
of vessels, when liable, 45.

CAPTION,
of inquisitions, 143.
forms of, 195, 222.

CARELESS DRIVING,
deaths from, 42.

CARRIERS,
for hire, 43.

CASUAL DEATH,
definition of, 95.

CAUTION,
to prisoner before receiving his statement, 105, 185.

CAUTIONS,
regarding cases of infanticide, 54.

CERTIFICATE,
of fine of juror or witness, 177.

CERTIORARI,
to Coroner, 192.
to executors of Coroner to certify record, 142.
form of, 192.

CHARACTER,
evidence of good, admissible, 106.
of wounds inflicted during life, 81.
made after death, 82.

CHARGE TO JURY,
after being sworn, 178.
after view of body, 178.

CHEMISTS.
how liable, 45.
fees, 166.

CHILDREN,
death of, from want or neglect, 46.
their subjection to parents, 30.
their capability to give evidence, 98.

CHLORIDE,
of mercury, symptoms of, 68.
antidote for, 78.
of lime, cautions regarding use of, 140.

CICUTA MACULATA,
symptoms of, 76.

CLEANLINESS,
necessity of, in performing *post mortem*, 139.

CLERKS OF THE PEACE,
should furnish lists of constables to Coroners, 23.

CLOSE OF INQUEST,
proclamation at, 186.

CO-CORONERS,
liability of Coroners for acts of, 26.

COERCION,
in committing crimes, 29.

COLCHICUM,
symptoms of, 72.

COMBINATION,
general, to resist all opposers, 41.

COMMISSION,
Coroner's, 172.

COMMITMENT,
of witness, 118, 180, 189.
form of, 180, 181, 189, 191.
for obstructing proceedings, 143.
of accused, 191.

COMPETENT SKILL,
deaths from want of, 42.

CONCEALMENT,
of birth, no presumptive evidence, 56.
should not be found, 53.

CONDUCT,
of parties in attendance at inquests, 127.

CONFEDERATES,
evidence of, 99.

CONIUM MACULATUM,
symptoms of, 76.

CONSENT,
of party killed, no excuse, 39.

CONSERVATORS OF THE PEACE,
Coroners are, 5.

CONSTABLES,
list of, to be furnished to Coroners, 23.
accounts of, how rendered, 154.
certificate to, 225.
fees of, 167.

CONTINUING,
and adjourning the inquest, 127.

CONTUSED WOUNDS,
remarks on, 82.

CONVICTS,
disposal of bodies of, 130.

COPPER,
symptoms of, 69.
antidote for, 79.

CORONERS,
several may take inquest, 9.
their rights, 21.
their jurisdiction, 18.
are conservators of the peace, 5.
authority of, 5.
duty of, 5.
their remedy for fees, 21.
liability of, 24.
removal of, 26.
misconduct of, 24.
Sheriffs cannot be, 26.
their court, 109.
when and where holden, 110.
who may attend, 111.
the jury, and how summoned, 112.
the witnesses, and how summoned, 117.
counsel at, 120.
opening of, 120.
viewing the body, 122.
continuing and adjourning, 127.
the medical testimony at, 132.
the depositions, 141.
obstructions, how punished, 142.
the inquisition of, 143.
publication of proceedings at, 151.
defraying expenses of, 152.
a court of record, 111 and note 5.

CO-CORONERS,
liability for acts of, 26.

CORRECTION,
by parents and others, 41.
killing by, 41, 59.

CORROSIVE SUBLIMATE,
symptoms of, 68.
antidote for, 78.

COUNSEL,
at inquests, 120.

CRIMES,
which come under notice of Coroners, 34.
capability of committing, 27.

CRIMINAL,
duty of Coroner on execution of, 8.

CROSS-EXAMINATION,
of witnesses, 106, 129.

D.

DATURA STRAMONIUM,
symptoms of, 76.

DEAF AND DUMB,
their accountability, 28.

DECLARATION,
of Coroner to his account, 225.

DECLARATIONS,
dying, when admissible, 103.

DE CORONATORE EXONERANDO,
writ of, 174.

DEFECT,
of will and understanding, 28.

DEFRAYING EXPENSES,
of inquests, 152.

DEFLECTION,
of balls, 89.

DEMENTIA ACCIDENTALIS,
definition of, 29.

DEMENTIA AFFECTATA,
definition of, 29.

DEMENTIA NATURALIS,
definition of, 28.

DEODANDS,
obsolete, 95,

DEPOSITIONS,
should be certified by Coroner, 141.
return of, 141.
when taken, in absence of accused, effect of, 142.
when evidence, 142.

DEPUTY,
power of Coroners to appoint a, 5.

DESCRIPTION,
of the crime, 149.

DETAINER,
warrant of, 191.

DIRECTION,
of a ball, how determined, 89.

DOCUMENTS,
proof of, 106.

DRIVING,
deaths from careless or furious, 42, 43.

DROPPING,
infants, 46.

DRUNKENNESS,
voluntary, 29.

DUELLING,
deaths from, 40.

DUTY,
of Coroners generally, 5.
as conservators of the peace, 5.
in inquests of death, 6.
to inquire into origin of fires, 9.
to return inquisitions, 11.
to execute process, 12.
other duties, 17.

DYING DECLARATIONS,
when admissible as evidence, 103.

E.

ECCHYMOSIS,
liability to mistake, 82.

ELISORS,
appointment of, 16.

ENEMIES,
killing of, 38.

ERSKINE,
his speech in defence of Hadfield, 29 note.

EVIDENCE,
competency of, 97.
primary, 100.
presumptive, 101.
matters of opinion, 102.
matters of privilege, 102.
hearsay, 103.
relevancy of, 105.

EXAMINATIONS. SEE UNDER DEPOSITIONS.

EXCUSABLE HOMICIDE,
remarks on, 58.

EXECUTION,
of criminals, murder by, 61.

EXECUTORS,
of deceased Coroner to certify record, 142.

EXPENSES,
defraying of, 152.

EXPOSURE,
deaths from, 46.

F.

FEES,
schedule of, 162.

FELO DE SE,
of, 34.
burial of, 35.
forfeiture of, 36.

FELONY,
killing to prevent, 62.

FEME COVERT,
crimes by, 30.
evidence of, against husband, 99.

FIGHTING, WRESTLING AND BOXING,
deaths from, 40, 57, 59.

FINING,
jurors, 117.

FIRES,
inquiries into origin of, 9.
jury on inquiries into, 113.
requisition to hold inquiry into, 223.

FLIGHT AND FORFEITURE,
of, 96.

FOOD,
deaths from want of, 46.
in stomach of infant, proves live birth, 50.

FOOT-PRINTS,
comparison of, 124.

FOREIGNERS,
examination of, 119.

FOREMAN,
oath of, 177.

FORFEITURE,
of, 96.

FORGERY,
Coroners guilty of, 25.

FORMS,
list of, 169.

FRACTURES,
of skull in infanticide, 55.

FURIOUS DRIVING,
deaths from, 42.

G.

GAOLER,
duty of, when a death occurs in his prison, 8.
killing prisoner by duress, 47.

GOOD CHARACTER,
evidence of, 106.

GREENWOOD,
case of, 125.

H.

HABEAS CORPUS,
form of, 192.

HADFIELD,
Erskine's speech in defence of, 29 note.

HANDWRITING,
proof of, 106.

HANGING,
various positions in cases of death by, 124.

HEALTH,
statements regarding, when evidence, 105.

HEARSAY EVIDENCE,
admissibility of, 103.

HOMICIDE,
upon provocation, 58.
excusable, 58.
by misadventure, 59.
in self-defence, 60.
per infortunium, 59.
se et sua defendendo, 60.
justifiable, 61.
in execution of law, 61.
in advancement of public justice, 61.
in defence of property, 60.

HUSBAND,
subjection of wife to, 30.
death of wife from neglect of, 46.
evidence of, against wife, 99.
coercing wife, 30.

HYDROCHLORIC ACID,
symptoms of, 66.

HYDROSTATIC TEST,
mode of performing, 91.
value of, 50.

I.

IDENTITY,
of vomited matter, should be preserved, 140.

IDIOTS,
their responsibility for actions, 28.
not capable of giving evidence, 98.
as to being, a question for jury, 29.

IGNORANCE,
no excuse for crime, 30.

INCAUTIOUS NEGLECT,
deaths from, 47.

INDEPENDENT CIRCULATION,
in infants, 50.

INDICTMENT,
for not taking an inquest, 174.

INFANTICIDE,
definition of, 48.
legal points regarding, 52.
by exposure, 53.
when is a child born, 48.
respiration best test of live birth, 49.
cautions regarding, 54.
evidence in, 55.
examination of suspected mother in cases of, 55.
concealment of birth is no presumptive evidence of, 56.

INFANTS,
when admissible as witnesses, 98.
their capability of committing crimes, 27.
deaths of, from exposure or want, 46.

INFIDELS,
are not admissible as witnesses, 99.

INFIRM PERSONS,
death of, from want or neglect, 46.

INFORMATIONS,
form of heading to, 183.
form of Coroner's certificate to, 183.
required before holding inquest, 9, 225.
and see under DEPOSITIONS.

INFORTUNIUM,
homicide *per*, 59.

INQUESTS,
when to be held, 6.
restricted to cause of death, and accessories before the fact, 9.
adjourning, 130.

INQUISITIONS,
to be returned, 11.
of, 151.
the various parts of, 142.
list of, 170.

INSANITY,
adventitious, 28.
excuses crimes, 28.

INSPECTOR,
of anatomy, 130.

INTENTION,
killing without, 41.

INTERPRETER,
examination of foreigners by an, 119.
form of oath of, 182.

INTOXICATION,
no excuse for crime, 29.
the insanity from, 29.

IRON,
symptoms of poisoning by, 71.

IRRITANT,
poisons, 65.

J.

JEOFAILS,
statute of, criminal prosecutions are not within, 156.

JUDICIAL POWERS,
of Coroners, 5.

JUNIOR COUNTY,
Coroners for, 3.

JURISDICTION,
general, of Coroners, 18.
particular, of Coroners, 18.
near boundaries of counties, 19.
in arms of the sea, 20.
in great rivers, 20.
in ships in harbour, 20.
upon high seas, 20.
between high and low water-mark, 20.
supreme, of Coroners, 20.

JURORS,
fees, 166.
Coroners are exempt from serving as, 22.
fining, 117.
not entitled to fees, 166.
how summoned, 116.
upon fire inquests, 113.
persons exempt from serving as, 113.
number of, on inquests, 116.
must not return a verdict from their own knowledge, 132.

JUSTICES,
of the Peace, Coroners cannot be, 25.

JUSTIFIABLE,
homicide, 61.

L.

LAUDANUM,
symptoms of, 73.

LAWFUL SPORTS,
deaths from, 58.

LEADING QUESTIONS,
when they can be asked, 106.

LIABILITY,
of Coroners, 24.

LIQUORS,
spirituous, deaths from, 45, 53.

LUNATIC ASYLUM,
persons dying in Provincial, 130.

LUNATICS,
when inquests are to be held upon, 6, 9.
their responsibility for crimes, 28.
their capacity to give evidence, 98.

M.

MACHINERY,
accidents from, 47.

MADMEN,
their capability of committing crimes, 28.
their competency to give evidence, 98.

MAGISTRATES,
cannot be Coroners, 25.

MALA PRAXIS,
of Physicians, 39, 45.
of Coroners, 24.

MALICE.
See MURDER.

MANDAMUS,
writ of, 22.

MANSLAUGHTER,
no accessory before the fact to, 33.
definition of, 57.
practical remarks upon, 57.
inquisitions in, 206.

MARKS,
on the body and clothing, 135.

MARRIED WOMEN,
their subjection to their husbands, 30.

MASTERS,
subjection of servants to, 30.

MAYHEM,
appeal of, 17.

MEANS OF DEATH,
not material in murder, 38.

MEDICAL,
practitioners and surgeons, how liable, 45.
who qualified as, 132, note 7.
testimony, 132.
witness, fees of, 166.
order for, 186.
summons for, 180.

MELIUS INQUIRENDUM,
award of, 157.

MENONISTS,
affirmation of, 118.

MILEAGE,
proof of, 163, 166, note 3.

MINISTERIAL POWERS,
of Coroners, 5.

MINOR,
how bound over to give evidence, &c., 156.

MISADVENTURE,
homicide by, 59, 60.

MISCONDUCT,
of Coroners, 24.
or jury, a reason for quashing the inquisition, 160.
of physician or surgeon, 39, 45.

MISDEMEANOR,
killing one accused of, 37, 62.

MISFORTUNE,
may excuse crime, 30.

MISNOMER,
of deceased, 146.
of party accused 148.

MISTLETOE,
accident to yacht, 157.

MODE,
of appointing Coroners, 3.

MONSTROSITIES,
destruction of, illegal, 52.

MORAVIANS,
affirmation of, 118.

MURDER,
definition of, 37.
of self, 34.
means of death not material in, 38.
death must happen within a year and a day, 38.
in, there must be malice, 39.
upon provocation, 40.
in mutual combat, 40.
in duelling, 40.
by correction, 41.
inquisition in, 205.

MUSQUASH ROOT,
symptoms of, 76.

N.

NATURALIS, DEMENTIA,
remarks on, 28.

NAVEL-STRING,
See UMBILICAL CORD.

NAVIGATING RIVERS,
accidents from, 44.

NECESSARIES,
deaths from want of, 46.

NEGLIGENCE,
deaths from, 42.

NEUROTIC POISONS,
remarks on, 73.

NEW INQUIRY,
of taking a, 157.

NITRIC ACID,
symptoms of, 66.

NON COMPOS MENTIS,
persons who are, 28.

NOTES,
taking of, at post mortem, 138.

NOTICE,
of bail, 193.

O.

OATH,
of allegiance, 173.
of office, 173.
of jurymen, 178.
of foreman, 177.
on the *voir dire*, 180.
of interpreter, 182.
of witnesses, 182.
of officer in charge of jury, 186.
of mileage, 194.
of correctness of account, 194.

OBSTRUCTIONS,
how punished, 142.

ODOUR,
on opening body, to be noticed, 139.

OFFENDERS,
of, 27.

OFFICE,
oath of, 173.

OFFICERS,
of justice, resistance to, 47.

OMISSION,
of duty, deaths from, 42, 46.

OMNIBUSES,
deaths from racing, 44.

OPENING,
the court, 120.

OPINION,
matters of, 102.

OPIUM,
symptoms of, 73.

ORDER,
for attendance of prisoner, 179.
for payment of medical witness, 186.

ORIGIN,
of office of Coroner, 1.
of fires, duty of Coroners regarding, 9.

OUTLAWRY,
judgment of, 17.

OUTLAWS,
may not be killed, 38.

OXALIC ACID,
symptoms of, 66.

P.

PACKING,
the viscera, 140.

PARENTS,
subjection of children to, 30.

PARTY,
jury, 112.
charged, 147.

PENITENTIARY,
inquests on convicts dying in the, 8.

PHOSPHORUS,
symptoms of, 66.

PHYSICIANS,
and surgeons, killing patients, 39, 45.

PLACE,
where the body is found, 123.
allegation of, 149.

PLEADING,
to inquisitions, 160.

POISONING,
deaths from, 47.
post mortem, in cases of, 138.

POISONS,
classification of, 64.
irritant, 65.
neurotic, 73.
sulphuric acid, 65.
nitric acid, 66.
hydrochloric acid, 66.
oxalic acid, 66.
phosphorus, 66.
alkalies, 67.
ammonia, 67.
arsenic, 67.
chloride of mercury, 68.
corrosive sublimate, 68.
salts of lead, 69.
copper, 69.
antimony, 70.
zinc, 71.
iron, 71.
tin, 71.
nitrobenzole, 71.
essence of mirbane, 71.
aniline, 71.
carbolic acid, 72.
vegetable and animal irritants, 72.
savin, 72.
colchicum, 72.
cantharides, 72.
opium, 73.
laudanum, 73.
prussic acid, 73.
alcohol, 74.
tobacco, 74.
spinal, 75.
strychnine, 75.
cicuta maculata, 76.
conium maculatum, 76.
æthusa cynapium, 76.
sium lineare, 76.
aconitum napellus, 76.
datura stramonium, 76.

POPULAR,
reputation, when evidence, 103.

POSITION,
of the body, 124.

POST MORTEM,
mode of performing, 136.

PRECAUTIONS,
deaths from neglect of ordinary, 42.

PRECEPT,
to summon jury, 175.

PREGNANT,
women. See INFANTICIDE.

PREMEDITATION,
drunkenness shews a want of, 29.

PRESUMPTIVE,
evidence, 101.
in infanticide, 56.

PRIMARY,
evidence, 100.

PRINCIPALS,
and accessories, 31.
in first degree, 31.
in second degree, 31.

PRISONER,
death of, from want or neglect, 46.
statement of, when evidence against him, 104.
caution to, before receiving his statement, 105.
evidence of, 105.
jury at inquests on body of, should be a party one, 112.

PRIVATE,
conducting inquests in, 128.

PRIVILEGE,
matters of, 102.

PRIZE FIGHTING,
deaths from, 40, 58.

PROCEEDINGS,
subsequent to inquest, 155.
with reference to the trial, 155.

PROCESS,
Coroners are to execute, 12.

PROCLAMATION,
before calling jury, 176.
for default of jurors, 177.
for attendance of witnesses, 179.
at adjourned meeting, 185.
at close of inquest, 186.

PROOF,
of handwriting, 106.
of documents, 107.

PROVINCIAL,
asylum, persons dying in, 130.
penitentiary, persons dying in, 130.

PROVISIONAL,
judicial districts, Coroners for, 4.

PROVOCATION,
homicide upon, 58.

PRUSSIC ACID,
symptoms of, 73.

PUBLIC,
duty, deaths from resistance to, 47.
rights of, to attend inquests, 111.

PUBLICATION,
of proceedings, 151.

PUTREFACTION,
in *utero*, sign of dead birth, 50.

Q.

QUALIFICATION,
of Coroners, 2.
of jurors, 112.
of medical men, 132.

QUAKERS,
affirmation of, 118.

QUARTER SESSIONS,
could not pass accounts for unnecessary inquests, 7.
could only be compelled to audit, 22.

QUASHING,
inquisitions, 159.

QUEEN'S BENCH,
judges of, Coroners *virtute officii*, 3.

QUEEN'S YACHT,
accident to, 157.

QUESTIONS,
leading, 106.

R.

RACING,
deaths from, 42, 43, 44.

RAILWAYS,
accidents upon, 47.

RECOGNIZANCE,
to prosecute, 187.
of jurors upon adjournment, 183.
to give evidence, 188.

RECORD,
Coroner's court is a court of, 111, and note.

REGISTRAR, DIVISION,
returns to be made to, 12.

REGISTRATION AND STATISTICS,
returns to be made to board of, 11.

RELEVANCY,
of evidence, 105.

REMOVAL,
of Coroners, 26.

REPUTATION,
popular, when evidence, 103.

REQUISITION,
to hold fire inquest, 223.

RESCUE,
killing in the attempt to, 62.

RESISTANCE,
deaths from, to public duty, 47.

RESPIRATION,
best test of live birth, 49.
absence of signs of, no proof of dead birth, 50.
wilful prevention of, 53.

RETURN,
of inquisitions, 11.
to Division Registrar, 224.

RIGHTS,
of Coroners, 21.
to fees, 21.
exemption from serving offices, 22.
privilege from arrest, 22.

RIOT,
what constitutes a, 62, note.

RIVERS,
accidents from navigating, 44.

ROYAL FISHES,
inquiries of, 17.

S.

SALTS,
of lead, symptoms of, 69.

SAVIN,
symptoms of, 72.

SCHEDULE,
of fees, 162.

SEA,
Coroner's jurisdiction upon the, 18, 20.
high and low water-mark, 20.

SELF-DEFENCE.
homicide in, 58, 60.

SELF-MURDER,
of *felo de se*, or, 34.

SEPARATION,
of counties, 3.

SERVANTS,
their subjection to their masters, 29, 30.
death of, from want or neglect, 46.

SESSIONS,
allowance of accounts at the, 7.

SHERIFF,
Coroners act as substitutes for the, 12.
judgment against, how levied, 12.
who forfeits office to execute process till successor is appointed, 12.
when, dies process must be awarded to deputy, 13.
process against deputy to be awarded to sheriff, 13.
arrest of, by Coroner, 14.
cannot be Coroner, 26.
return to writ, 175.

SHOOTING,
death from, at targets, 58.

SIUM LINEARE,
symptoms of, 76.

SKILL,
deaths from want of competent, 42.

SOLENT,
disaster on the, 157.

SOVEREIGN,
Coroners, 3.

SPECIAL,
jury, Coroners not to summon, 14.

SPINAL,
poisons, 75.

SPIRITUOUS,
liquors, deaths from, 45.

STABS,
remarks on, 82.

STARVATION,
deaths from, 55.

STATEMENT,
of prisoner, when evidence against him, 104.
caution to prisoner before his, 105.
relating to health and suffering, when evidence, 105.

STATUTES,
Coroners are not entitled to, 23.

STEAMBOAT,
accidents from, 47.

STRANGULATION,
of infants by umbilical cord, 53.

STRUGGLING,
mortal wound, prevents, 86.

STRYCHNINE,
symptoms of, 75.

SUBJECTION,
persons in, to others, 29.

SUFFERINGS,
statement regarding, when evidence, 105.

SUFFOCATION,
deaths of infants by, 54.

SULPHURIC ACID,
symptoms of, 65.

SUMMONS,
for jurors, 176.
to witnesses, 178.
for medical witness, 180.

SUNDAY,
inquisition should not be taken on, 110.

SUPER VISUM CORPORIS,
inquests must be, 122.

SURGEONS,
how liable, 39, 45.

SURROUNDING,
objects should be noticed, 126.

SWORD-PLAYING,
deaths from, 41.

T.

TARGET,
deaths from shooting at a, 58.

TAKING UP,
bodies, power of Coroner, 110.

TECHNICAL,
words, 150.

TENURE,
of office, 4.

TESTS,
for blood, 92.

TIME,
required for analysis, 141.
allegation of, 149.

TOBACCO,
symptoms of, 74.

TRAVERSING,
of, inquisitions, 158.

TREASURE-TROVES,
inquiries of, 17,

TUMOURS,
of the head in children, 55.

TUNKERS,
affirmation of, 118.

U.

UMBILICAL CORD,
point of insertion, no evidence of degree of maturity, 52.
omission to tie the, 53.
twisting of, round the neck, 54.
ends of, should be examined, 54.
attempts to sever the, cause wounds, 55.

UNAVOIDABLE,
necessity, killing from, 61.

UNITED BRETHREN,
affirmation of, 118.

UNLAWFUL,
sports, deaths from, 41.

UNNECESSARY,
inquests condemned, 6.
accounts for should not be passed, 7.

UTERINE AGE,
of a child, 51.

V.

VENIRE.
to amend inquisition, 194.

VENUE,
the, in inquisitions, 144.

VERDICT,
the, is equivalent to an indictment, 147.

VIEW,
inquest can only be taken on, of the body, 9.
of the body, 122.

VIRTUTE OFFICII,
Coroners, 3.

VISCERA,
observations on packing the, 140.

VOIR DIRE,
examination on the, 98.
oath on the, 180.

W.

WANTON,
conduct, deaths from, 41.

WARRANT,
to constable to summon jury, 175.
to gaoler to summon jury, 175.
against witness for contempt, 179.
to bury the body, 184.
to bury a *felo de se*, 184.
to take up a body, 190.
to apprehend accused, 190.
of commitment of accused, 191.
of detainer to gaoler, 191.

WILL,
defect of, 27.

WITNESS,
how summoned, 117.
fining for non-attendance, 118.
manner of swearing, 118.
should sign his depositions, 119.
fees of, 166.
oath of, 182.
affirmation of, 183.
competency of, 97.
the medical, 132.
payment of, 166.
order for payment of, 186.
form of information of, 183.

WIVES,
death of, from want, 46.
how bound over to give evidence, 155.
subjection of, to husbands, 30.
evidence of, 99.

WRECKS,
inquiries of, 17.

WRESTLING,
deaths from, 40, 41, 58.

WRITING,
proof of, 106.

WRITS,
return of, by Coroners, 15.
direction of, to Coroners, 15.

WOUNDS AND BRUISES,
examination of, 80.
characters of, inflicted during life, 81.
made after death, 82.
remarks on, 82.
contused, 84.
gun shot, 87.

Z.

ZINC,
symptoms of, 71.

COPP, CLARK & CO., PRINTERS, COLBORNE STREET, TORONTO.

CORONER'S BLANKS.

		$ c.
INFORMATION of Witnesses	Per 100	1 50
Inquisitions	"	1 50
Recognizances	"	0 75
Coroners' Bills	"	1 50
Summons to Jurors	"	0 75
Summons to Witness	"	0 75
Warrant to Constable	"	0 75
Warrant of Commitment	"	1 50
Summons for a Medical Witness	"	0 75
Recognizance of Jurors upon an Adjournment	"	0 75
Warrant to Bury the Body	"	0 75
Warrant to Bury a *Felo de se*	"	0 75
Order for Payment of Medical Witnesses	"	0 75
Warrant to Apprehend Accused	"	0 75
Caption of a Fire Inquest	"	1 50
Requisition to Hold a Fire Inquest	"	0 75
Information to Hold Inquest	"	1 50
Return to Division Registrar	"	
The Oaths required to be used at Inquests, printed altogether in a convenient form for reference	each	

☞ *Any form not in Stock Printed to Order.*

CPSIA information can be obtained at www.ICGtesting.com
Printed in the USA
LVOW111303100313
323543LV00012B/164/P

9 781278 916095